DATE DUE

The
Iconoclastic
Deity

Also by CLYDE A. HOLBROOK

Faith and Community (1959)
Religion: A Humanistic Field (1963)
Original Sin (1970). Ed., vol. 3, *Works of Jonathan Edwards*
The Ethics of Jonathan Edwards (1973)

The Iconoclastic Deity

Biblical Images of God

Clyde A. Holbrook

Lewisburg
Bucknell University Press
London and Toronto: Associated University Presses

Associated University Presses
440 Forsgate Drive
Cranbury, NJ 08512

Associated University Presses
25 Sicilian Avenue
London WC1A 2QH, England

Associated University Presses
2133 Royal Windsor Drive
Unit 1
Mississauga, Ontario
Canada L5J 1K5

Library of Congress Cataloging in Publication Data

Holbrook, Clyde A.
  The iconoclastic Deity.

  Bibliography: p.
  Includes index.
  1. God—Biblical teaching.   2. Image (Theology)
3. Symbolism.   4. Worship.   I. Title.
BS544.H65   1984   231   83-45948
ISBN 0-8387-5069-9

Printed in the United States of America

Being then God's offspring, we ought not to think that the Deity is like gold, or silver, or stone, a representation by the art and imagination of men.

Acts 17:29

When thou settest thyself to meditate on the Joys above, think on them boldly as Scripture has expressed them: Bring down thy conceivings to the reach of sense. . . . Both Love and Joy are prompted by familiar acquaintance: When we go to think of God and Glory in proper conceivings without these spectacles, we are lost and have nothing to fix our thoughts upon.

Richard Baxter, "The Saints' Everlasting Rest,"
in Robert Daly, God's Altar

Quite simply: I want honesty.

Sören Kierkegaard,
Attack on Christendom

Contents

Acknowledgments

I owe a considerable debt not only to the many authors consulted, but also to several former colleagues at Oberlin College, particularly Professors Andrew Bongiorno, Keith Boone, John Hobbs, Robert Pierce, and Grover Zinn. My ruminations have been inflicted on a small group of students who occasionally met in my home. They provided a sounding board for my poorly articulated ideas, and they did not hesitate to question my efforts. Of course, none of the above are to be held accountable for any failure on my part to profit by their knowledge and advice. The libraries of Oberlin College and the First Church in Oberlin have been of great assistance. My wife rendered into readable form my nearly illegible handwriting. The book is dedicated to one who more faithfully than I has understood and responded to the noblest images of God—my sister, Madge I. Burke.

Introduction

This book began with my uneasiness about the fact that Christian worship and theology employ only a few of the many images of God found in the Bible. From that point I was drawn into speculation about literary images generally and religious images in particular. I realized that the latter were expressions less of theological speculation than of worship, in which human beings believed themselves most directly and intimately engaged with the deity. Accordingly, I did not set out to write a theological treatise as such, but a book whose theological character would arise from the study of the biblical images themselves, viewed from the perspective of worship. That intention soon found itself involved with the question of how far I should bring to bear my acquaintance with the technicalities of biblical criticism and interpretation. I answered that question in a way that biblical scholars may well regard as presumptuously simple-minded, by refusing to be chained to biblical commentaries except in rare instances. I preferred for my purpose to let the survey of biblical images include all images seen from the standpoint of a "second naiveté" that presupposed a technical biblical criticism into which I would not here enter. Because I did not intend to explore the problems of biblical language, I did not take on the role of literary critic, for which I was ill fitted. That interest has been well served by G. B. Caird's book *The Language and Imagery of the Bible* (Westminster, 1980). Another self-imposed limitation has been my use of only one English source, the Revised Standard Version of the Bible. Other translations, however, have been used occasionally, but in the main I have accepted the risks involved in trusting the work of the scholars who translated that version. In the explication of the images I have followed a narrow path between a literalism that would destroy the poetic character of the images and the equally dangerous tendency to poeticize God into the realm of unbridled imagination. I see these images as rooted in this worldly experience, yet not confined to flat, unnuanced prose. At the same time, to avoid stratospheric claims about God, the images are regarded as tethered to the identifiable worldly characteristics the images contain. Contradictions among the images have been allowed to stand naked, only occasionally mediated by the too-often-used term *paradox*. Images deemed unworthy of the deity have been included since, I take it, they were not

11

originally framed to suit modern religious and ethical sensibilities. So neither traditional confessional interests nor contemporary theological positions have been allowed to limit the exposition of the divine images.

Truth seldom comes into the world unadorned by imaginative constructions, since, as it has been said, people more often live their lives in the light of images, symbols, and myths than by abstract ideas and doctrines.[1] This observation has guided my treatment of the biblical images and, I hope, justifies it, but I have also been aware that images bear a cognitive element as well, without which they would be intellectually and religiously vacuous. Consequently, I have wrestled with the question of their truth value, with the understanding that their principal function is the inciting of the imagination. As one modern theologian has commented, "One might suppose that the decisive errors which grip contemporary spirituality are largely failures or corruptions of the imagination. This great faculty of the soul can be redeemed only through a rebirth of images."[2] So truth, imagination, and images may be seen as constituting a whole by which the religious life is ordered.

In Part I of the book consideration is given to the topic of images in general, and religious images and symbols in particular. The sources and functions of images have been explored, after which a distinction has been drawn between religious images and symbols (chap. 4). The contention that images are best understood in the context of worship next called for a treatment of two principal foci of worship in connection with the idea of transcendence. The explicitly theoretical segment of the book concludes by addressing the problem of the truth of images. The phenomenological or descriptive purpose of the study in Part II is realized in an exposition of the images themselves, concluding with observations on the eventual transcriptions of some of them into metaphysical or theological image-symbols. The wide variety of biblical images of God and his attributes has demanded illustrations of them in sufficient quantity to establish their importance. However, many examples of a particular image have been eliminated, lest the reader be benumbed by the sheer mass of citations. Nevertheless, I must admit that in spite of my pruning efforts, a certain literary turgidity occasionally occurs, but I hope that the evidential weight of these citations will excuse any infelicity of literary expression. Equally, I hope at this point that my adoption of a "secondary naiveté" in approaching these images will not be confused with simple-mindedness or fundamentalism. It has been a device to let the images appear in their own right without reduction of the resonance ascribed to them in Part I. In a sense that I hope will not repel the reader, Part II may be understood as an uncommonly persistent and thorough attempt to catch a glimpse of "what God looks like" as seen through the spectrum of images offered by Jewish and Christian authors and editors. In the conclusion I return to the questions of why only certain images or symbols have become authoritative for worship and in what this authority consists. At the end I propose that the image of God as the Iconoclastic Spirit incorporates many other images and symbols and best reflects the heights and depths of Christian experience.

NOTES

1. Cf. Amos Niven Wilder, *Theopoetic* (Philadelphia: Fortress Press, 1976), 44.
2. Julian N. Hartt, *Theological Method and Imagination* (New York: The Seabury Press, 1977), 5.

The
Iconoclastic
Deity

Part I

1

An Approach to Images

The commandment is clear: "You shall not make yourself a graven image, or any likeness of anything that is in heaven above, or that is in the earth beneath, or that is in the water under the earth" (Exod. 20:4). The strictures of this verse once and for all put an end to talk of physical images of God. God was to be imageless so that his transcendence to all earthly and finite realities would be clear. Nothing from this world could adequately represent him or be substituted for his invisible nature. But finite realities are not simply physical objects. There are the finite "objects" entertained by the mind, and if by extension of the prohibition against graven images these are also eliminated, little if anything remains by which to grasp whatever God is. If graven images lead to the idolatry of the senses, so also the images of the mind can lead to the deeper idolatry of the spirit. And warnings against this idolatry have not been uncommon. In his speech on the Areopagus Paul warned his hearers not to think that God is "like gold, or silver, or stone, a representation by the art and imagination of man" (Acts 17:29). The imagination, no less than the senses, can beguile people into false belief, as Jonathan Edwards reminded his readers: "Oftentimes when the imagination is too strong, and the other faculties weak, it over-bears them, and much disturbs them in their exercise."[1] Protestantism has often taken the prohibition against images to extend to mental images. Thus the Heidelberg Catechism (1563) crisply states, "God may not and can not be imaged in any way." And later the Puritan William Perkins is heard to say, "So soon as the mind frames unto it selfe any forme of God (as when he is popishly conceived to be like an old man sitting in heaven in a throne with a sceptre in his hand) an idol is set up in the mind . . . a thing faigned in the mind by imagination is an idol."[2] To follow this line of thought would presumably foreclose all study of the biblical images of God, for no images of God would be found in Scripture. Yet the Jewish Scriptures tell of God's making man in "our image, after our likeness" (Gen. 1:26). And Christian Scriptures dare to speak of Jesus Christ as "the image of the invisible God" (Col. 1:15) with no thought of idolatry, al-

19

though a human, physical being must be involved in the concept. A survey of the biblical record, furthermore shows literary images of God's nature and attributes to be plentiful.

How difficult, if not impossible, it is to reverence a being who is absolutely imageless, lacking any identifiable features! Such a being could scarcely be called a being at all. But the Bible did not shrink from giving literary form to its apprehension of God, and in so doing pictured God to the mind and also retained the sense of God as different from the images. For Christianity the tension is illustrated by this comment: "The difficulty is that while Christian theology asserts that God is unknowable, it simultaneously asserts that God can be known."[3] Without some concept, some idea or image, one could not say anything of a cognitive nature about God. What would be the sense of calling a person a believer, an atheist, or an agnostic, unless some reasonably definite idea or, if you will, image, is in question? Even believers are atheists in respect to the ideas of God they repudiate. And an agnostic or an atheist may suspend judgment or negate God only if he or she holds to some conception of deity. Since no image of a God was found in the Holy of Holies in Jerusalem, we are told, Pompey decided that the Jews were atheists. And he was correct, according to what he thought was necessary to the worship of a deity. Pseudo-Dionysius, on the other hand, like other radical mystics, could call God "nothing," that is, beyond all possible descriptive imagery. But in his case a tradition replete with descriptions of divine activities led to and framed the idea of this "nothing." The "nothingness" of God did not take place in a conceptual vacuum. So we find the irrepressible Hume, in his "Dialogues on Natural Religion," discomfiting one of his pious colleagues by charging him with being a mystic. He asked, "Or how do you mystics, who maintain the absolute incomprehensibility of the Deity, differ from Sceptics or Atheists, who assert that the first cause of all is unknown and unintelligible?"[4] As Hume and many others have seen, there is little point in believing in or denying the existence of a being of which nothing can be said.

The innumerable verbal images of God in the Bible did give a purchase on "the imageless one." But the fact that we find images rather than clear, prosaic descriptions reminds us that a "gap" between the reality and the image comes with every image.[5] The distance between the two is not one to be eliminated by any literary sleight of hand. The poet, to be sure, may rhapsodize about creating "reality" by literary invention, and constantly denounce heavy-handed efforts to determine the truth of a poem in terms of anything except itself, but biblical imagery does not come to rest in aesthetic narcissism. For the Bible, only God's words create reality, not the words of mankind. Religious faith does not enjoin us to admire what went on in the heads of poets or what they wrote. More is at stake than that, for the images remind us that the intervening distance between literary figures and the reality they express forbids one from casually strolling with slovenly intimacy into God's presence. Yet these images do bridge the gap to the degree that one can be sufficiently confident that whatever is expressed reports some aspect of an engagement with the reality of God. They call to mind, with all the limitations they place on religious experience, that access to reality is primordial to knowledge of it. Martin Buber made excessive claims for the I-Thou relation, but he did forcefully tell us a homely truth in claiming that life is not a string of metaphors for something never to be realized. The bounds of language were not to be taken as the definitive limits of our deepest engagements with the real.[6] At some points such preeminent power or authority confronts us, making evasion impossible without placing in jeopardy our sanity and very existence. Our fervent denials and worrisome doubts pay silent tribute to the reality from which we would free ourselves. Our very capacity for denial or doubt presupposes a reality with which we must live. And it is by words, figures of speech, and ideas that the reality of our situation is brought home to us, ultimately if not at first.

Religious language may not be entirely reducible to poetic language, as Paul Ricoeur has maintained, but we shall turn to poets and interpreters of poetry, from whom we expect a clarifying and expert word on images. The word *image* has a wide variety of meanings, depending on context, but for the present the testimony of those engaged in purely literary pursuits is sufficient.[7] When we first inquire of those who treat of literature as to the definition of *image*, we find, for example, the following: "An image is a literal and concrete expression of a sensory experience or an object that can be known by one or more of the senses . . . a sensation through the process of being a 'relict' of an already known sensation." Or again, as to its function we read that it is "the means by which experience in its richness and emotional complexity is communicated, as opposed to the simplifying and conceptualizing processes of science and philosophy."[8] An image, it seems, originates in sensory experience, which provides knowledge of that which is imaged. The image, however, is a "relict," or perhaps a surviving imprint left in memory, of that which is "known by the senses." But if it is a "relict," presumably having lost its original vivacity, how then can the image communicate the "richness and emotional complexity" of the experience from which it originated? Perhaps the poets themselves, rather than their interpreters, are better qualified to answer the question.

C. Day Lewis begins in a straightforward fashion to define an image as "a picture made out of words." But then, expanding upon this simplified version, he points out that an epithet, a metaphor, or simile may create an image, but in such a fashion that it is "something more than the accurate reflection of an external reality. Every poetic image, therefore, is to some degree metaphorical." A whole poem may itself be an image. We come closer to the center of his meaning when he unleashes an academic turn of mind only at last to confess that he has said too much. "The poetic image," he writes, "is a more or less sensuous picture in words, to some degree metaphorical, with an undernote of some human emotion in its context, but also charged with and releasing into the reader a special poetic emotion or passion—No, it won't do," he interrupts, "the thing has got out of hand."[9] Here the sensory element is again emphasized, along with the emotional coloration that suffuses the "picture." But there is also a more metaphysical truth that the image brings before us. While admitting that the image cannot reproduce the soul of things, nevertheless, "by the force of its own vitality, and our own answering sense of revelation," it is able "to persuade us that there is beneath the appearance of things a life whose quality may not be apprehended in our everyday intercourse nor to be gauged by the instruments of science." So, he writes, "all these word pictures—and here perhaps we have hit upon a law of imagery—are only something more than word-pictures," and *only become images in relation to a general truth.*"[10] We have come some distance when we hear the poet, in pondering upon the meaning of *image*, stating that there is a reality that images open to us that lies beneath the commonplaces of existence. It is the image that, in its vivacity, presents to us something like a revelation of a domain that escapes the limits of our ordinary language.

Contrary evidence comes from another poet. In describing an image, Octavio Paz claims that it characteristically contradicts the fundamental law of logic, dispensing with it altogether. "The image shocks because it defies the principle of contradiction: the heavy is light. When it enunciates the identity of opposites, it attacks the foundations of our thinking. There- fore, the poetic reality of the image cannot aspire to truth. The poem does not say what it is, but what could be. Its realm is not the realm of being, but that of Aristotle's 'likely impossible.'" Like the Eastern thought forms, which assert "this is that," and unlike the Western mode, which says "this *or* that," the poetic image makes a shambles of the neat categories of reason. Nevertheless, Paz points out, "poets persist in affirming that the image reveals what is and not what could be. Moreover, they say that the image re-creates being. . . . Poetic images have their own logic," whatever that may be.[11] This poet's contention clearly moves in a different direction from that of Lewis. Poetic imagery seems in this case to be in a world of its own, unanchored either in sensuous or rational reality. It is a unique world of its own that it reveals, but it is a world of possibility, not of some substantive metaphysical reality. Yet Paz, whatever value his insights may have for poetry, does not seem at first to shed light upon the imagery we find in biblical poetry or prose.

When we listen instead to the French poet and phenomenological philosopher Gaston Bachelard, it is clear that he is out of patience with those who would attempt to understand images in terms of psychology or rationalistic philosophy. Images, he argues, are not to be understood in terms of some general or fundamental principle. For example, they escape the category of causality altogether. In the proper sense the poetic image is not caused. Rather it "flames up" in the imagination, thereby escaping investigative efforts. In its simplicity, it is not an object or a substitute object of some kind. Instead it calls upon one to seize the specific reality of the image itself. Its very pristine quality as the product of a naive consciousness does not even demand a knower, for in the poetic image the soul bespeaks its presence. Whereas the psychologist or psychoanalyst intellectualizes the image by searching for its origin and translating it into another language, the phenomenologist, as Bachelard holds himself to be, brackets everything extraneous to the image itself, and offers in justification a phenomenology of the poetic consciousness or imagination.[12] This author lets us know that the way to understanding the meaning of *image* does not lie in the path of Freud or Jung, but in an objective consideration wherein the "reality" of the image is taken seriously for its own sake, supported only by the development of a metaphysic of the imagination. It appears also that the image not only is to be seized in its integrity, but that it also seizes upon some aspect, if not of "reality," at least of subsistence. There is a world that images occupy, and it is not one to be dismantled by the tactics of rationalistic analysis. But one is left once more, as with Paz, wondering whether images convey truth, or whether they satisfy only the aesthetic imagination or the pride of their creators.

Among phenomenologists and historians of religion, Mircea Eliade has given much attention to images. His line of interpretation parallels at certain points that of Bachelard, but in significant ways diverges from it. Each has a different interest: religion for Eliade, poetry for Bachelard. For Eliade, symbols, myths, and images are the very substance of the spiritual life.[13] As such they may be disguised, degraded, and militated against, but they never can be eliminated. "Images, symbols, and myths are not irresponsible creations of the psyche: they respond to a need and fulfill a function, that of bringing to light the most hidden modalities of being."[14] In this statement Eliade breaks with Paz's contention that images have nothing to do with "being" or truth and with Bachelard's autonomous domain of images. In company with Bachelard, however, he mounted an attack upon "psychologism" and upheld the irreducibility of images. "To 'translate' the images into concrete terms is an operation devoid of meaning . . . the reality that they are trying to signify cannot be reduced to such 'concrete' references." The search for the origin "of the images is a problem that is beside the point." And to analyze the multiple meanings inherent in the image is to annihilate or annul it as an "instrument of cognition."[15] The important turn that Eliade makes is to invest the term *images* with a psycho-ontological significance not usually found in the interpreters of poetic imagery. Images are not simply the play of the imagination attempting to say in words what more prosaic language fails to express. They are imaginative, but they are imitating exemplary models or archetypes. They reproduce, reactualize, and repeat these models endlessly.[16] Here a Jungian "racial unconscious" seems to be implied, and we have moved back into psychologism. The question of the origin of images, which earlier we were informed was a dead-end enterprise, has been answered. However, Eliade has yet another string to his bow besides that of a racial unconscious filled with archetypes. There is a "transconscious" level of the self. As he put it, "Indeed, if an ultimate solidarity of the whole human race does exist, it can be felt and 'activated' only at the level of the Images (we do not say 'of the subconscious' for we have no proof that there may not also be a Transconscious)."[17] This line of thought does not allow him to escape the charge of psychological reductionism, because the term *transconscious* is no less "psychological" than *subconscious*. It is woefully weak to argue that there may be a "transconscious" on the basis that there is no proof that there isn't one!

Eliade's treatment of images shows up the difficulty of harnessing them to the subliminal world of archetypes, from which "grab-bag" all manner of both beneficent and horrible images emerge, although Eliade seems inclined to believe that only "good" archetypes subsist. Furthermore, Eliade is a prime example of the error later to be discussed, namely, the surreptitious conversion of psychology into ontology. He does it by way of the images, but serious questions remain as to the validity of this tactic, for which no evidence is adduced. To deposit so much intellectual and spiritual capital in the subconscious (or transconscious) is to rob any inquirer of the possibility of validating the contention that archetypes are themselves the "hidden modalities of being."

Naturally, the philosophers have also addressed the problem of images. Hume believed that the imagination reproduced impressions made on the senses after the things that had made the impressions were no longer present. Although creative and free in its own right to the degree that it could rearrange the data that came to it from the senses, the imagination was limited by custom and by what the senses brought to it. "Nothing is more free than the imagination of man; and although it cannot exceed that original stock of ideas furnished by the internal and external senses, it has unlimited power of mixing, compounding, separating and dividing these ideas, in all the varieties of fiction and vision."[18] But even in our everyday perceptions of our surroundings, the imagination does its work, unfortunately, as the previous quotation suggests, often leading us into inappropriate reaction and false beliefs about our world. Or as Mary Warnock observed, "imagination is not only the helpful assistant; in this chapter [on scepticism] it has turned out to be the deceiver which gives us an altogether unwarranted sense of security in the world."[19] If this be the upshot of Hume's philosophy, the imagination and its images can never be surely depended upon to provide a basis for correct belief or knowledge. However, it seems that Hume managed to avoid this conclusion by distinguishing between just and unjust exercises of the imagination, the former being founded upon custom, productive of ideas truly related to the proper impressions, and thereby providing the means by which to interpret experience and thus enable the reason to make use of them.[20] Yet Hume leaves us in some doubt as to whether the images produced by the imaginations themselves convey a true or a fictitious account of the world. The bridge between sensation and reason that imagination presumes to offer is rickety. It was Kant who fixed more firmly and explicitly the mediating function of the imagination. It is that function of the mind which permits us to apply concepts to sense experience. It spontaneously produces images according to the schema or structure inherent in the mind itself. It is to the structures of the mind that the sensed data must conform.[21] Sense data are filtered through the imagination on their way to the understanding. On the one side, imagination partakes of the sense manifold, and on the other it participates in the rational structure of the mental faculties; consequently it does form the bridge between sense and understanding. In Kant's scheme the contribution to truth by the imagination is enhanced by virtue of the fact that the complex structure of the mind, of which it is an active part, determines what truth is, as it works over the deliverances of the senses into rational form in conformity with the Forms of Intuition, the Categories of the Understanding, and the Ideas of Reason.

But we stray some distance from religious images in listening to Hume and Kant, whose studies of the imagination and images have more to do with epistemology than with the practices of the devout. Yet we learn, at least by indirection, the importance of the image-making faculty of the mind, and that images may convey truth, even if the philosophers' concepts of truth apparently diverge from those which religious images purport to offer. These thinkers show that not only does the world sensuously experienced as present call the imagination into play; so also does nonsensate experience. On the face of it, that should provide an opening for the imagination to work upon religious "reality," for is not God absent to the senses and yet counted to be real?

Briefly, one other track concerning images can be followed, that offered by Jean Paul Sartre in his "The Psychology of Imagination." Here an existentialist philosopher tells us that images express the nonbeing of the object they reflect. "However lively, appealing or strong the image is, it presents its object as not being. This does not prevent us from reacting to the image as if its object were before us. It is possible for us to react to an image as if it were a perception, but "we seek in vain to create in ourselves that the object really exists. . . . We can pretend for a second, but we cannot destroy the immediate awareness of its nothingness."[22] Applied to religious images, this conclusion is devastating. If images always introduce the unreal, or the "nothingness" that Sartre lovingly embraces, then the quest for images of God is again forestalled. Like Paz, Sartre divorces imagery from any relevance to personal existence, to say nothing of the more inclusive realm of being. And it is done, in this particular case, by transforming the psychological fact that the image is analogous to or representative of something that does not appear in literally construed language, into a metaphysical element called "nothingness." Absence in any case is not the same as "nothing," nor is invisibility identical with the unreal. Sartre is not much help in coming to grips with the images of God in the Bible, where the presence of God as real is overwhelming.

The legacy of Kant in respect to images and symbols was accepted and interpreted by Ernst Cassirer. He argued in the Kantian manner for the structure of the mind that he called symbolic forms. Unlike empirical or pragmatic theories of language, which either fail to grasp reality or reduce all knowledge, language, and art to a kind of fiction, this philosopher held that the structures or the forms organize experience so that it becomes reality. As he put it, "Instead of measuring the content, meaning and truth of intellectual forms by something extraneous which is supposed to be reproduced in them, we must find in these forms themselves the measure and criterion for their truth and intrinsic meaning." Only then can there be "reality, any organized and definite Being at all." And to make the point even clearer, Cassirer added, "Thus the special symbolic forms are not imitations, but *organs* of reality, since it is solely by their agency that anything real becomes an object for intellectual apprehension, and as such is made visible to us. The question as to what reality is apart from these forms, and *what are its independent attributes, becomes irrelevant here.*"[23] When this type of thinking is applied to the area of religion, Cassirer discusses the "mythic consciousness," where, as with certain poets, names and images create reality. In one place he claims that "whatever has been fixed by a name, henceforth is not only real, but is Reality," and in another, in company with Paz, he holds that "The 'image' does not represent the 'thing'; it is the thing."[24] In this view, obviously, the power of language and the symbolic forms is tremendous. They constitute reality, so we need not look behind the words or images to discover the reality being represented, since the structures of the mind in both secular and religious areas determine what reality is to be, not simply the truth about reality.

If Cassirer's ideas be followed through in the quest of the meaning and function of the image, we are left with the question of what constitutes the object known. Is the presence of an "object" only the product of a mind and, in this sense, a psychological function that swallows up ontological relations? Is "object" only a product created by epistemological activity? Is the "reality" to which Cassirer repeatedly refers only a philosophical indulgence in a world that Hans Vaihinger once denoted as the realm of "as if," a way of treating the world "as if" it were real?[25] We may anticipate that for the biblical authors their images signified something more than a veiled attempt to treat God as a product of mental and linguistic structures. They seem to have been aware of the distance between God and the images they used, a fact that once more reminds us that access to reality was not for them the same as the ability to grasp it linguistically or epistemologically.

Another philosopher who occupied himself with verbal images and "reality" was the Idealist Wilbur M. Urban, who was especially interested in the religious use of images and symbols. In his view "Images are taken from the narrower and more intuitable relations and used as expressions for more universal and ideal relations, which because of their pervasiveness and ideality cannot be directly expressed."[26] However, an image is not a pure re-presentation of the truth or reality in question. Whatever is intuited cannot be directly set forth in the image. Some distortion of the intuition is necessary if the original is to be indirectly reflected in the image.[27] In this sense an image or a symbol always tells a "lie" about its object. It is and yet it is not the conveyor of truth. One might liken its function to that of perspective in a painting, which conveys the sense of depth by offering an illusion as lines seem to converge in the distance. It is doubtful that Urban would leave the matter there. Although distortion enters into symbolic language, there is in religious language a basis of nonsymbolic knowledge in connection with the metempirical. However, "The religious symbol is always supernatural in all the possible meanings of this word," he writes, and therefore has "no literal significance in the sense of reference to empirically observable entities."[28] The religious image has knowledge value, and therefore he maintains that there is some nonsymbolic knowledge at the root of the religious image, and that without it "symbolic knowledge is an illusion."[29] Yet, if the image is translated into its nonsymbolic form, its impact is lost. The emotional and dramatic effect of the image is blanched out into the speculative terms of philosophy and theology. The knowledge-value of an image thus hovers between a literal, or at least a speculative knowledge, and a knowledge that depends largely upon the imagination. As such, it mutely seeks a cash value forever denied it. It is not a literal truth, if by that is meant reference to sense-apprehended objects, but neither is it a forceful illusion. The image occupies the territory of "deeper truth."

In certain respects Urban assists us in understanding the biblical images, but there are limitations here also. One gathers that Urban's theory, which largely rests upon an idealistic reading of the world, fails to catch the more earthly vigor that lies at the base of some biblical images. His use of the word *supernatural* is also disturbing, because the Old Testament, at least, knows nothing of the modern distinction between nature and supernature. As one scholar put it, "all nature was supernatural, and the supernatural natural."[30] However, on the other hand, Urban's reading of the nature of images and symbols and their dependence upon some nonsymbolic knowledge seems accurate—although I would prefer a noncognitive term in place of *nonsymbolic knowledge,* such as *existential engagement,* to emphasize the impact of God on human beings. Perhaps Urban observed the distinction when he wrote, "Doubtless it cannot be said that that which cannot be expressed is not 'real,' but surely that which cannot be expressed cannot be said to be either true or false."[31]

H. Richard Niebuhr's perceptive comment on the dangers of leaving experience uninterpreted speaks to this problem. He saw that speculative reason does not determine reality, but he also saw the possible dangers when experience of reality was not informed by the appropriate images of the practical reason. "The consequences of declaring any part of human experience and action to be beyond reason is not to eliminate it from existence, but to leave it subject to unregulated passion, to uncriticized custom, or to the evil imaginations of the heart."[32] Consequently, he went on to offer one of the most fruitful theological examinations of the nature and function of images in respect to Christian revelation. He distinguished, as did Kant, between the "pure" or scientific, impersonal reason and the practical or participative reason, but he went on to show that both employed the imagination. The images or patterns by which experience of the external world conveys to the mind various sensations are paralleled in the history of participating selves by images that organize and interpret the affections, which are the data of our internal histories. Affections never remain uninterpreted. We use our imaginations to respond rightly or wrongly "to a whole of reality of which this affection is for us a symbol and a part." And the appropriate images by which we form our responses are usually personal rather than impersonal ones, as the merely observant mind suggests. "The images of the observational method are so out of place in the life of participation that they must be abandoned in favor of other ideas or surreptitiously modified when employed by moral agents in moments of decisive action."[33] One estimates the validity of personal images by their capacity to make existentially involved life intelligible and coherent, and their invalidity by the isolated subjectivity of selves, who become humanly impoverished or are even destroyed. Inept reactions, stimulated by false and misleading images, leave one without any meaning as to socially involved history, as well as to the private histories of individual lives.[34]

The values of Niebuhr's insights are most obvious in respect to his demonstrating that imagination plays its part in respect to knowledge of the external world as well as of our social and personal histories. He rescues imagination and the realm of images from being the sheer play of fantasy, and elucidates the manner in which images come to grips with the most persistently important issues of existence. He also gives an account of the way in which images can be evaluated as they focus and interpret human life. At the same time, however, he tells us little about the way images are formed in respect to internal or participative history. Nor, in the light of his theory of revelation, are his pragmatic criteria for images markedly Judaic or Christian, although they are certainly humane. His criteria appeal to the best sense of a broad liberal culture informed by biblical insights. Although the danger is great that the meaning of religious images be circumscribed by the precincts of a community of faith, he showed the possibility of a universal relevance of its images for the interpretation of life by all persons. However, his emphasis on the point that "personal images" are alone capable of carrying the weight of participative history is subject to correction, since religious involvement sometimes uses transpersonal or nonpersonal images that are better able to express the more intense moments in the dialectic of piety.

As we might expect, theologians like Niebuhr, who undertake to deal with images, find their theological viewpoints coloring the way they interpret the images in which their theology is couched. But some go beyond speaking of a theology that merely uses images to one in which the images themselves become the theology itself. Such an orthodox thinker as Austin Farrer comes closest to this position. As a Christian theologian he chose certain dominant images, such as "Kingdom," "Son of Man," and "Israel," as central to setting forth the supernatural mystery at the heart of Christ's teaching. The biblical images in his hands are transmuted into the essence of Christian faith itself. For example, "Israel" stands for "the human family of God" and then by a further twist of ingenuity we learn that Christ was himself "Israel," who appointed twelve men to be his typical "sons." In explaining revelation, Farrer writes that "the great images interpreted the events of Christ's ministry, death and resurrection, and the events interpreted the images; the interplay of the two is revelation."[35] We are furthermore told that as the God-given images continued to live in the mind of the early church, they revealed "the nature of the supernatural existence of the Apostolic church."[36] The images apparently have the authority of God behind them, and so anchor the church in divine reality. It is the images themselves that count in the spiritual life, for although the theologian may confuse the images and metaphysicians speculate about them, "the Bible-reader will immerse himself in the simple image on the page before him, and find life-giving power in it, taken as it stands."[37] But obviously, given Farrer's imposition of a traditional theological exegesis upon the images, he did not just immerse himself in images as they stood on the page. There is still the possibility that others immersing themselves in images will not read off the theology he offers. He is confident that revelation comes to us by the interplay of image and event, as seen in Christ's life, death, and resurrection, but one is forbidden to look for reality behind the image. In the images themselves we have a foretaste of a supernatural life, for the veil that images provide is not a blank. "It is painted with the image of God, and God himself painted it, and made it indelible with his blood. . . ." There is an indelibility about the master-images that made it impossible for prophets and apostles to devise new ones. They, like us, do not invent them *de novo*. The images comprise an interlocking system whereby the

whole world of images determines the meaning of each. Thus they constitute the world in which the devout person lives in the fellowship of the
church, and they provide the locus for the theologians' proper task.[38]

The theology of images that Farrer offers is baffling to one who finds the
talk about the "supernatural" and "God-given" images virtually meaningless. The ambience in which Farrer works is quite removed from that of
Niebuhr, and it has an esoteric quality that smacks more of the cloister than
of the realistic atmosphere common to much of the Bible. When the reality
of God or Christ is so wreathed in imagery, or at times identified with the
images themselves, a poetic fantasy-land opens before one. In one respect,
however, and it is a most important one, Farrer knows where the heart of
imagery lies for the religious person. It is in the life of worship, not in the
unscrambling of images or the speculative wanderings of the philosopher
or theologian, when the latter has lost contact with the participative existence that Niebuhr delineated.

Whereas Farrer's view of images scarcely comes to grips with the sec-
ularism of the present, Langdon Gilkey sees a crisis in theology precisely
because in an age of secularity the meaning of religious and theological
language has been thrown into jeopardy. He hopes to salvage the meaning
of religious affirmation by showing that the secular world, so often taken
for granted as constituting the limits of our knowledge, is actually shot
through with intimations of the transcendent or ultimate.[39] Thus the symbols and images employed in theological discourse are rooted in the felt
experiences of these intimations. "No symbol or proposition can *mean* for
us, and so communicate to us and be intelligible, unless it is a thematic
expression of some lived experience. This is, to be sure, an 'empirical' view
of meaning. In this view, symbols can not just be 'revealed' and communicate anything to us."[40] Out of the lived and felt experience that silently
apprehends the larger dimensions of human existence, symbols or images
take on their essential task—a task that psychology or philosophy cannot
carry through.[41] It is important to Gilkey that the grounds for religious
symbols be found in ordinary experience, and through that experience he
discovers what he calls "the unconditional ground of coherence," which
does not appear on the surface of secular life where nothing sacred, numi-
nous, and ultimate shows itself. But if ordinary experience is the ground of
symbols, it seems clear in a secular age that one is permanently shut off
from transcendence or "the unconditional ground of coherence" by the
same ordinary experience. It must rather be that an uncommon type of
experience is possible if one is to advance to the felt experience of the
transcendent. Gilkey admits as much when he notes that "when men have
become aware of it [the sacred], it has never felt like ordinary experience,
as if it were merely a part of the ordinary sequence of natural or historical
events." The sacred, although experienced in connection with the profane,
has been "demarked as a special kind of experience."[42] So our awareness of

the ultimate has a transcendent sense and a knowledge that the surface experiences of life do not yield. But Gilkey wants to make his point even clearer. He states that "the sacred is apprehended in and through the structural elements of secular life." To put the matter even more precisely, the symbolic forms take on meaning only if they are understood to be answers to the questions of ordinary life. In summary, the author lays out the function and the sole meaningful usage of religious symbols: "To point beyond the finite referent of which it is a sign to the sacred and the ultimate that is there manifest: to 'disclose' through this manifestation the ultimate questions and crises of life; and lastly, to provide models and norms by which our freedom, individual and cultural, can guide itself."[43]

Gilkey presents a richly fashioned case for the importance and function of symbols or images in relation to the secular. However, we notice that much of what is symbolized does not apply to God. Rather, we are repeatedly referred to experiences of transcendence, coherence, the sacred or ultimate, which themselves need not necessarily be taken as references to God, since in their symbolic character these terms may apply to realities other than God. In fact, religious discourse, as Gilkey concludes, is not "directly talk about God," and he blames this need for indirection on the fact that human beings cannot know God as he is in himself, and therefore have no "experienced base or content" upon which to draw. If this assumption is accepted, the possibility of ascertaining the truth of symbols or images of God would be precluded, since one would not know if even indirect talk about God was pointed in the right direction. But if transcendence and the sacred, which he maintains are experienceable, are appropriate to God's nature, then it must be that there is some "content" upon which that judgment is based.

A theme that recurs in Gilkey's work particularly applies to biblical images of God. It is the common-sense observation that religious reality appears only in secular or worldly experiences. In contrast to Farrer's elaborately filigreed theology of images, Gilkey centers on the relevant fact that symbols and images originate in and do their work within the commonplace structures of human life. If there is a supernatural domain completely separate from the world we know, it is impossible to conceive it without the aid of the natural world. And in fact, it always appears in that natural world. But if we intend to use the word *supernatural*, it seems best to employ it to refer to that sense of this word where broader and deeper meanings suffuse the immediacies of what Heidegger called "everydayness." In this sense Gilkey could appropriately designate the experiences of transcendence, coherence, or sacredness as supernatural if he so chose.

The Christian ethicist James M. Gustafson finds that religious symbols and images "interpret the significance of circumstances and events in which human action is required." Because they emerge from the religious experience, "they enable the interpreter and others to perceive profoundly important dimensions, characteristics, and meanings in what is occurring. These dimensions are intrinsically related to the perceptions of the reality of God."[44] Even more important is Gustafson's claim that these perceptions are confirmed by religious experience.[45] But this claim is far too naive to enjoy the author's indiscriminate approval. Thus he lays aside as the primary question of Christian moral action the inquiry "what is God doing?" because, since every experience of God is mediated and not direct, "all perceptions of his presence are opaque."[46] In this judgment he is at one with Gilkey's notion of the sacred as refracted through ordinary and secular events. The uncertainty about God's actions, however, is compounded by Gustafson's insistence upon what he calls the "multidimensional" character of the experience of God's reality.[47] It would appear, and our study of biblical images themselves will confirm it, that the human experience of God is indeed multidimensional to the point of confusion—although that is not the conclusion to which Gustafson came. Rather, in spite of the mediated, multidimensional character of the experience of the deity, he does assert that God is real, purposive, powerful, and good.[48] In a context derived from this understanding, symbols are developed and used to clarify moral and human values when these are at stake and for which action is deemed necessary.

Gustafson does not spend time on the question of how symbols are formulated, but rather, like Niebuhr, he discusses the criteria for the selection of symbols. What is especially important is the rationalistic and pragmatic way in which he treats this subject. There is little of the poetic in his method. First he speaks of selecting symbols. Although they may be taken from the Bible, tradition, and general experience, the author's primary interest does not rest there. Selection is made in the light of several criteria. After demonstrating the inadequacy of several alternative grounds for selection, Gustafson offers four tests. First is the theological norm of God's good will for creation, and the ways in which the symbols elucidate the fact; second, the symbols must be relevant to the events and circumstances that they interpret; third, the symbols ought to be tested by ethical concepts "warranted by the symbols and the experiences of the religious community"; and finally, there is a social test, which means that symbols must be open to the investigation and criticisms of other interpreters who are engaged in the same kind of study.[49] He admits that this method is relative, private, and insufficiently rational, but within the limits of his academic discipline of ethics, Gustafson has come to grips with the possibility of bringing symbols under some theological and ethical control without disturbing their authentic literary integrity. Images or symbols are the means by which the experience of God takes form in such a way as to provide the interpretive and invigorating structures for the Christian moral life.

In a book that purports to defend the truth of the "faith once and for all delivered to our fathers," Julian N. Hartt also offers a compelling and articulate case for the use of the imagination and images in religious knowledge. He strongly opposes the notion that "world-viewing" by means of images is essentially aesthetic. Christian faith, he maintains, is a world view that employs the image of the kingdom, a world in its entirety under the sovereignty of God. Whether this image, or any other found in the Christian faith, is of human invention or of divine derivation, the author puts aside. But also in sympathy with Farrer, he claims that there is no logical anomaly involved in calling an image God's gift or even the substance of revelation. However, he is not ready to travel the whole distance with Farrer's interpretation, since he admits that the significance of such claims is not clear. Hence the issue must be left hanging. Hartt's treatment of images in connection with the problems of theological method, which he addresses, is perceptive and impressive, for he ranges through literature and assorted alternative views of the theological enterprise, but the substantiation of the validity or truth-bearing power of images is never satisfactorily made. What we have at last is a functional view of images—certainly not a view to be lightly spurned—as they play their part in helping us to make sure of existence in the fullest and deepest sense, even when human existence is faced with catastrophe. "Images," he concludes, "are the ordained instruments for organizing the elements and energies of the self in the face of incomprehensible events, the better to preserve, or attain, that unity without which the world itself is a 'sound and fury, signifying nothing.' "[50] But by whom or by what power are images "ordained"? And do images come into play only when "incomprehensible events" lower over human life? There is no satisfactory answer to the first question, unless we are to believe that Hartt has indeed accepted Farrer's idea of God-given images.[51] If events are incomprehensible, then what happens to the truth-yielding capacities of images? The truly incomprehensible, it would seem, could not even be envisioned in an image, to say nothing of constituting the substance of a concept. Since Hartt's aim is to make a case for a fairly orthodox theology, whose objective is "to discover and propagate the truth about ultimate reality," such truth certainly should not at last be revealed to us as the incomprehensible.[52] Nor, by his sophisticated and skillful handling of argument does he leave the case in such straits. But one may still be confused as to the origin and validity of Christianity's dominant images, even when a rational demonstration of the existence of God is offered.

A further matter that concerns our inquiry arises when, as in the case of both Hartt and especially Farrer, an orthodox position fixes certain images once and for all as the criteria of Christian or religious faith. The possible discovery of other more appropriate symbols and images would seem to be necessary for a living faith. This possibility Gustafson pointed out when he wrote, "There is a continuing process of resymbolizing and reconceptualizing the reality of God and his relation to creation and history in the light of new experiences." For this reason the authority of religious symbols can never be absolutely fixed, once and for all.[53] It is entirely in conformity with the development of biblical images of God that the dynamic interplay between human life and the deity assumed certain forms in specific situations that were in other settings put aside. When some images become dominant in a religious faith, we probably should be alarmed at the threat of a rigidity that has not only seized upon the mind, but by that means has also succeeded in harnessing the intractibility and dynamism of deity. Perhaps one of the functions of religious images is that they provide the novel and freer expressions of human engagement with God, thus preventing living experience from premature hardening into dogma, or beyond that into an intransigent dogmatism, a disease not unknown among liberal as well as more orthodox religious folk.

A survey of the interpreters of images and symbols shows that no one definition of either has clearly won the field. We do find that for several of the authors symbols and images are treated as identical, but in spite of differences of opinion, some agreement among the parties has emerged. Images arise from both sensate and nonsensate experiences, and in both cases the imagination is the instrumentality by which the image or symbol is formed. For some, these literary figures well up spontaneously without cause, while for others they are carefully crafted metaphors. Images, more than symbols, are likened to "pictures" in the mind, which vigorously seize the attention of human beings, swaying the emotions and will as prosaic language fails to do. Images distort what they purport to represent, but they are also held, in differing ways, to convey truth about the objects of experience. They are not mere fantasies operating in a mental and social vacuum. They are grounded on experiences of the world, even when they speak of "realities" transcending those experiences. As such they can direct thought and behavior, subject to criteria drawn from the communities and traditions by which they are surrounded. Religious images arise naturally in worship situations, where they convey the impact of engagement with the sacred or ultimate afforded by those situations. Therefore they are the media by which religious faith lives a truth borne out by biblical images of God.

NOTES

1. *Works of Jonathan Edwards*, vol. 4, *The Great Awakening*, ed. C. C. Goen (New Haven and London: Yale University Press, 1972), 236.

2. Cf. Frances A. Yates, *The Art of Memory* (Chicago: The University of Chicago Press, 1966), 278. On Puritan use of images, see Robert Daly, *God's Altar* (Berkeley, Los Angeles: University of California Press, 1978).

3. Edwyn Bevan, *Symbolism and Belief* (New York: The Macmillan Co., 1938), 25. "After the Iconoclastic Controversy of the eighth and ninth centuries, the Mosaic prohibition of images was qualified by maintaining that the Old Testament had forbidden idolatry because God is

not visible, but that the coming of Christ had revealed the physical nature of God." John Phillips, *The Reformation of Images: Destruction of Art in England, 1535–1660* (Berkeley, Los Angeles, London: University of California Press, 1973), 14.

4. Cf. Charles Hartshorne and William L. Reese, *Philosophers Speak of God* (Chicago: The University of Chicago Press, 1953), 419.

5. "There is a kind of sacred distance between man and God that is violated whenever a form of character connectible to human life is attributed essentially to God." Robert C. Neville, *God the Creator* (Chicago and London: The University of Chicago Press, 1968), 199.

6. Cf. Martin Buber, *I and Thou*, trans. Ronald Gregor Smith (Edinburgh: T. and T. Clark, 1950), 112. In another context Whitehead supports a similar view as he writes, "Hard-headed men want facts and not symbols," important as symbols are. Cf. Alfred N. Whitehead, *Symbolism, Its Meaning and Effect* (Cambridge: Cambridge University Press, 1928), 60, 61–62.

7. Cf. David Pellauer, "Paul Ricoeur on the Specificity of Religious Language," *The Journal of Religion* 61, no. 3 (July 1981): 264ff. For examples of the varied use of "image" among early church fathers, see Robert Javelet, *Image et ressemblance au douzième siècle* (Paris: Editions Letouzey et Ané, 1967), xxii; among poets, see Octavio Paz, *The Bow and the Lyre*, trans. Ruth L. C. Simms (Austin and London: University of Texas Press, 1973), 84ff.; in the Bible, see *Dictionnaire de spiritualité* (Paris: Beauchesne, 1977), 7, pt. 2, cols. 1401–6.

8. William Flint Thrall and Addison Hibbard, *A Handbook to Literature*, rev. and enl. C. Hugh Holman (New York: The Odyssey Press, 1960), 232.

9. C. Day Lewis, *The Poetic Image* (London: Jonathan Cape, 1947), 17, 18, 22.

10. Ibid., 107, 139.

11. Paz, *Bow and Lyre*, 85, 87, 92.

12. Cf. Gaston Bachelard, *La Poétique de l'espace*, 2d ed. (Paris: Presses Universitaires de France, 1958), 1–16.

13. "All religious facts have a symbolic character . . . every religious act and every cult object aims at a meta-empirical reality . . . every religious act . . . is endowed with a meaning which, in the last instance, is 'symbolic,' since it refers to supernatural values or beings." *The History of Religions, Essays in Methodology*, ed. Mircea Eliade and Joseph M. Kitagawa (Chicago and London: The University of Chicago Press, 1974), 95.

14. Mircea Eliade, *Image and Symbol*, trans. Philip Mariet (London: Harvill Press, 1961), 12.

15. Ibid., 15.

16. Ibid., 20. Paul Ricoeur also wanted to guard against the notion of the image's dealing only with the unreal. He wished to distinguish the play of imagination from image, "if by image is understood a function of absence, the annulment of the real in an imaginary world. This image-representation, conceived on the model of a portrait of the absent, is still too dependent on the thing that it makes unreal. . . . A poetic image is much closer to a word than to a portrait." *The Symbolism of Evil*, trans. Emerson Buchanan (New York, Evanston, London: Harper and Row, 1967), 13.

17. Eliade, *Image and Symbol*, 17.

18. Hume, *Selections*, ed. Charles W. Hendel, Jr., (New York, Chicago, Boston: Charles Scribner's Sons, 1927), 137.

19. Mary Warnock, *Imagination* (Berkeley and Los Angeles: University of California Press, 1976), 25.

20. Ibid., 26.

21. Cf. Frederick Copleston, S. J., "Kant," in *A History of Philosophy*, vol. 6, pt. 2 (Garden City, N.Y.: Doubleday Image Book, 1964), 51; Warnock, *Imagination*, 34.

22. Cf. Warnock, *Imagination*, 162–63, 198–99.

23. Ernst Cassirer, *Language and Myth*, trans. Susanne K. Langer (New York: Dover Publications, 1946), 8. Italics added.

24. Ibid., 58; *The Philosophy of Symbolic Forms*, trans. Ralph Manheim (New Haven, Conn.: Yale University Press, 1955), 2:38.

25. Several other lines of evaluation of Cassirer can be suggested by the following comment: "Scholars who have proved at length that primitive man has a 'prelogical' mode of thinking are likely to refer to magic or religious practice, thus forgetting that they apply the Kantian categories not to pure reasoning, but to highly emotional acts." H. and H. A. Frankfort, John A. Wilson, Thorkeld Jacobsen, *Before Philosophy* (Hammondsworth, Middlesex: Pelican Books, 1951), 19; or the authors of *Vico's Science of Humanity*, ed. Giorgio Tagliacozzo

and Donald P. Verene, also complain of Cassirer's failure to provide a logical basis in the image between the particular and the universal. (Baltimore and London: Johns Hopkins University Press, 1976), 315. See also articles by Susanne Langer and Wilbur M. Urban in *The Philosophy of Ernst Cassirer* ed. Paul A. Schilpp (Evanston, Ill.: The Library of Living Philosophers, Inc., 1949), vol. 6.

26. Wilbur M. Urban, *Language and Reality* (New York: The Macmillan Co.; London: George Allen and Unwin Ltd., 1961), 580.

27. "All symbols, that is, all images taken from intuitive domains and applied to other domains of experience, require that the intuition shall be moulded so that there shall be some distortion of the intuition if it shall represent symbolically or indirectly that which itself is not immediately intuitable." Wilbur M. Urban, *Humanity and Deity* (London: George Allen and Unwin Ltd., 1951), 103–4. Cf. also his *Language and Reality*, 582ff.

28. Urban, *Language and Reality*, 582, 613. "Thus, while both the names for God Himself and for His attributes and activities have a symbolic element, there is an element in all religious knowledge which is non-symbolic, namely the direct knowledge or intuition of this reference to an 'overworld.'" 606.

29. Cf. Urban, *Humanity and Deity*, 238, 220.

30. E. C. Rust, *Nature and Man in Biblical Thought* (London: Lutterworth Press, 1953), 81.

31. Urban, *Language and Reality*, 12.

32. H. Richard Niebuhr, *The Meaning of Revelation* (New York, Boston: The Macmillan Company, 1941), 107.

33. Ibid., 106.

34. Cf. Ibid., 99–102.

35. Austin Farrer, *The Glass of Vision* (Westminster: Dacre Press, reprint ed. 1958), 43.

36. Ibid.

37. Ibid., 61.

38. Cf. ibid., 136; also Farrer, *A Rebirth of Images* (Boston: Beacon Press, 1963), 13, 18.

39. Cf. Langdon Gilkey, *Naming the Whirlwind* (Indianapolis and New York: The Bobbs-Merrill Co., 1964), 306ff.

40. Ibid., 273.

41. Cf. Ibid., 391, 419.

42. Ibid., 446.

43. Cf. ibid., 456, 464.

44. James M. Gustafson, *Can Ethics Be Christian?* (Chicago and London: The University of Chicago Press, 1975), 130.

45. Ibid., 123.

46. Ibid., 157.

47. Ibid., 138.

48. Ibid., 139. "The heart of religion is the experience of the reality of God, mediated through all sorts of other experiences." 179.

49. Cf. Ibid., 142–43; see also 130–43.

50. Julian N. Hartt, *Theological Method and the Imagination* (New York: The Seabury Press, 1977), 250. Cf. also 14, 15.

51. Cf. Ibid., 16.

52. Ibid., 18.

53. Gustafson, *Can Ethics Be Christian?*, 129.

2
Biblical Images of God: Sources and Functions

What has been said of images generally bears upon biblical imagery. In respect to the mental processes that create images, as to literary structure, purpose, and function, biblical images exhibit no peculiar features. They, like all images, could be said "to stand for some larger meaning or set of meanings which cannot be given or not fully given in perceptual experience itself."[1] Yet biblical images of God inhabit a different world from that of exuberant poetic creativity. Theirs is a realm where God is a reality encountered, and the profundities of human life are at stake. And this sphere evokes quite extraordinary claims while arousing deep loyalties and passions. It is not the place for calm, dispassionate reason, for it is freighted with the pathos of deeply felt concerns. "Pure thought," as Paul Ricoeur observes, "makes no appeal to any myth or symbol," for it leaves "everyday reality outside."[2] But biblical imagery does not leave everyday realities "outside"; they are integrated into its very essence. They are part and parcel of the domain of worship, which suffuses even the most prosaic parts of Scripture.

This religious ambience has led historians of religion to seek within it for the source of the images it spawns. In spite of warnings that the search for sources of images is a fruitless one (e.g., Bachelard, Eliade, Ricoeur),[3] the quest has gone on. Eliade, for example, has himself claimed that religious images bring to light certain primordial archetypes somehow embedded in the "transconscious."[4] These archetypes are the "modalities" of being itself, which the images exhibit. But the "being" to which he refers stands at some distance from the lively, vigorous God depicted by the Bible. And one biblical scholar takes exception to such an attempt when he points out, "The symbol does not arise from the primordial experience of man as man, but rather from the historical experience of the community for which the symbol has meaning. . . ."[5] Furthermore, Eliade's view leaves unexplained the apparent mutual inconsistencies and transitoriness of images that supposedly are based upon permanent, normative archetypes.[8]

Nor is the search for the sources of biblical images of God more successful when the theologian Farrer shortcircuits the process by asserting that
Christian images are God-given. His conviction is a human judgment and
does not bear on its face any compelling reason for its acceptance beyond
that with which tradition invests it. The fact that images have been
changed or eliminated by human use suggests that God has failed to protect them from manipulation or interpretation in the course of history. In
the light of this undeniable fact Farrer's insistence that the images he
selects are not subject to change has a hollow ring. "Neither prophets nor
apostles," he claimed, "are inspired to devise new master-images. That is
an impossibility."[7] But this way of thinking leads to a creedal formulation
that would constrict the freedom of the God to which the biblical images
attest.

So the puzzle about sources remains, never better expressed than by
Augustine in his "Confessions." "I found Thee not there among the images
of corporeal things; and I came to those parts to which I have committed
the affection of my mind, nor found Thee there. And I entered into the
very seat of my mind . . . neither wert Thou there. . . . Place there is none;
we go forward and backward and there is no place . . ." (10:25–26). Yet he
was convinced that it was from the senses that images took shape. "Who
can tell how these images are formed," he wrote despairingly, "notwithstanding that it is evident by which of the senses each has been fetched in
and treasured up?" (10:8). Here he offered one clue to the source of images
that applies to the Bible. Even images of God take from the sense world a
major portion of their data, without which they would lack comprehensi-
bility and communicative power. It has been observed that "the revelatory
sphere of special history cannot be wholly discontinuous either with the
nature of finite being who is to receive it or with the finite experience and
language through which he must express and interpret it." So, for example, to image God as loving "it is necessary to have some understanding of
what love means in man's experience."[8] With this truism the quest for the
sources of biblical images must begin. If God is experienced or revealed, as
the biblical images surely show, it is not first of all by access to some
supernatural realm, but rather in the world of sense and time-space.[9] To
whatever heights one may be lifted by the experience of God, the elements
of the daily world are never cast aside. They continue to give substance to
religious ecstasy and frame the literary reports of it.

Three principal ways in which life experiences have been the source of
images may be detected in the Bible. First among these is the naturalistic
realm. This term is intended to encompass two related elements, objects
possessing mass but subject to cultural creativity, such as towers, houses,
shields, and the like, all of which depend upon the second element, nature
untouched by human fabrication or control. Nature in its proper sense
includes two types of entities, the human, physical body and nature as

external to human corporeality. In various ways God is imaged in all these aspects. In fact, the realism, particularly of the Jewish Scriptures, is so manifest that to read off its images of God is to recite the daily life of the Hebrew people as interpreted by the biblical authors. In so doing a network of images appears that vividly communicates even today.

When God is imaged in the form of a human body, the second source of divine images is found. This is the area of anthropomorphism, in which God is pictured as having physical form and features. Passages that represent God in this way are often passed over or explained away as the products of a crude stage of religious development found only in the earliest strata of biblical writings. The more "spiritualized" or "idealized" ideas of God are presumed to be superior to those which stress the physical or sensate aspects of the deity. The result has been to accept a less realistic understanding of the Bible and a deprecatory view of the natural world, which limits God's sovereignty to the spiritual and moral needs of humanity. The New Testament, which in part is responsible for this view, was not itself above daring to make of the human Jesus the incarnate God, and it recites examples of his physical resurrection. Apparently the idea of God in human form was not demeaning to God, but a way of dignifying mankind's physical nature.

Anthropomorphism did not bear the full weight of God's impress upon the people of the Bible. It was, however, the third, and in many ways the most important source of images. The imagery of this kind had its origin in human personality, although that was never far from anthropomorphism. The capacities of reason, wisdom, will, and feeling were laid under tribute, as were the ethical aspects of human beings. Nor were these capabilities always seen as exercised in a morally elevated way. Many images of God ascribe reprehensible acts to him, acts that are reprehensible in human beings. And it will not do for Christians to reserve to the New Testament only those features of God palatable to the modern conscience. A Jewish scholar points out that the Bible begins with a loving God of the Covenant and ends with "depart from me and there will be a weeping and gnashing of teeth."[10] Growth in religious and ethical sensitivity apparently does not go hand in hand with chronological development.

Anthropopathism enters into another phase when sociohistorical roles are used for imagery. Preeminent among these is that of king. Understood against the background of Near Eastern conceptions of kingship, this image includes notions of creatorship, guardian, or lord over a particular people and land, as well as power and glory associated with sovereigns. Thus the political experience of biblical peoples provides a crucial interpretive device for their experience of God. "The concept of Yahweh as a king," writes one Old Testament scholar, "would hardly be adopted by the Israelites until they themselves had got a king, and, with him, an obvious occasion to bestow on Yahweh this highest title of honor."[11] By parity of reasoning it is legitimate to suggest that the images of God as warrior, judge, lawgiver, and covenant-maker are drawn from the social experience of various historical periods as known to the biblical authors and editors. The importance of these images lies in the emphasis they provide for a God of history, not simply one approached by individuals in isolated privacy.

In pursuing further the source of images, we encounter a formidable difficulty, because we lack the means of reproducing the mental processes by which the images have been created. And in that sense the search for sources ends in a blind alley, for we have only the products of religious imagination, separated from us by centuries. That fact has not hindered scholars from diligently seeking out the thought world of the ancient Hebrews and early Christians, but in doing so conjecture must be piled upon conjecture, each of which, once regarded as "the assured results of biblical scholarship," has a way of being eroded by new or different insights and sources of information. But a fundamental uncertainty about biblical thought processes haunts this scholarship, carefully wrought though it is. Manuscripts, scrolls, books, monuments, and relics are consulted, and comparative judgments based on similar products of cultures contemporaneous with the biblical sources are made. And everything turns upon guesses as to whether minds worked then as now. To adopt this principle is not to claim that the materials with which the ancients found their world furnished are identical with those now employed. The images themselves count against that supposition. Rather we are forced to assume that the processes of the human mind have not markedly changed from biblical times to our own, lest we give over all possibility of understanding the images of God, and lock ourselves into the limits of our own historical epoch. We may never successfully enter into the moment of intuition when, for example, an ancient Hebrew pictured God as a rock, but we can understand the meaning of the image.

However, one source of images stands out on the pages of Scripture, that of worship. By that word is signified not only formalized worship in a temple or church, although some parts of the Bible bear the indelible marks of cultic activity. In a broader sense worship penetrates all levels and literary genres found there (historical writings, narrative, legal prescriptions, poetry, gospel, epistle, and homily). Worship means a sense of divine presence before whom destiny-filled issues are raised and answered. The biblical authors believe that they themselves or those about whom they write have been confronted by deity in an impressive manner. An objective reality has impinged upon them in so convincing a way that even prosaic language as well as poetic utterance can give vent to their experience. As John Oman once expressed it, "religion is an illusion, unless it has an objective reality which has witness convincing to ourselves, and not merely heard of from others."[12] So it must have been with the creators of images who, whatever their doubts, felt compelled to write of God with vigorous imagery. No arguments for his existence or attributes intervene between believer and deity. He was present, at least at some points, in such awe-inspiring authenticity and power that He could not be denied[13]—except for the fool, whose corruption blinded him from witnessing what for others was evident (Ps. 48). To describe this state of affairs no word is more suitable than *worship*.

Worship led in two related but distinct directions. One was that of soteriology, expressed by the question, "What shall I or we do to be saved?" God, imaged as covenant-maker, lawgiver, judge, or savior, was the answer to cries for freedom from the myriad dangers and evils that affect human existence. The other direction is the enjoyment and glorification of God, the one by whom the promise of salvation is fulfilled. And again, in the mood of self-transcendence that marks worship, images break forth that are traceable to their origins in worship. But images express worship in many forms as well. They are functions of worship. These images function like all images: they particularize and make determinative what otherwise would be expressed in less arresting forms or mere ejaculatory utterances. In brief, dramatic form, appealing to the imagination of the reader, they give insight and illumination. However, in accomplishing this they simplify, in this case the experience of the divine. Irrelevant details are excluded from the image. God imaged as a rock stresses the shelter, not the weight of the rock. Christ as the lamb of God does not emphasize the stupidity of a sheep, but its defenselessness. By the constriction the image places on sensuous and ideational materials, it focuses and clarifies what is to be said about God or Christ. It brings together in one literary unit disparate elements of experience where the subjective response to the deity takes place. It is a "clearing" in the thicket of a language made virtually inchoate by sheer richness of experience. The function of illumination can be understood only against a background that itself is dark or opaque. It is by virtue of that darkness or opaqueness that the light of the image may be seen to shine. Mystery provides the necessary contrast. But mystery is not unintelligible. The image, as it were, radiates significance. It sends out rays of understanding that bring into intelligible focus that which it does not totally "com-prehend." Thus the biblical images of God, while clarifying his nature, also determine what kind of mystery is manifested in the religious encounter.

Biblical images also serve as mediators. They link experience of the world and the self together with the experience of God, and the latter is interpreted within the context of the former. This is the point made by emphasis upon the thisworldly source of images. Admittedly, an interpretive act has intervened, since it is doubtful that experience of anything, including God, remains uninterpreted. However, the underlying reality affects the way in which the interpretation will go. The image provides a middle step between sheer immediacy and inference or conceptualization.[14] Latent within the image lies a cognitive function. The image, in spite of its limitation or distortion, claims to tell some truth about God. This truth is not the kind of propositional truth found in discursive language, but comes from a pictorial representation. As Aristotle said, "The soul never thinks without a mental picture."[15] In this sense those who defend images or symbols as vehicles of revelation may be correct, since imageful and symbolic rhetoric, rather than discursive locution, conveys truth in Scripture. This is what Hartt meant when he stated, "Nowhere in the Old Testament is knowing God primarily an intellective-cognitive affair."[16] Knowledge or truth is too intimately felt to be subject to abstract reasoning (see chap. 5). Yet there are those who would emphasize the intellective aspect of images by treating them as embracing hypothetical claims. Images as metaphors are seen as awaiting further confirmation.[17] Others would deny the importance of the cognitive aspect of images because of the great investment that personal faith puts in them.[18] The tentativeness that hypothetical reasoning calls for is far removed from the deep involvement the religious believer has in the image prior to any "experiment" or verification. However, images are fertile in hypotheses for philosophers and theologians. But in the context of worship this hypothetical factor is suppressed.

Images function in still another way. They are essential to the communal memory of a people. They are ingredients in what H. R. Niebuhr called internal history, first of the Hebrews and then of the nascent Christian community. They bind together the past and present and become the practical devices of communication, as well as norms of thought and practice. Thus in the history of Christian doctrine what has been called the Old Roman Symbol was transmuted into the Apostles' Creed, serving to highlight those beliefs held to be crucial to Christian faith and restricting membership to those who accepted those beliefs. The images found in this symbol provided coherence of belief, molded the affective life of believers, and in some instances shaped the social organization of the church. The contentions of a sociologist are not far wrong when he argues that "the organization of social life is importantly related to prevailing imagery about 'God' and imagery about man." Although he does not limit the term *God* to its biblical connotations, he contends that such imagery "rationalizes" and maintains "social solidarity and stability." These images warrant and sanction social structure and provide compensatory mechanisms.[19] In spite of this author's overemphasis upon God "as a sanctioner of social values and organization," his interpretation of one of the functions of images cannot be denied. The images of God have far too often been reduced to that level without thought of the prophetic and revolutionary imagery that abounds in the Scripture.

NOTES

1. Philip Wheelwright, *Metaphor and Reality* (Bloomington: Indiana University Press, 1962; Midland Book ed. 1968), 92. For this author's typology of symbols, see Norman Perrin, *Jesus and the Language of the Kingdom* (Philadelphia: Fortress Press, 1976), 84–85, n. 91.

2. Paul Ricoeur, *The Symbolism of Evil* (New York, Evanston, London: Harper and Row, 1967), 347.

3. Cf., e.g., Francis M. Higman, *The Style of John Calvin in his French Polemical Treatises* (London: Oxford University Press, 1967), 124–25.

4. In referring to Jungian theories of archetypical images, Hartt remarks, "A preference for images of depth rather than for images of height may tell us more about psychocultural predilections than about anything else." Julian N. Hartt, *Theological Method and Imagination* (New York: The Seabury Press, 1977), 257, n. 5. This insight bears directly upon Eliade's view.

5. Norman Perrin, *Jesus and the Language of the Kingdom* (Philadelphia: Fortress Press, 1976), 62.

6. Cf. James M. Gustafson, *Can Ethics Be Christian?* (Chicago and London: The University of Chicago Press, 1975), 128.

7. Austin Farrer, *The Glass of Vision* (Westminster: Dacre Press, reprint ed. 1958), 136.

8. John E. Smith, *The Analogy of Experience* (New York, Evanston: Harper and Row, 1973), 20, 44.

9. "We are finite creatures and cannot be anything else. Whatever we know of God will also be finite." John Y. Fenton, "Being-Itself and Religious Symbolism," *The Journal of Religion* 45, no. 2 (April 1965): 81.

10. Cf. Robert Gordis, *Judaism in a Christian World* (New York: McGraw, Hill, 1966), 136–37.

11. S. Mowinckel, *The Psalms in Israel's Worship* (New York, Nashville: Abingdon Press; Oxford: Basil Blackwell, 1962), 1:125. Cf. Perrin, *Jesus and the Language,* 80.

12. John Oman, *The Natural and the Supernatural* (New York: The Macmillan Company, and Cambridge, England: The University Press, 1931), 26.

13. Cf. G. Van Der Leeuw, *Religion in Essence and Manifestation,* trans. J. E. Turner (London: George Allen and Unwin Ltd., 1938), chaps. 1 and 17.

14. Cf. John E. Smith, *Experience and God* (New York: Oxford University Press, 1968), 52ff. Smith introduces the idea of interpreted experience, wherein the medium of disclosure is "related in an intimate way to the reality it discloses."

15. Cf. Frances A. Yates, *The Art of Memory* (Chicago: The University of Chicago Press, 1966), 32: In mythopoetic language "the imagery is inseparable from the thought." H. and H. Frankfort, John Wilson, and Thorkeld Jacobsen, *Before Philosophy* (Harmondsworth, Middlesex: Penguin Books, 1951), 15.

16. Hartt, *Theological Method,* 139.

17. Cf. Earl R. MacCormac, *Metaphor and Myth in Science and Religion,* Durham, N.C.: Duke University Press, 1976), 93; cf. Lyman T. Lundeen, *Risk and Rhetoric in Religion* (Philadelphia: Fortress Press, 1972), 192–93.

18. John E. Smith, *Experience and God,* 53–54. Cf. Clyde A. Holbrook, *Faith and Community* (New York: Harper and Brothers, 1959), 36, 37.

19. Cf. Charles Y. Glock, "Images of 'God,' Images of Man and the Organization of Social Life," *Journal of the Scientific Study of Religion* 1, no. 1 (March 1972): 3, 4, 5.

3
Worship, Transcendence, and Biblical Images

The contention that worship provides the ambience in which images of God flourish is most clearly supported by those passages of Scripture where God is directly addressed as present. Many of the Psalms, sections of the prophetic literature and Gospels, where prayers for help or adoration of the deity occur, illustrate the intensity of fervent worship. The intensity of these passages found its characteristic literary form in vivid images of God. But images growing from I- or We-Thou relations also find their way into accounts of God's dealing with Israel and the Christian community. In these passages, couched in less poetic language, God is referred to in the third person. Yet they are replete with the same images to be found in portions of Scripture when God is regarded as immediately present. Thus it may be concluded that the atmosphere of worship suffuses much of the Bible. As Wohlfahrt Pannenberg says, "All biblical speech about God . . . is rooted in adoration and is in this sense doxological."[1] In both cases, people are made aware that they stand in the presence of the determiner of their destiny, or more precisely, that God has serious business to transact with them. Whether in rebellion or in acquiescence to his will, the central point of reference is God. And the images used reflect the fact that the meetings with God have taken place where people have been in a state of elevated consciousness, beyond that of normal consciousness, best described as transcendence of the self.

Worship in Scripture can be found oriented to two poles. One, to be designated subjective worship, directs attention to the human individual and social situation. The human subject or the group, with its purposes, needs, hopes, and fears, receives the emphasis. Benefits are sought from God, among them freedom from danger or death, release from frustration, disappointment, and moral debility, or victory over foes, peace, courage, and wisdom. The common signs of this kind of worship are petitions and intercessions. "Hear our prayers, O God"; "Save this people"; "Remember us for good"; "Give us this day our daily bread"; "Deliver us from evil";

"Teach us"; "Grant us," etc. The worship of God in passages of this type is not an end in itself. Rather God is worshiped as the one from whom some good is anticipated, and at its lowest level this worship becomes a form of religious utilitarianism in which God is primarily regarded as a means to the satisfaction of human desires and needs.

The other pole of biblical worship finds God worshiped for his own sake. Attention is not centered upon human subjects, but upon the divine object. The intrinsic worth of God fills the religious horizon. Nothing is sought, no effort is expended in manipulating God's will or human emotional states. God is adored for his glory, power, beauty, and sheer existence. As the Westminister Confession put it, one "enjoys" *God*, rather than the feelings that ensue from this kind of worship. The height of worship is reached in giving over oneself unreservedly to the deity. This objective worship expresses itself in such phrases as "Praise the Lord," "Hallowed be thy name," "Thine is the power and the glory forever," or the words of Jesus in Gethsemane, "not what I will, but what thou wilt." The words of Habbakuk best express it. "Though the fig tree do not blossom, nor fruit be on the vines, the produce of the olive fail and the fields yield no food, the flock be cut off from the fold and there be no herd in the stalls, yet I will rejoice in the Lord, I will joy in the God of my salvation (3:17, 18). Precisely because objective worship points away from the human dimension toward the One who stands over against mankind, it produces profound and lasting effects upon the worshiper. A. E. Taylor had the right of it when he claimed, "The regenerating moral effect of our religion on our conduct is most genuine and profound when the direct object of our attention is not the self and its tasks, but God."[2] Similarly, Jonathan Edwards could write, "the first objective ground of gracious affections is the transcendentally excellent and amiable nature of divine things, as they are in themselves, and not any conceived relation they bear to self, or self-interest . . . what makes men partial in religion is, that they seek themselves, and not God, in their religion, and close with religion, not for its own excellent nature, but only to serve a turn."[3] It was his objectivistic preaching and theology, he thought, that had had the most powerful emotional effects upon the sensibilities of his hearers, rather than appeals to their affections.

Probably there are few examples in public worship in the Judaic or Christian traditions where only one of the poles of worship is manifested. Ordinarily the two emphases appear together. For example, a prayer in the Scottish Collect of 1595 reads in part: "Most Potent King of Kings and Lord of Lords, whose glory is incomprehensible, whose majesty is infinite, and whose power is incomparable: maintain thy servants in quietness and grant that we may be so settled on the certainty of thy promises. . . . " Here the glorification of God for his own sake directed the believer's mind away from the self, and yet it is followed immediately by petitions. A cynic might conclude that effusions of tributes like these, poured out upon the deity, are unnecessary, he being whatever he is without need for anything from finite human beings. They might be seen as flattery, a low form of sycophancy, demeaning to both God and worshiper. But this concentration upon subjective worship does injustice to human needs. Subjective worship to be sure has bulked large in the history of religions because, as we have seen, the soteriological question is a prominent part of religion. The hope and confidence that salvation in some form is to be expected from the gods or God cannot be ruled out. However, it is unfortunate that some sociologists of religion have fastened upon subjective worship as the only true clue to the interpretation of all religion. Regarded in this way, Edwards's talk of the worship of God as an end in itself would be absurd. And the austere glorification of God for his own sake, posited by the biblical religions, would be otiose. Consequently, if objectivistic worship is taken account of, it is regarded as merely a respectful introduction to the petitions soon to follow. Yet, without the presence of objectivistic worship, religious faith could easily sink to the depths of crass utilitarianism and forfeit its highest and most compelling moments. Certainly worship as presented in Scripture blends the two emphases and, for the most part, escapes the baser level to which subjective worship can descend.

Whether it is considered subjective or objective, biblical worship involves transcendence. But transcendence, from which images spring, is itself difficult to describe, for its significance lies on both sides of the subjective-objective polarity. On the one hand, it applies to an attitude of the self, and on the other, it summons up the idea of the Transcendent as an object of thought or worship. True, both terms, self-transcendence and the Transcendent, bear the sense of "going beyond" some time-confined present patch of sense or mental datum to a new datum previously unavailable or unrealized. So in mental acts such as the exercise of memory, self-awareness, imagining, or the invention and manipulation of signs, symbols and images, we are in the precincts of self-transcendence. Without them we would be less than human.[4] Self-transcendence has been persuasively described as "the belief that there is more in our experience of the world than can possibly meet the unreflecting eye. . . . " Without it "even at the quite human level of there being something which deeply absorbs our interest, human life becomes perhaps not actually futile or pointless, but experienced as if it were."[5] By means of self-transcendence, the imagination opens indefinite ranges of experience, among which are the images found in worship.

The term *the Transcendent* conveys a different meaning from self-transcendence. It refers to "a beyond," a realm usually contrasted or paired with "the Immanent." The Transcendent is viewed as an object of consciousness, an ontological reality, rather than consciousness itself. Beyond the precincts of the secular, the ordinary, or the worldly, the Transcendent exists or subsists, not however always treated as a religious reality. Thus the transcendentals of Medieval Philosophy stood for the basic structure of metaphysical realities, although they were not in themselves sacred or holy objects. However, *the Transcendent* has come to be used in a religious or theological context as a substitute term for God, although Scriptures give scant support for this usage. A further confusion crops up when self-transcendence is elided with *the Transcendent,* or more vaguely, transcendence. Whereas self-transcendence as an act of human beings seems empirically comprehensible, *the Transcendent,* used of God, causes a gap between that which is clearly experienceable in daily life and that which one theologian identified as incomprehensible by definition.[6]

A variety of efforts has been made to close the distance between self-transcendence and the Transcendent. William A. Johnson, for example, holds that there is little difference between the two views. "Whether transcendence is conceived of in a philosophical sense (as that metaphysical realm above the rational) or in an ordinary sense (as that phenomenon or experience found within the natural world, but which appears to point beyond that world), the meaning is about the same."[7] If this is the case, then ontological transcendence is collapsed into self-transcendence or perhaps vice versa. The metaphysical gap posed in the religious experience simply vanishes. However, it can be noted that a gap still exists when Johnson allows that self-transcendence points beyond the world. In this opinion he is joined by Peter L. Berger, who counted self-transcendence as providing "pointers to" or "signals" of the Transcendent.[8] In a similar vein Hans Küng believes that human self-transcendence posits a "really other dimension" unavailable on the merely human level, in his rhetorical question, "Does not genuine transcending presuppose genuine transcendence?"[9]

Certain difficulties immediately emerge. In the case of Johnson's solution, where the distance between self-transcendence and the Transcendent itself is lost or overcome, we have a psychological function quietly transformed into an ontological dimension or reality. This conversion smacks of the idealism of Bishop Berkeley's dictum, "To be is to be perceived." Thereby the psychological act of perception assumes a causal character, a debatable issue at best. It confers reality upon the Transcendent, although we are familiar with the fact that perception does not of itself guarantee or create the reality of that which is perceived. The case is no better with language that interprets self-transcendence as offering clues to the Transcendent. We would have to know in advance that the "pointers" or "signals" correctly direct us in the right direction, but in terms of traditional theological wisdom, this prior knowledge is impossible, unless the mystic's claim is justified.[10] Furthermore, since self-transcendence offers so many confusing claims, many of which lead to tragic and evil ends, it becomes difficult to decide which among these pointers directs us to a "good" Transcendent. Ambiguity persists, especially when one attempts to sort out those which point to a personal Transcendent as opposed to an impersonal Transcendent.[11] As one author observed, "Experiences of transcendence are not all experiences of creativeness."[12] In fact, "the Transcendent" would seem to be a mass of contradictions or have opaqueness and indefiniteness patient of anything the religious imagination cares to deposit there. Self-transcendence certainly plays a large part in worship, but it does not of itself certify the presence of the Transcendent as such.

Another attempt to bridge the gap between self-transcendence and the Transcendent is offered by a theologian who has given much thought to those matters. Roger Hazelton has laid down a fundamental principle about transcendence generally. It "no longer can be used by theologians to mean God's total otherness from everything natural and human," in order to refer "to that which is beyond all time and space, unknowable and absolute and eternal." It does not serve to distinguish between "man" and "God."[13] The gap between man and God is closed because being transcended and transcending, as well as immanence and transcendence, are always given together in experience. "Why may not man's self-transcending capacity be properly expressed as God's immanent activity in him?" Hazelton asked in his presidential address before the American Theological Society (Homo Capax Dei). In a conciliatory move in Feuerbach's direction, he was willing to maintain "that God, or, better, transcendence is what human experience means."[14] The process of translating the divine into human terms, he admitted, is not a simple task, but by giving up the notion of an "outsider God" apart from self-transcending humanity, one does not surrender a whole range of meanings.[15] Apparently some remnants of an independent God remain after the translation is effected. What the differences are between human qualities and this God is not clear, but Hazelton is confident that "transcendence, even if its right name should turn out to be God, has nothing to fear from self-transcendence."[16]

When held up to the perspective given by the biblical images of God, some compatibility can be seen between this view and the Bible. By containing transcendence in both senses within a thisworldly ambience, Hazelton has approached the mind-set of many of the biblical authors. God, as he sees it, is experienced as transcendent within the world—what other alternative is there? However, we are also less than sure that in the last analysis he has shed light on biblical imagery. He may assert, without substantial grounds, that immanence and transcendence are always given in one and the same experience, but how does one tell the difference between them? This is no more than to state the obvious fact, mentioned above, that all experience takes place in the world. It tells us nothing of the nature of that which transcends us, not even that God is different from our sense of self-transcendence. Biblical imagery largely rests upon the supposition, or better, the experience, of a God at some distance from man. There is a radical difference between the means by which man experiences God (self-transcendence) and the object of that experience. Instead of converting psychological functions into ontological reality, as the previous authors have done, Hazelton seems to have reversed the process by virtually converting an ontological reality into self-transcendence, and thereby offering an anthropocentric rather than a theocentric perspective.[17] Or to put the matter differently, no way remains to distinguish God from mankind, either in thought or worship. Transcendence has become immanence in spite of the veiled implication that self-transcendence cannot, without remainder, be identified with God. We are not sure in what way the independent reality of God has been salvaged. In arguing that immanence is a new way of talking about the Transcendent, we may have been treated to the common fallacy that supposes to perceive or experience things differently amounts to perceiving and experiencing different events and objects. By rearranging the meaning of self-transcendence, giving it his own interpretation, this author has led us to believe that we are dealing with a different God, not merely a different idea of God. In the process the impression persists that the terms *the Transcendent, transcendence,* and *immanence* are devoid of any specifiable differentiated meanings. Certainly no objection can be made to the development of new ideas of God, but something is strange when the word *God* becomes another word for human experience. But Hazelton offers good advice in respect to his own position when he writes, "Language must not be taken to legislate reality questions."[18]

The gap between God and the world of humanity, which the preceding views have attempted to bridge or ameliorate, has been treated as an ontological breach. But biblical images, being literary conventions, suggest not only the ontological gap, but also a verbal one, in which, as poets and worshipers know, words are seldom capable of carrying the full weight and richness of experience. The recognition that flat, literal prose does not do justice to the heights and depths of experience, including religious worship, is not only a truism, but it indicates the discovery of a gap that symbols, ritual, and images strive to overcome. Insofar as they accomplish this purpose for religious faith, they do not serve as fanciful adornments, but as interpretations creating new attitudes and situations. They report what is taken as reality, as being worthy of reverence and productive of hope, awe, fear, sadness, and so on. However, it is important to see that the gap between expression and experience, between image and "fact" is not necessarily indicative of an ontological gap. The verbal gap between words and the fullness of experience exists whether or not there is a transcendent being or realm. The ontological gap postulated in much religious literature is itself based upon a mental picture or image, if you will, of the universe's having an "outside." This cosmological picture, which has nurtured the idea of "the Transcendent," is apparently not to be regarded as a piece of antiquated mythology. Modern common sense has not cast it aside; it still colors the religious imagination, whatever the astrophysicists may say. But as a modern philosopher has pointed out, "If the universe is everything that is, then to think of the other side of it is always to think of nothing. If God is a being, then he is part of the universe in this sense. The other side of existence is necessarily empty."[19] The remarkable fact, at least for much of the Old Testament, is that the images that suggest transcendence are obviously earthbound. The "more than" of which their self-transcendence was aware did not drive the people we find depicted in those passages to positing an ontological reality separate from their world. Except in apocalyptic literature, they did not create, for the most part, an unbridgeable gap between themselves and the deity. "The underlying support and reinforcement of the Jewish sense of God lies . . . profoundly in a this-worldly and present life experience of theistic reality."[20] In short, much of the Old Testament imagery, although it contains the verbal gap, is not based upon an "outside" God or a two-world background. Where God is pictured as transcendent, it is not a metaphysical transcendence that is in question; it is the religious and moral distance from God that is expressed. God is independent; he is not swallowed up in self-transcendence; he is objectively real as that power which stood obdurately over against Israel. The scenes of wonder, the physical aches and pains, the healings as well as storm and drought, are evidence of One who is in and with his world, even as he looks at it "from above." He transcends, but he is not "the Transcendent." Israelites did not worship the Transcendent; they worshiped a living God.

New Testament imagery, as we would expect, retains the verbal gap, and with it something of the Hebrew Scriptures' sense of God's intimate relation to and care for the world, probably best expressed in the parables and sayings of Jesus in the Synoptic Gospels. The transcendence of God is assumed, as in "Our Father, who art in Heaven," but where distance of God from his world or people comes to the foreground, for example, "Why hast thou forsaken me?", spiritual and ethical rather than ontological distance is present. God is present, although hidden. But the metaphysical gap comes to dominate the thought world of Paul and other New Testament writers, where the mediating presence of Christ alone between man and God emphasizes the fact that God exists in a transcendent realm. From this perspective, the early Barth launched his attack on liberal theology with talk of "the vertical dimension" from which God in Christ "strikes into history," as if there were an "outside." Within the Christian Scripture the Gospel of John perhaps best exemplifies this two-world idea, although even there the imagery is confused. Christ, a sometimes strange, unearthly figure, yet occasionally revealing human qualities, stalks its pages. He comes into the world from an "outside," overcoming the gap, and by that fact at the same time underlining its existence. Those who believe in him will be saved out of the world, even if it is not clear what "world" is meant. To be saved from the world with its disbelief and blandishments is the goal of the new life, but a foretaste of the new eternal life is possible within this world. Reference to "the spiritual hosts of wickedness in the heavenly places" (Eph. 6:12) underscores the two-world view, as well as the dangers lurking in the transcendent realm, which is not always benign.

The ambiguities attendant upon the word *transcendent*, used in a religious sense, moved one author to conclude: "Clarity of thought will dictate that God should not be mentioned in connection with radical transcendence. . . ."[21] Perhaps in a less than radical sense of transcendence one may be permitted to refer to God as transcendent without adoption of a transcendent cosmology. Worship certainly involves self-transcendence in the creation of its images. In some parts of Scripture the images used did assume a transcendent realm external to the world known in everyday experience. In these instances a gap is present between the earthly basis of the images and God. In other parts of the Bible, most notably in the Hebrew Scriptures, transcendence is not metaphysical or ontological, but rather a way of expressing spiritual and moral differentiation between God and human beings. In both cases, whatever form of transcendence is intended, the images of God bespeak the irreducibility of deity to an aspect of human consciousness. His transcendence in Scripture is the objective reality of an "other than," not the "distance from" that cosmology suggests. It is with that transcendence that worship is engaged. It is from self-transcendence that images flow in attempting to describe it.

NOTES

1. Quoted by E. Frank Tupper, *The Theology of Wohlfahrt Pannenberg* (Philadelphia: The Westminster Press, 1973), 59.

2. A. E. Taylor, *The Faith of a Moralist* (London: Macmillan and Co., ltd., 1951), 2:68.

3. *The Works of Jonathan Edwards*, vol. 2, *Religious Affections*, ed. John E. Smith, (New Haven, Conn.: Yale University Press, 1959), 393–94.

4. Cf. Clyde A. Holbrook, "The Ambiguities of Transcendence," *The Christian Century* 92, no. 43 (December 24, 1975), 1118.

5. Mary Warnock, *Imagination* (Berkeley and Los Angeles: University of California Press, 1976), 202–3. "There is in all human beings a capacity to go beyond what is immediately in front of their noses. Indeed, there is an absolute necessity for them to do so." 201.

6. Bernard Cooke, "The Current State of Theological Reflection," *The Bulletin of the Council on the Study of Religion* 10, no. 2 (April 1979): 39.

7. William A. Johnson, *The Search for Transcendence* (New York: Harper-Colophon, 1974), 2.

8. Peter L. Berger, *A Rumor of Angels* (New York: Doubleday Anchor, 1969), 55ff. Also "Cakes for the Queen of Heaven: 2500 Years of Religious Ecstasy," *The Christian Century* 91, no. 43 (December 25, 1974): 1220.

9. Hans Küng, *On Being a Christian*, trans. Edward Quinn (Garden City, N.Y.: Doubleday and Co., Inc., 1976), 58.

10. See Ronald W. Hepburn's use of this argument in his devastating attack upon Karl Barth's interpretation of the Grünewald painting of Jesus, believers, and the realm of God, *Christianity and Paradox* (London: Watts, 1958), 79.

11. Cf. Rudolph Otto, *The Idea of the Holy*, trans. John W. Harvey (London, New York: Humphrey Milford, Oxford University Press, 1925), appendix V.

12. Roger Hazelton, *Ascending Flame, Descending Dove* (Philadelphia: The Westminster Press, 1975), 59.

13. Ibid., 97, 113. "A theology of creative transcendence will have no new limits to draw between God and man; that will be the least of its concerns." 125.

14. Ibid., 107.

15. Cf. ibid., 107–8.

16. Ibid., 125.

17. For the moment I bracket the question raised by those interpretations of Christ which see him as overcoming the "gap" by his entry into history "from above."

18. Ibid., 113.

19. Robert Roberts, "The Feeling of Absolute Dependence," *The Journal of Religion* 57, no. 3 (July 1977), 253, n. 1. Cf. Gabriel Marcel: "Beyond all experience, there is nothing; I do not say merely nothing that can be thought, but nothing that can be felt." *The Mystery of Being*, ser. 1, *Reflection and Mystery* (Chicago: Henry Regnery Co.; London, The Harvill Press Ltd., 1950), 47–48.

20. Cf. John Bowker, *The Religious Imagination and the Sense of God* (Oxford: Clarendon Press, 1978), 102. "It would make no sense to say that the human transcends the physical world, or that God transcends the universe, if in each case they were not involved in that which they transcend." G. W. H. Lampe, *God as Spirit* (Oxford: Clarendon Press, 1977), 207.

21. Roberts, "Feeling of Absolute Dependence," 266.

4

Images or Symbols?

No attempt has been made thus far to distinguish between images and symbols. Both can be easily subsumed under the category of metaphor. In verbal form and literary function they appear to be similar. So in dealing with figures which are at least verbal cousins, it would seem to be hair-splitting to seek distinctions where no substantive differences occur. Yet everyday use of the words *symbol* and *image* suggest a distinction that carries a difference. People are accustomed to speak of an entity as *symbolizing* something else in situations where the less common word *imaging* would be out of place. On the other hand, *symbol* is not used where *image* is suitable. A son's resemblance to his father does not *symbolize* the parent, but *images* him, so there is the colloquialism, "He is the 'spitting image' of his father." In some respects it appears that the two terms function in different ways, in spite of their obvious similarities.

Theories about the distinction are not uncommon. Unfortunately, one term is sometimes defined by the other. "A symbol is an image which evokes an objective concrete reality and has that reality suggest another level of meaning."[1] Here, *symbol* uses an image to bring about a *reality*, but little is clarified about either term. Similarly, a literary critic holds, "A literary symbol is a way of directing the reader's intellectual and emotional attention . . . by means of an image . . . to an area of experience that cannot be directly described in any other way without loss of meaning."[2] In both instances the word *symbol* is inclusive of *image* by having a broader meaning. On the other hand, a clear distinction between the two is suggested by C. Day Lewis. "An intense image is the opposite of a symbol. A symbol is denotative: it stands for one thing only. . . . Images in poetry are seldom symbolic, for they are affected by the emotional vibrations of the context so that each reader's response to them is apt to be modified by his personal experience."[3] Schelling's distinction between the two terms describes an image as a "concrete, particular thing or picture" deliberately used as an illustration, whereas a symbol "is not deliberately chosen. It is naturally symbolic."[4] Another philosopher takes a different tack in describing symbols, when he argues that attempts to explain every expression in language or art as a "symbol" are misguided. "The symbol is a final abstraction, a rational simplification of something more differentiated. . . . Symbol is always a means and always a means for an end, its so-called signification. . . . As a symbol, a limited entity stands for another limited entity, and it is just this which makes the symbol accidental, conventional, and arbitrary." He continues by stating that "symbols simplify in substituting a part for a more complicated whole, make the part a whole and let this whole stand for the other whole which is meant."[5] It is doubtful that this rendering of symbols would be totally acceptable to Cassirer or Urban, or more particularly to religious thinkers like Eliade, who with his "modalities of being" revealed in images, contended that images or symbols are not arbitrarily or conventionally chosen. What he calls "the exemplary models," an expression that seems to stand for the enduring symbols, are initiated in images that reproduce, reactualize, and are repeated "without end." Instead of simplifying by bringing into one focus the reality imaged, the image as such, Eliade believes, has a whole bundle of meanings, no one of which is completely true.[6]

The distinction between image and symbol may be better clarified in Paul Tillich's treatment of religious symbols. His analysis, sometimes in contrast to those of the interpreters of poetic imagery and symbolism, has the advantage of being squarely set in the framework of the religious quest. Philosophical theologians of persuasions other than his, of course, may reveal the nature of this fundamental religious orientation by alternative analyses of religious symbols. This is to be expected, since no theological treatment of symbols or images is capable of escaping entirely the presuppositions of faith with which they are organically united. Symbols in general, Tillich maintained, point beyond themselves, while at the same time they participate in that to which they point. They open levels of reality otherwise closed off, and unlock dimensions and elements of the soul that correspond to the various levels and elements of reality. They are not produced intentionally. Rather they grow out of the individual or collective unconscious. Nor can they effectively function unless they are accepted by the unconscious dimension of selves. Symbols grow, develop, and even die, in the last case not because of scientific or practical criticism, but because they no longer produce response in the group wherein they originally found expression.[7] Tillich further contended, as he moved into the area of religion proper, that religious symbols were necessary expressions of man's ultimate concern on the grounds that "the true ultimate transcends the realm of finite reality infinitely." Faith has no other language than that afforded by symbols. The word *God* is itself "the fundamental symbol for what concerns us ultimately." Indeed, if the word *existence* refers to what can be found within the whole of finite reality, no divine being "exists." The qualities we attribute to God, such as love or justice, are drawn from the realm of finite experience, but they are applied symbolically to that which is beyond finitude.[8] When these ordinary features of the mundane world are employed symbolically, they must never be taken in a literal sense. Rather, in Tillich's view, "every religious symbol negates itself in its literal meaning, but affirms itself in its self-transcending meaning."[9] This insight is tellingly used in his development of the meaning of Jesus Christ for Christian faith.

Only one nonsymbolic statement can be made about God, we are told in the first volume of his *Systematic Theology*. There he wrote that God as being-itself is "a non-symbolic statement," since it does not point beyond itself.[10] However, in the face of criticism of this assertion, and upon further thought, he relinquished that position when he wrote in his second volume that "everything we say about God is symbolic."[11] With this later affirmation he seems to have drifted off into the realm of pansymbolism, and thereby lost, as Urban contended to the contrary, the possibility of affirming anything directly or nonsymbolically about either God or Being-itself.[12] Critics have pointed out that these two terms are not necessarily identical in meaning, but Tillich went on to identify Being-itself with God. God is the "ground of the ontological structure of being, without being subject to this structure himself. He is the structure; that is, he has the power of determining the structure of everything that has being."[13]

The personal pronoun *he* has now been introduced, affecting the other characteristics of God. But warning is given that it is improper to refer to God in any nonsymbolic fashion. Thus if it is said, "God lives," symbolically we mean "insofar as he is the ground of life." However, when God is spoken of in a religious mood, a shift from the ontological language is proper. Anthropomorphic symbols are adequate for speaking of God religiously.[14] In fact, "man cannot be ultimately concerned about anything that is less than personal." But reference to a personal God is a confusing symbol, for what one actually means to say is that God is the ground of personality. But having conceded this much to personalistic symbolism, Tillich nevertheless contended that "only that which is unconditional can be the expression of unconditional concern. A conditioned God is no God."[15] But personalistic symbols come into play when this unconditioned Being is described with words such as creativity, love, and justice, terms that in turn are symbolized as Lord and Father. However, in his sermons and his book *Love, Power and Justice*, theological and ontological language gives way to concrete examples, stories, and images expressive of the divine nature.[16]

Tillich's treatment of the idea of God in relation to symbolism could be used as a way of showing that it is impossible to be an atheist, although some critics have charged him with being responsible for the "Death of God" movement and being himself an atheist! His way of outflanking the radical doubter, and those who could no longer believe in what they took to be the absurdities of Christian doctrine, was to direct their attention to what he called the God above God. This Being beyond the gods of the theists, the one whom the atheists denied, remained unscathed by criticisms. The phrase *the God above God*, he held, was not intended as a suggestion to surrender all traditional symbols and to escape to a direct encounter with the transcendent Being. Rather, "the term is meant as a critical protection against attempts to take the symbols literally and to confuse the images of God with that to which they point, the ultimate in Being and Meaning."[17] While protecting the imageless character of the deity, he continued to defend the use of symbols and images. The terms *symbol* and *image* appear to be identical when he addresses those in radical doubt who are uneasy about "the Christian images of God." "Transcend the symbols," he counsels; "they themselves want you to do so. That is what they demand."[18] To those who would claim that God is only the projection of the self, he used the term *image* to explain that the realm against which the divine images are projected is not itself a projection. It is the experienced ultimacy of being and value. Here the mystical element comes to the foreground. When a direct, intuitive apprehension of God beyond all symbols and images is emphasized, a flood of images might be anticipated, since the mystical consciousness is notoriously prolific in translating the indescribable into vivid figures of speech. Important as the mystical strain was to Tillich's total position, he nevertheless maintained a critical and selective attitude toward it.[19] Hence images do not crowd the pages of his *Systematic Theology*, although at times they surreptitiously intrude in the midst of technical argument.

His theory of symbols is so intimately intertwined with his theology that unless a critical look is directed at some aspects of his theology, the problems that symbols present would remain unclarified. In the end, the distinction between images and symbols would also be less intelligible. The controlling presupposition of Tillich's entire theological undertaking is that there is one entity, the ontologically transcendent, available to human experience, yet distinct from the realm of identifiable finite beings. "Being-itself is beyond finitude and infinity" is one way he had of expressing this insight.[20] Without it the whole theory of religious symbols falls to the ground. It is not defended philosophically or theologically. It is the *pou sto* situated outside the framework of the theoretical structure he has erected. Once more a "gap" may be detected between the realm of finite beings and the ontologically transcendent domain, and insofar as it can be bridged, symbols are the only legitimate means available. How they do so is not clear. The "participation" he attributes to symbols lies essentially beneath the linguistic form of the symbols. It may be asserted that "participation" exists, and it may well be the case, but how this participation takes place is never clarified. It is merely affirmed. The explication of the participation in Being-itself is the task of symbols. No universal language can accomplish this task without turning Being-itself, or God, into a finite being alongside all other finite beings in the world, that is, without turning God into no-God, in Tillich's view. But this figurative notion that the "world" or the "universe" has an "outside," a world beyond the world, although commonly held in various forms in both Hebraic and Christian traditions, is an odd way of expressing transcendence, and it creates problems for establishing the validity of symbolic language.

One of the consequences of such a position is that the relation to this world of the unconditional transcendent becomes moot. As one critic put it, "It is false piety to place God beyond the realm of beings, for that places him beyond the reach of those philosophical principles we need to relate God intelligently to the world and to our situation."[21] In the same vein another critic says, "The much noted extremity of Tillich's views on symbolism seems to stem from the extremity of his view on God's transcendence."[22]

Furthermore, since Tillich seems launched upon a course of pansymbolism, all talk of God falls into circular argument, since no nonsymbolic statement can be made about the deity.[23] He has turned his back upon the contention of Urban, who insisted that all symbolic religious knowledge incorporates an element of the nonsymbolic. That author claimed that without "some literal knowledge of divine things symbolic knowledge is an illusion."[24] From a similar point of view Tillich has been criticized because he has provided no nonsymbolic method of interpreting symbolic statements by which to decide whether such statements refer to anything at all. If they do, one is not enabled to discriminate between more or less adequate symbols of God or Being-itself. "No sense can be made of symbolic statements unless we know *how* they refer. If no non-symbolic rule of interpretation is provided, we are unable to distinguish more appropriate symbolic statements about Being-itself from less appropriate symbolic statements about it. God could not be distinguished from a stone."[25] To claim, as Tillich does, that symbols point to a referent and at the same time that the referent is not a being but Being-itself, provides little aid in solving the problem. We are left with what one critic saw as a *via negativa*. Tillich's criteria give little basis for determining the direction in which the symbols point. The negative criterion of "not being a being" is too unspecific. Because of this imbalance this critic concluded, "Tillich's *via symbolica* becomes a *via negativa*."[26]

Tillich was well aware of such criticisms, and particularly those which charged him with failure to do justice to biblical language, which as I have already intimated, arises in a different atmosphere from that found in theological constructions. "The philosophical language I am using in my theological work," he wrote, "has often been critically contrasted with the concrete imagery of the biblical language." The essence of his defense against this charge was to argue that biblical symbols, as he called them, drive one to ontological questions, for example, questions about Being-itself, and to remind his readers that theological answers necessarily contain ontological elements.[27] Here he refers to his method of correlation, whereby the questions implied in human existence are formulated and answered by theology in the light of divine self-manifestation.[28] Biblical symbols and imagery do presuppose ontological considerations for the philosophical theologian. Whether they did so for the biblical authors is another matter. Tillich's attempt to legitimatize his translation of symbols and images into ontological terms, on the grounds that ontological factors are implicit in the symbols and images, fails to take account of the meaning such figures had in their own time and continue to have for some people today. The effort to convert biblical language into another idiom blanches out the vividness with which God is portrayed in the Bible. As theologian, Tillich offered Being-itself in place of the dynamic deity of Scripture, a concept that brought down upon him the kinds of criticism we have seen. The Transcendent God beyond God we are invited to contemplate is a singularly vacuous and colorless entity, of which either nothing or everything can be said. It is a magician's hat from which any number of symbols or images can be drawn at random unless there is some controlling principle. And interestingly enough, as we shall see, it is biblical imagery that introduces that principle of interpretation. Tillich, of course, recognized that biblical images of God could not easily be incorporated into his idea of God. "A static ultimate and the living God are obviously incompatible. But being-as-such has neither static nor dynamic implications. It precedes any special qualification. It points to the original fact that there is something and not nothing, and to the power of that which is to resist non-being."[29] It might be noted that the idea of "power" here assigned to God has its rootage in the images of power repeatedly used in Scripture. It may further be noted that a God as being-as-such, possessing neither static nor dynamic attributes, that is, having no determinate qualities except power (and if it is power it must manifest itself in particular ways) is scarcely identical with the biblical deity.

Tillich's way of meeting this difficulty is to claim that no type of religion operates without personifying the encounter with the holy. Items of finite reality mediate this experience. And in fact, everything in various degrees can become a medium of revelation. So objects in nature, culture, and history, as well as principles, categories, essences, and values may be intermediaries of the encounter.[30] But when they are so, a personal imagery intrudes. Biblical ideas of nature and history, however, are never first inert and then personified. The world they inhabited, especially as seen in the Old Testament, was not inflexible. It was always alive and filled with evidences of God's personal will. When the Frankforts contrasted modern with ancient man, they argued, as did Buber, "for modern, scientific man the phenomenal world is primarily an 'It'; for ancient—and also for primitive man, it is a 'Thou.' "[31] It need not be assumed that the Bible, without remainder, represents the thought of primitive men, nor need it be supposed that the term *primitive* refers to some past chronological period. It remains with us if we choose to use the word, as a part of human experience of the world, as it was of the biblical authors. If the world does not seem to the modern consciousness to be invested with personal attributes, it and God do exist as active, as the thought of Whitehead and his successors have made clear. To this degree they come closer to biblical imagery than does Tillich.

I have previously alluded to Tillich's contention that nothing less than the personal can be of ultimate concern to human beings. He was willing to go as far as to argue that we do not first of all know what "person" means before applying the term to God. "In the encounter with God," he stated, "we first experience what 'person' should mean and how it is distinguished from, and must be protected from, everything a-personal."[32] He is skeptical of using the term *personification*, since here he accepts the personal encounter as being real and genuine in religious experience. One need not, therefore, fabricate the idea of "person" and then impose it upon God. If this is the case, why translate the idea of God back into the sober language of being-as-such? The proper locale of the word *God*, it might be held, is in religious experience, that is, worship, not in metaphysics.[33]

Tillich well knew that the personal terminology of the Bible did not agree with his own. In his list of the ways God and man interact, he recounts some of the biblical images of God. "God commands; man obeys or disobeys. God plans; man cooperates or contradicts. God promises; man believes or disbelieves. God threatens; man reacts with fear or arrogance or change of heart. And God's attitude changes accordingly."[34] It is difficult to escape the conclusion that if words mean anything, it is simply nonsense to claim that being-as-such or "the power of being" does all this. What we actually see here is that for Tillich images must be brought to the speculations of philosophical theology for authentication. When one deals with biblical religion, the concreteness of images takes over. Nothing better illustrates this truth than the sermons of Tillich, where the images come into play in the context of the pulpit and worship. The underlying theology is still present, but it takes on substance and vitality as Tillich the preacher uses biblical images and stories, and offers illustrations to round out the texts he employs.[35] He turns to the Bible when the existential issues of life are at stake. Certainly there is nothing wrong in translating theology back into images. What is important is the emphasis that must be placed on images as the instrument by which the translation takes place when dealing with religious, in distinction from philosophical and theological matters. Although the two arenas of experience should not be totally cut off from each other, neither should they be totally assimilated to each other. Ontological factors are implicit in imaginative language, but neither does the job of the other.

One example of the way images enliven even the most abstract speculations of a philosopher is found in the cosmological reflections of Whitehead. Like Tillich, this philosopher found that the best way to clarify his formidably dense prose was to describe God's consequent nature in figures drawn from human emotions. "The image—and it is but an image—the image under which this operative growth of God's nature is best conceived, is that of a tender care that nothing be lost." The judgment of God in the world, he further suggested, is "a tenderness which loses nothing that can be saved—a judgment of wisdom which uses what in the temporal world is mere wreckage." This is a God of "infinite patience."[36] Here the philosopher called upon the deposits of worship nurtured by awareness of biblical images.

Has this exploration of Tillich's treatment of symbols in connection with his theology brought us closer to the answer to the question of "symbol or image?" Pansymbolism invites problems. At times Tillich drew a line between symbols and images. And his sermons indicate that imagery, as well as symbolism, is pertinent to the expression of the religious consciousness. These clues are significant, but nowhere does Tillich carefully draw out the differences between symbol and image. In fact images, at times, seem swallowed up in the category of symbol. They are alike linguistically as metaphors, but images seem to have a sharpness of focus and a precision of reference that is lacking in symbols, as Tillich used that term. For example, in one place he referred to the word *God* as a symbol. As such, as we have seen in his theology, it is a term with a wide variety of meanings. It brings into focus no particular aspect of deity. To take another example, which Tillich might call a symbol, the cross; if anything in Christianity is a symbol, it is the cross. But of what is it a symbol? It expresses sacrificial love, love to the point of suffering, pain and anguish, humility under suffering, and death. It brings to remembrance the life and ministry of Jesus. It provides a pattern for the Christian life. It brings into view the new life of the resurrection through death. It can also depress the mind by its accent upon the sins of mankind, which bind Jesus to the cross and cause his death. It reminds humans that crucifixion is the fate of innocence and virtue in this world. The cross also acts as a symbol for those outside the Christian fold. It symbolizes the persecution and death carried out in its name upon infidels and Jews. Wide, indeed, is the range that this symbol manifests. From it radiate innumerable meanings, no one of which exhausts its meaning, nor does any one or a group of meanings produce complete agreement among Christians. So also the Apostles' Creed is a symbol, which does its work best when its meaning is not too clearly and dogmatically defined. Best leave it unanalyzed and uninterpreted! As Edwyn Bevan put it, "To say that all religious beliefs about events in the time-process are to be understood as symbols is really to assign value to the general, as against the particular."[37] It is the particular that the image gives.

But something is gained in the symbol that is lost in the image. By its imprecision of meaning, the symbol wins a generality and universality of acceptance that images lack. With the universalism of a symbol also comes a greater longevity or endurance than the image often enjoys. It perhaps better preserves for thought some remnants of "the felt characteristics of lived experience."[38] Images contract and focus meanings; symbols expand them. Images flesh out in pictorial and auditory ways the concreteness and vividness that symbols hint at or suggest. In this way they often operate as controls over the several meanings of symbols, now bringing to the foreground one aspect and then later bringing to the mind another meaning. Images force themselves upon the mind directly in the present; symbols resonate to the traditional historical authority vested in them. Symbols impinge the past on the present, whereas images rely for their effect on spontaneous recognition in the moment. Biblical images arise from direct contact with the world; they describe God as immediately accessible to the religious imagination.[39] Symbols, lacking the vivacity of images, tend to produce a less direct relation to the deity because their focus is less sharp. Symbols develop their power over time; images simply occur, compelling assent and understanding. The sharpness of detail in the image catches the imagination of the reader or listener; the symbol, deeply embedded in the traditions of the religious community, incites reflective interpretation and emotional attachment. Once created, images in some cases may, by continued use, become symbols, although in the first instance not intentionally created as symbols.[40] Symbols may be created out of images, but images are not created out of symbols. By a selective process, scarcely consciously undertaken, the symbol succeeds in maintaining itself, feeding upon the particular image from which it is drawn, by giving a wider yet less definite meaning to what the image presented. But no Christian symbol ever exhibits humor, as an image may. For example, there is a world of difference between the direct appeal made by Jesus' humorous image of the rich man's failure to enter the Kingdom (like the camel trying to go through the eye of a needle), and the symbol of Jesus on the cross. Indeed, for much of Christianity Jesus himself is universalized and has become a symbol. Even as no symbol invites laughter, neither does a demeaning or vulgar image of God make its way into the symbolism of Judaism and Christianity, although such images are frequently met in the Bible.

That symbols and images sometimes merge, that the term *symbol* often includes what properly can be called image, is not denied. However, in the light of biblical passages and the several distinctions noted between symbols and images, for which there seems to be adequate evidence in both Scripture and the works of Tillich and Whitehead, the word *image* seems to be the more satisfactory term to guide the selection and treatment of those biblical figures of speech which set forth the nature of deity.

NOTES

1. Wilbur Flint Thrall and Addison Hibbard, *A Handbook to Literature*, rev. and enl. C. Hugh Holman (New York, The Odyssey Press, 1960), 478.
2. C. Day Lewis, *The Poetic Image* (London: Jonathan Cape, 1947), 40–41.
3. David Daiches, "Myth, Metaphor, and Poetry," in *Essays by Divers Hands* (London: Oxford University Press, 1965), n.s. 33:48.
4. Mary Warnock, *Imagination* (Berkeley and Los Angeles: University of California Press, 1976), 68.
5. Cf. Martin Foss, *The Idea of Perfection in the Western World* (Princeton, N.J.: Princeton University Press, 1946), 71–72.
6. Cf. Mircea Eliade, *Image and Symbol*, trans. Philip Mairet (London: Harvill Press, 1961), 20, 15.
7. Cf. *Dynamics of Faith* (New York: Harper and Brothers, 1957), 41–43; *Theology and Symbolism in Religious Symbolism*, ed. F. Ernest Johnson (New York: Harper and Brothers, 1955), 108–11; *Religious Experience and Truth*, ed. Sidney Hook (New York: New York University Press, 1961), 301–21.
8. Cf. *Dynamics of Faith*, 44–47 passim; cf. William L. Rowe, *Religious Symbols and God* (Chicago and London: The University of Chicago Press, 1968), 129.
9. Paul Tillich, *Systematic Theology* (Chicago: The University of Chicago Press, 1957), 2:9. Hencforth ST.
10. ST, 1:238.
11. ST, 2:9.
12. "For those who claim that the justification of religious language is to be found in its symbolic nature, the acknowledgement that all language is symbolic turns their contention into a trivial one." Earl R. MacCormac, *Metaphor and Myth in Science and Religion* (Durham, N.C.: Duke University Press, 1976), 90.
13. ST, 2:239. Cf. Robert C. Neville, *God the Creator* (Chicago and London: The University of Chicago Press, 1968), 173. The author unconvincingly argues, in company with Tillich, that the power of being produces "determinations."
14. ST, 1:242.
15. Cf. ibid., 244, 245, 248.
16. Cf. ibid., 252–86ff. passim. *Love, Power, and Justice* (New York, London: Oxford University Press, 1954), 24–34.
17. The *B.B.C. Listener*, August 3, 1961, 172.
18. Ibid. "With the God above God Tillich tries to do what he elsewhere deemed impossible. He tries to express the *symbolizandum* of the symbol 'God' by another more explicit, less symbolic term, 'God above God.' The attempt fails." Adrian Thatcher, *The Ontology of Paul Tillich* (London: Oxford University Press, 1978), 86.
19. ST, 1:212. "Mystical exerience or experience by participation is the real problem of experiential theology," 44–45. Cf. James R. Horne, "Tillich's Rejection of Absolute Mysticism," *The Journal of Religion* 18, no. 2 (April 1978): 130ff.
20. ST., 1:237.
21. Lewis S. Ford, "Tillich and Thomas: the Analogy of Being," *The Journal of Religion* 46, no. 2 (April 1966): 244.
22. Robert C. Neville, "Some Historical Problems about the Transcendence of God," *The Journal of Religion* 47, no. 1 (January 1967): 7. Neville does concede that Tillich's theory of symbols "has served better than any contemporary alternative to keep before us an awareness of God's transcendence and mystery, while at the same time articulating a sense of the presence of mystery and transcendence in our lives."

23. Cf. John Y. Fenton, "Being-Itself and Religious Symbolism," *The Journal of Religion* 55, no. 2 (April 1965): 79.

24. Wilbur M. Urban, *Humanity and Deity* (London: George Allen and Unwin, Ltd., 1951), 238. Urban accepts what he takes to be Aquinas's meaning of the word *literal*, i.e., a synonym for "unconditional truth," as strictly and properly applicable to God. 240.

25. Fenton, "Being-Itself" 79–80. A similar conclusion is drawn by Paul Edwards, who argued that since Tillich's theology is compatible with any and all states of affairs, and his metaphors are irreducible to anything that makes literal sense, the whole enterprise is meaningless. Cf. Paul Edwards in *Philosophy of Religion, Contemporary Perspectives,* ed. Norbert O. Shedler (New York: The Macmillan Co., Inc., 1974), 186–205. Answers to Edwards may be found in William L. Rowe, *Religious Symbols and God* (Chicago and London: University of Chicago Press, 1968), 183–94.

26. Ford, "Tillich and Thomas," 244.

27. Paul Tillich, *Biblical Religion and the Search for Ultimate Reality* (Chicago, University of Chicago Press, 1955), p. vii. Henceforth BR. His scorn of what he terms "biblicism" is evident. "The attempt of biblicism to avoid non-biblical, ontological terms is doomed to failure as surely as are the corresponding philosophical attempts. The Bible itself always uses the categories and concepts which describe the structure of experience. . . . Biblicism may try to preserve their popular meaning, but then it ceases to be theology." ST, 1:21. But biblical authors were not, for the most part, trying to write theology in Tillich's sense of the word.

28. ST, 1:61.

29. BR, 16.

30. BR, 22–23.

31. Henri Frankfort, Mrs. Henri Frankfort, John A. Wilson, and Thorkeld Jacobsen, *Before Philosophy* (Harmondsworth, Middlesex: Penguin Books, 1951), 12.

32. BR, 27. See also 22–25.

33. The word *God,* John Wren-Lewis maintained, originates in worship, not from abstract thought. "The Doctrine of the Trinity," *B.B.C. Listener,* May 11, 1961, 837.

34. BR, 30.

35. Cf. *The Shaking of the Foundations* (London: S.C.M. Ltd., 1949); *The New Being* (New York: Charles Scribner's Sons, 1955).

36. Cf. Alfred N. Whitehead, *Process and Reality* (New York: The Social Science Book Store, 1941), 525. Examples of his distaste for divine images of coercive power, such as king or tyrant, and his preference for the persuasive aspects of deity are found in his *Religion in the Making* (New York: The Macmillan Co., 1926). Cf. 55–57, 67–76. "The ascription of mere happiness, and of arbitrary power to the nature of God is a profanation. . . . The various attempts at descriptions are often shocking and profane." *The Philosophy of Alfred North Whitehead,* ed. Paul A. Schilpp (Evanston and Chicago: Northwestern University Press, 1941), 697, 698.

37. Edwyn Bevan, *Symbolism and Belief* (New York: The Macmillan Co., 1938), 264.

38. Cf. Roger Hazelton, "Theological Analogy and Metaphor," *Semeia,* no. 13, pt. 2 (Missoula, Mont.: Scholars Press, 1978), 161.

39. G. E. Wright was in error when he claimed that man in the Old Testament "does not encounter the world directly. He creates, or has created for him, a world of symbols through which he experiences, interprets, and perceives 'truth' in the objects, processes, people, nations and cultural heritage in the midst of which he lives." Cf. *The Old Testament and Christian Faith,* ed. B. W. Anderson (London: S.C.M. Press, 1964), 183. The ancient Hebrews encountered nature and history far too directly in their daily lives to be interpreted now as gazing forever through a haze of symbols at what actually confronted them.

40. "Is there any important sense in which 'symbol' differs from 'image' and 'metaphor'? Primarily, we think, in the recurrence and persistence of the 'symbol.' An image may be invoked once as a metaphor, but if it persistently recurs, both as presentation and representation, it becomes a symbol, may even become part of a symbolic (or mythic) system." René Wellek and Austin Warren, *Theory of Literature,* 3d ed., a Harvest Book (New York: Harcourt, Brace and World, Inc., 1970), 189.

5

The Truth of Images

To raise the question of the truth of images invites the criticisms and warnings of the exponents of "poetic truth." Fearful lest rude hands be laid upon this unique province, they hasten to warn of dangers ahead. "The long course of literary activity," cautions one, "is strewn with the wreckages of artists lured to their doom by the siren songs of intellectual truth."[1] The conversion of poetic truth into the flat prose found in philosophical argument not only desecrates the literary form, but also leads to cloudy speculation to which there is no end. It is a throwing of dust into the air, which ends in the complaint that nothing can be seen. Instead of the clarity of truth which images bring, the investigator of their truth is left no wiser than when he started. And if, as some have claimed, the images are themselves divinely sanctioned, the attempt to ferret out their truth is nothing less than blasphemy. Did not the Lord say, "As I live . . . I will not be inquired of by you"? (Ezek. 20:3) In the face of these dangers is it not better to let images alone rather than to embark on a trail doomed to frustration from the outset?

The trail may indeed be hazardous, but images themselves implicitly purport to tell the truth about God once experienced. They lure one to ask the nature of that truth, as does religious faith itself. So it has been said that religion "loses its nerve when it ceases to believe that it expresses in some way truth about our relation to a reality beyond ourselves which ultimately concerns us."[2] Or in respect to the early Christians it has been observed that they wanted "to be reasonably well assured that the revelation of Christ and the holiness of the Spirit are really one with ultimate transcendent reality, if they were asked to count the world well lost for them."[3] When the weight of human destiny has been invested in the biblical images, the question of their truth is bound to emerge. Without truth the spiritual life languishes, for human beings live by knowledge as well as hope and faith. It may well be that no justification persuasive to all people will be found, but at least the grounds upon which images at some time were believed to be true can be explored in the light of present knowledge.

The first step toward ascertaining the truth of images would seem to be a

64

study of the original languages in which they were couched. However, this study has purposely been limited to one translation, and therefore, for good or ill, it depends almost entirely on the scholarship of its translators. One gratefully seizes upon the words of a biblical critic who admits that "the fundamental points of biblical assertion will normally be visible to those who do not know the original languages."[4] Mastery of the biblical languages may clear up meaning, but it does not follow that philological acumen decides the truth of what the Bible says. The meaning given to certain words by the translation is the basis of truth-judgments, but equally important is significance. If E. D. Hirsch, Jr., is to be believed, significance is to be distinguished from meaning. Whereas the meanings of words of statements do not vary, significances do. Hence, he claims, the meaning of an ancient text can be ascertained, whereas significance, properly used to refer to the relation between the meaning and a person, conception, or situation, changes in accordance with context.[5] Important as context is for significance, even that factor does not strike to the question of truth. An image understood in its religious and social context may have both meaning and significance, but reliance upon these to determine the validity of an image does not establish its truth. "It is one thing to see that language, even biblical language, has meaning; it is another thing to see it is true."[6]

Granted that context is important to understanding images, one feature of the biblical context is the world or cosmological picture. Biblical texts are not laden with speculation about the world scene, but behind the images there lurks an inclusive cosmic framework. In rough form this is understood to be a three-tiered structure made up of heaven above, the earth, and an underworld, more or less indeterminate in nature (sheol, watery deep, sustaining pillars). In this scenario God inhabits heaven and man the earth. This portrayal has so deeply entered into the sphere of piety that God's relation to what goes on in the world is cast in terms of a metaphysical metaphor. God's being "above" the earth translates into a transcendence that in turn makes difficult the possibility of discovering the truth of images about him. If God enters the world only at specific times and places, and then only obscurely, it is hard to see how any dependable knowledge or truth about him is possible. Thus to say that he only intermittently has connection with the world, or that he is "essentially hidden" or "indeterminate"[7] raises the question as to whether he is present to human consciousness long enough to provide sufficient acquaintanceship for these terms themselves to have any cognitive value.[8] If the cosmological background that informs such affirmations leads to these theological conclusions, one asks whether in fact the images support that view.

A more inclusive way to insure the truth value of biblical images is to pronounce that the entire Bible is the Word of God. Thereby all speculation about truth is answered by making all images of the deity true. This way is open to the literalist, but it burkes the question altogether. Liberally inclined scholars, taking the path of distinguishing the words of the Bible from the Word of God, also run into trouble in attempting to salvage the authority of the Bible. So one can write, "What authorizes the use of symbols and concepts is not the location of words (that is, in the Bible), as in fundamentalism, but God's decision to reveal what is 'real' through the events there recorded."[9] But this statement scarcely moves the question of truth any nearer to solution. The need to defend the authority of the Bible in this way still suggests that it is not so manifestly authoritative as to make the truth of its images immediately convincing. And if tradition is added to biblical authority, the case is not improved. The weight of centuries use of biblical images may give an impressive inevitability that may easily be taken for truth, but acceptance over time alone has not established truth. Tradition legitimizes the images, but does not vouch for their truth.

Theology may also be put forward as the proper judicatory of truth in religious matters, since "theology is not and never has been uncritical of its own subject matter,"[10] but to depend upon theologians is to wallow in a morass of conflicting claims. One theologian disdains "academic" theology, claiming that theology "is not done best in scholarly forms and artifices of the learned." Instead its purpose, at least in Christian terms, is to construe the Bible "as though it were addressed to sinners, not the curious . . . ," and this is a project in which the understanding emanating from historical study of the Bible is relatively useless. "Theology tells us what Christianity is and what and who God and we are," as addressed to "the passions of the human heart." As such, its final purpose is to make people godly.[11] The protest against the aridities of disengaged theological speculation is well taken, but the cavalier, if not dogmatic spirit, of the author in respect to the total theological enterprise serves to narrow the focus of theology. Like some other theologians, this one takes for granted that the revelation of God in the Bible is true. His conception of theology does not show how revelation is true, but how, given its truth, it is to be understood. On the one hand, he sticks to the fundamental religious nature of what in our case would be the images, but on the other, leaves the question of their truth unanswered. Theologians, he claims, are in no position to justify the processes by which words have acquired their meanings—"for justification is entirely out of order here."[12]

Another theologian freely admits that when Scripture is employed in theology, it is prefaced by a judgment made in independence of the study of Scripture. It is a decision made in entering upon theology as to what Christian theology is "and that is determined, not by the results of historical-critical biblical study, but by the way in which he tries to catch up what Christianity is basically all about in a single, synoptic, imaginative judgment."[13] The authority of Scripture enters the picture, and with it whatever justification for the truth of its images it gives, only in the light of presuppositions about Christianity as a whole. The source of this "synoptic" vision of all Christianity is left vague except by the further assertion that the church's common life is the "occasion and mode of God's presence," and therefore Scripture has authority over it.[14] This position is impervious to any "lack of theological unity" in Scripture, or to any cultural changes.[15] Biblical authority in this sense is not only integral to the church's existence, but also in fact depends upon the church's acceptance of it as authority. However, this seems at most to be an attempt to guarantee the authority of Scripture by an appeal to tradition and the conviction that God acts in the church.

One does not enter upon the theological enterprise simply with a holistic view of what Christianity is about. For some theologians another antecedent judgment has also been made, that about God. For our purposes that means that one must set about determining the truth of images in possession of the right idea of God. Otherwise, with ideas like that of an arbitrary tyrant or a kindly old man, human well-being and ethical conduct will be destroyed.[16] This "right idea," forged from centuries of religious experience and thought, serves as a criterion by which images can be tested. It has been known as the classic theistic view. In brief, it holds that God is a supernatural, supreme, eternal, omnipotent, omniscient, divine being, possessed of all good. He is a personal being who desires the salvation of his creation, and to that end has sent law and the prophets for Judaism, and decisively revealed himself in Jesus Christ for Christianity. Entirely different from nature and human beings, he dwells in deep mystery, yet he is filled with justice, mercy, and love for all. He is invisible to human eyes, and cannot be known by any means common to human understanding, which he infinitely surpasses. How then does the validity of biblical images fare when set against this theological outlook? Those images depreciative of God are immediately to be ruled out as false or at best inappropriate. But certainly it is wrong to impose the criterion of classical theism upon the biblical images, since it is the product of a historical and religious process in which certain ideas of God have already been winnowed out and others given pride of place. The Bible, however, knows no such criterion, and with apparent equanimity offers images of God ranging from the disreputable to the most elevated. Insofar as the classical view has achieved normative status, it has done so by drawing upon biblical images selectively, but at the same time claiming for itself the authority of the Bible. Modern religious persons may well be justified in repudiating some images and accepting others, but they can scarcely legitimate their selection by reference to the Bible. Other determinants have come into play, but the images selected in the classical view suffer from the problems already mentioned in connection with tradition or the church.

Attempts to harness the true value of images to biblical authority seem destined to fail. And theology, in its present state of disarray, promises little better. Theologies now rampant uncritically seize upon whatever in

Scripture is of use to their purposes, and loudly proclaim what Christianity is "all about." Black theology, liberation theology, feminist theology, narrative theology, process theology—all make their discordant claims, and in the confusion the magisterial influence of theology is lost. And a lament goes up that theology has sold out its classical stance to modernity.[17] As far as piety and worship are concerned, some comfort can be drawn from this state of affairs by remembering that theology is a second-order discipline at some distance from the urgencies of the religious life itself.

A long tradition of mysticism in Judaism and Christianity has laid claim to truth about God. By immediate, unmediated relation to God in vision or union, an empirical test of truth would seem to be forthcoming.[18] The reports of this direct relation to deity, including images, symbols, and paradoxes, should possess an evidential value far beyond that provided by inferences drawn from God's activity mediated by events in the world. The mystics characteristically claim knowledge of God, not simply knowledge about God—although this distinction is less clear-cut than its proponents admit.[19] However, when it is claimed that mystics, regardless of their respective religious traditions, participate in a common world of experience, the variety and conflicts of the images they offer cast doubt upon the veridical status of their reports. Prior religious beliefs shape the resultant images and cannot therefore be accepted at face value.[20] The more extreme mystics, in spite of their volubility, of course, are among the first to disparage the adequacy of their images. The meeting with God is ineffable and can never be adequately expressed. Or maybe, as Ninian Smart maintains, the mystic does not have any mental images or perceptions, so there is nothing in the mystic state to describe.[21] As a result there is a strong tendency to revert to silence or negations, thus moving beyond intelligible communication. Then this inadequacy of language becomes in turn a metaphysical assertion about God himself. In his essential nature he is the Unspeakable. One defender of mysticism argues that the mystic "unnames" God to show that he is beyond the gods of culture that language denotes. Accordingly, the "entire symbol system" the world uses must be rejected.[22] But a God imaged as "nothing," as Meister Eckhart taught, is scarcely informative when the details concerning His nature have been obliterated. It must be admitted, however, that when imaging does come into play, a certain plausibility about the mystics' reports gains persuasive power. Although their claims fail to meet the ordinary criteria of intellectual truth, they are impregnable within the bounds of their purported intuitions of God. Only when they come into the open arena of philosophical and theological discourse and defend their insights by reference to the "good deeds" their mystical insights have produced, or by extended epistemological argument, are they laid open to the criticisms that have dogged mysticism wherever it has appeared. The best answer, then, may be "try it and see for yourself!"

The criticisms of mysticism are not the present purpose in respect to biblical imagery. Rather it is the failure of the mystical tradition to find a place in the Bible. There are traces of the mystical spirit in the Scriptures, especially in the Gospel of John and in some of Paul's writings, but in general it is foreign to the texts. "The fact is," said one biblical scholar, speaking of modern interest in mysticism, "that contemporary mystics do not find what they want in either the New or Old Testament."[23] The mystical tradition appears to have been grafted onto the Bible by treating it in a symbolic manner, as did the medieval mystics, rather than by a study of images in their historical and religious settings. There, without mysticism, direct experiences of God are found amid the occurrences of daily life.

Set over against the mystics' way to truth is that of faith. Union is not sought, nor a vision of the Holy One, but fellowship with the deity. Faith regards God as objective to humanity, yet in communication with it. Typical of this faith posture are the words of Micah, "What does the Lord require of you but to do justice and to love kindness, and to walk humbly with your God" (6:8). Norman Perrin, in reference to the New Testament, developed within this framework his idea of "faith-knowledge." He claimed that faith-knowledge was "knowledge of Jesus of Nazareth which is significant only in the context of specifically Christian faith, i.e. knowledge of him as Lord and Christ." This kind of knowledge pertains to a particular historical person "who comes to be of special significance in terms of revelation, religious experience, or religious belief." Through this historical person the nonhistorical reality of God's actions in Jesus is made apparent. This knowledge, although dependent upon faith, is valid because "it grows out of religious experience and is capable of mediating religious experience." It is communicable and intelligible. Furthermore, it can only be tested by methods appropriate to it, namely by "the understanding of ultimate reality it mediates, the kind of religious experience it inspires, the quality of personal and communal life it makes possible."[24]

Perrin's emphasis upon faith brings to mind the role it plays in the knowledge of God. But faith is not an organ of knowledge by which alternative cognitive functions are bypassed. Faith properly is to be referred to the existential realm—the whole set of the self in trust towards God as a way of being or living.[25] It disposes toward knowledge of God, but never produces it by itself. The certainty it brings does not of itself validate the beliefs that arise from it. It can neither do so nor aim to do so, partly because it is a way of living before God rather than a knowledge about God and partly because faith in its very nature includes an element of doubt or uncertainty whereby it is distinguishable from clear comprehension of its object of devotion. "I believe; help my unbelief" (Mark 9:24)—this is the cry of faith.

Since Perrin limited his idea of faith-knowledge to the figure of Jesus Christ, it is less useful in understanding the Old Testament images or those people in the New Testament who are devout apart from the agency of Christ, for example, the centurion (Luke 7:9), the criminal (Luke 23:40, 41), Joseph of Arimathea (Luke 23:50, 51), John and his disciples (Luke 11:1; John 3:25), Nathanael (John 1:47), and Nicodemus (John 3:10). Yet in all these cases faith undergirds the devotion that is expressed. And in the Jewish Scriptures expressions are found that bear a vivacity that witnesses to an apprehension of God's presence, in which Christ plays no part. Consequently Perrin's position, whatever value it has for a Christian knowledge of God through Christ, fails to embrace the entire field of biblical images.

Faith-knowledge, we have been told, can be tested, and this observation opens a larger question that may be applicable to biblical images. Are we to understand that such testing is available only by what Perrin and others have called methods appropriate to religious experience, or are criteria external to the religious community also applicable? Holmer, for example, asserts that to have knowledge of God "you must fear him and you must love him. There is no knowledge of God otherwise."[26] If this be the case, "testing" consists of the changes that faith produces in the self, the overcoming of despair, the incitement of hope, contrition, repentance, and conversion, and the sense of God's nearness. It is the quality of the heart, mind, and will that has the last word in the knowledge of God.[27] In short, the test of knowledge of God lies strictly within the subjective realm, and correct belief fades in importance.

This kind of testing, if it be such, implies that any search for truth of images can properly be carried out only within a religious community where devotion is at a height. As D. Z. Phillips put it, "the criteria of the meaningfulness of religious concepts are to be found within religion itself."[28] The use of criteria from a nonreligious context can only lead to error.[29] When "a single paradigm of rationality to which all modes of discourse must conform" is used, violence is done to religious conviction.[30] And since the word *God* stands for a reality, totally eternal and unique apart from the physical world, knowledge of him must be distinguished from all other types of knowledge.[31] The corollary advanced by Phillips is that "God's goodness does not entail good things happening to those who believe in him." What happens in an individual's life has no bearing on whether or not God is good. Because God is supernatural, "the search for assurances and guarantees, the desperate attempt to argue on behalf of God, the desire for justification, all this" is foreign to religious belief. Events in the world do not constitute evidence for God's goodness, "since the essence of the believer's belief in divine goodness consists precisely in the fact that the meaning of life does not depend on how it goes."[32] Nothing that happens in the world outside religious discourse counts for or against the truth of God's existence or nature, and so religious faith seems to be safely immured within its own precincts. "Religious beliefs are ir-reducible."[33]

Yet Phillips was not altogether happy with this conclusion. External criticism of religious beliefs is possible when beliefs are found to be mis-taken, confused, or distorted, but he draws a distinction at this point between "checks" and "criteria of verification or falsification." The latter falsely assumes one paradigm of rationality, whereas the former is appro-priate to the language game he wishes to play. Religious beliefs by the external criticism of coherence may be coherent, but still be mistaken in the light of a "check." But verification by worldly standards is helpless to decide in what way. This attempt to safeguard religious faith and its im-ages from contamination by criteria external to them has always had a respectable following. And it is a position that receives support from philosophical arguments that maintain methods of testing or proof are functions of the communities to which they are appropriate.[34] Undoubtedly if criteria for the truth of images are drawn from the world of experience external to the worshiping community, the significance and functions of the images would be endangered. On the other hand, the biblical authors do look to how the world goes in framing many of their images. The evidence of God is in the world, and in what transpires within human beings in relation to that world. To a large degree rewards and punish-ments take place within the world and their history in it, not in some transworldly sphere. Faith, as the images show, did depend on the move-ments of nature and history. Religious beliefs are not reducible to these external factors, but neither are they totally bound by religious criteria alone, as Phillips argues.

The search for the truth of images would seem to lead inexorably to the matter of consequences as a test of validity. Perrin, for example, did not justify faith-knowledge solely by the fact that it produced reverential emo-tions. The personal and social life it makes possible was also to be taken into consideration. As biblical images form an essential part of faith-knowledge, it need not be denied that they both express and beget reli-gious feelings, but it must also be insisted that a cognitive element is one ingredient in the complex nature of these images. Sheer intensity of feeling cannot be substituted for truth, but feelings and will have a part in the whole process. These aspects, no less than intellective functions, bore heavily upon the capacity images had in producing individual and social behavior. And it may be that these consequences clarify the truth pos-sessed by the images. If by them moral sensibilities are heightened, ethical and religious actions are engendered, and character elevated and en-hanced, a clue is at hand for pronouncing at least some of them as valid.

This is the line that H. Richard Niebuhr took in his interpretation of the images produced by revelation. We deal with the understanding of God and selves not by the pure reason, he held, but, following Kant's distinction, by the practical reason. Whereas the former treats impersonally of external realities, the practical reason, which includes both emotion and will, has to do with the internal history of individuals and social groups. The form that these dealings assume is that of images. Thus revelation, when used as the basis of our reasoning, seeks "to conquer the evil imaginations of the heart and not the adequate images of an observing mind."[35] Evil imaginations expressing themselves in individual and communal conduct are shown to be evil, "just as erroneous concepts and hypotheses are shown to be fallacious by their results."[36] The evil images betray their nature in the conflict set up within and among selves. Impoverishment and destruction of persons occur as egocentrism and arbitrary subjectivity take over. The world becomes distorted in the light of these images where individual egos are pridefully inflated along with the estimates of their respective groups. Paradoxically, the meaning of life shrinks in proportion to the degree that this inflation expands, or it ends in despair, when inevitable disappointments shatter the images that have guided expectation. Images are evil because they destroy the integuments that bind together human life, only to leave in their path unredeemed pain and conflict.[37] On the other hand, the images of revelation show their validity by integrating life in and between selves. When one reasons by means of them, they show their truth by their consequences. They make past events intelligible by bringing to mind past individual and social histories, even those of darkest hues which have been repudiated or forgotten. At last these strands of the past are appropriated and integrated into a coherent story in which a fresh vitality comes to birth through repentance. But equally important, ever ongoing histories must be integrated with the histories of other individuals and groups. Thereby the skein of human histories is enriched and deepened as provincial memories are left behind.

Niebuhr, as a Christian, believed that these functions inhered in the figure of Christ, who is both "parable and analogy." The Christian reads his own life, and life about him, in the light of the teaching, life, death, and resurrection of Christ, for Christ is the "rational image." The rationality of the image is seen in its capacity to illuminate the heights and depths of human existence, making of it a comprehensible pattern that in turn yields doctrines and concepts of ever greater inclusiveness by which life's vicissitudes can be understood and redeemed. Revelation, through the image of Christ, thus opens itself to progressive validation "as ever new occasions are brought under its light, as sufferings and sins, as mercies and joys are understood by its aid."[38]

In describing how images work and how their validity may be ascertained, Niebuhr actually laid out a phenomenology of images that was not confined to his Christian orientation. Like Perrin and Holmer in their respective ways, he directs us to the consequences that images bring about.

Images are true when they make sense of private and social histories, when they incorporate into a whole the vexations and anxieties of daily life, and when they produce the trusting equanimity and hope with which to meet its buffetings. Implicit in estimating the validity of an image is the degree of inclusiveness or comprehensiveness it possesses. If images serve as a kind of paradigm for human existence, then MacQuarrie is correct in suggesting that as "some particular limited area of reality" becomes a paradigm, "its proof or disproof, so far as there is any, demonstrates its truth as it is extended to wider areas of experience."[39]

The appeal to consequences and comprehensiveness would seem to be an attractive way in which to determine the truth of biblical images. It would be strange if the report given by biblical images of confrontation with God did not produce both striking personal and social effects. Jesus warns that false prophets will be known by their fruits (Matt. 7:16, 20), and Paul contrasts the works of flesh to the fruit of the Spirit (Gal. 5:19–23), and again, the early Christians were told to "test everything" (1 Thess. 5:21), and to "test the spirits" (1 John 4:1). Both results and testing seem to have a legitimate place in estimating spiritual truth.

Comprehensiveness, on the other hand, is less obviously a germane test of images, since the biblical images have been struck off in particular situations that often do not lend themselves to generalization. They are relative to those situations and may lose their effectiveness when withdrawn from that framework. They are infected by time and history. Their truth value then might be regarded as episodic, depending upon the duration of time in which they have been accepted as true. In this way we are forced to admit either that the images were true for the time in which they originated, or that they are dependent upon social acceptance over some period of time. The failure of some images to stand the test of time argues for the first alternative, since some of the more debasing images of God have been relegated to early cruder states of religious and moral development. But this position puts in jeopardy not only objectionable images, but also those most cherished in religious traditions. Relativity knows no distinction between "bad" and "good" images. It is ironical that those who wish to salvage the comprehensiveness or universality of some images and not others exempt the noble images of God from this relativity. But if we are to believe that the Jewish authors wrote "The Lord will reign for ever and over" (Exod. 15:18), or that the author of Hebrews could say, "Jesus Christ is the same yesterday and today and for ever" (13:8), with the intent of uttering universal truths, the particular time and place of their speaking does not determine the validity of what they express. In fact, some images, thought once to have been safely stowed away as antiquarian novelties, have survived and come back into use when no better idea or image has been found. Images are time-dependent as to origin and meaning, but they are often implicitly comprehensive and universalizable as to significance. The God of the Bible may act in different ways in various circumstances, and even in a contradictory fashion, but in whatever way he acted, those who first experienced him believed that they were expressing what was universally true in the variety of these experiences, and they expected others to understand them as such.

If one were to estimate the truth or falsity of an image by its consequences, the time factor is important. Consequences may take time to develop, but it does not follow that the truth or falsity of an image is determined only when all the consequences are known and judged. Apart from the practical impossibility of ever knowing when all the consequences are in, those consequences which can be traced to the impact of an image operate only retroactively in respect to the validity of that image. If it could be decided that certain consequences flowed more or less directly from the image, those consequences at best could only testify to the fact that the image was true antecedent to the consequences. In the case of the *cogito* of Descartes, by which he hoped to establish the reality of his own existence, the *cogito* revealed only that it *was* true that he *had* existed. Insofar as Descartes' *cogito* succeeded in establishing the certainty of his existence, it assisted him in getting on with his philosophy, but "the certainty of his existence was not dependent on the consequences to which it led."[40] In a similar manner, it may be argued that an image's truth or falsity does not entirely hinge on the consequences it produces.

In any case, consequences as such can only weigh in the balance between truth and falsity, if criteria are introduced by which their adequacy may be estimated. The evidential value of consequences depends upon a further judgment made in the light of these criteria. Whether the criteria are to be drawn from within the religious circle, as Phillips insisted, or from a wider range of experience remains to be seen. But of these problems the Bible tells little except to affirm that God is to be obeyed and trusted.

Once more in the face of the failure of the varied ways of attempting to establish satisfactorily the truth of biblical images, the effort must be made to penetrate the sense in which these literary figures are true. It seems clear that the biblical authors intended to express the truth about the God they experienced, although amid the diversity of images they employed, many included evaluations rather than prosaic descriptions about his nature.[41] Consequently their validation must take into consideration the worshipful mode of self-transcendence they express. Within limits the contentions of Holmer and Phillips must be accepted, for they place the origins of images within that orbit. "Conceptual meaning," Holmer argues, "is achieved and often discerned within the science or the religion, not by an outsider, a philosopher or even a theologian."[42] Yet, on the other hand, since images do produce models or paradigms of behavior observed by those outside the religious community, they cannot be bottled up within the privacy of individuals or communities where they originate and are used. They incorporate cognitive features, or what one philosopher calls "theory fragments" that call for substantiation.[43] The fact that images operate in a poetic milieu should not eliminate this need. "Ultimately," it has been observed, "questions of truth are very much at issue, as much in the religious as in the scientific arena, and certainly nothing is gained by reassigning religious utterances to the category of poetry, if that reassignment involves ignoring the fact that a very large number of religious utterances are propositional in appearance and are apparently, even though expressed poetically, about putative matters of fact. . . ."[44]

Once more those who speak for poetry must be heard. One form in which poetry claims truth is illustrated by the title of Wallace Stevens's poem, "Reality is an Activity of the Most August Imagination."[45] But can "reality" without remainder be the product of the imagination? Must not the imagination have "material" upon which it does its work? An answer is found in the conviction that "reality" impinges upon the mind from outside, giving "the sense that we can touch and feel a solid reality which does not wholly dissolve itself into the conceptions of our own minds."[46] An image, as a poetic metaphor, is " 'true' only insofar as it contains such a reality, or hints at it."[47] In this sense of the word *true*, an image begets and transmits the powerful impact of God upon the human mind. It brings about what the Psalmist called "truth in the inward being" (51:6). But to call this truth merely subjective is to omit from consideration the power of an objective reality that has brought it about. Truthfulness "in the inward being" is response, not self-initiated. Furthermore, the charge of subjectivity reckons without the fact that subjectivity is not by definition false or incommunicable. To identify truth as subjective is a shorthand way of stating that truth has affective and volitional components. What the image does is to become the "bearer of reality" that invades, and sets in motion, these deeper tonalities of the self. It shocks the imagination into a vision of what is signified.[48]

Verification of the truth of images in any purely scientific or intellective sense is impossible. This is not due to God's transcendence, if by that term one continues to mean that he is "outside" the universe in some non-metaphorical sense. His transcendence is his objectivity recognized as "other than" mankind, nature, and history, but never disconnected from them. Nor is the failure of verification due to human finiteness that cannot penetrate his essence or essential being. To speak in terms of essence is to fall under the spell of a metaphor that likens God to a being in which hides a kernel of reality forever separate from and inaccessible to human beings. In this way it is believed that his mystery is safeguarded. But, to change to an idea better suited to biblical images, it can be claimed that God is what he does.[49] Among his actions are those in which he is experienced as hidden, as well as active in human affairs and nature. Certainly there is mystery enough about God in the dialectic of presence and withdrawal to satisfy the most ardent believers in a supernatural realm, and no interpretation of the biblical images dares rule out the mystery that enfolds the knowledge they convey.

If proof of the truth of images in any strict and universally accepted sense of that term is ruled out, the concept of plausibility is not. Plausibility lacks the definiteness that proof might give, but it may be used to refer to a broader range of experience that produces validation. And at least some images are so manifestly based on empirical evidence convincing to the believers that to speak of them as containing only vague "symbolic truth" is to distort their essential character. Plausibility maintains the cognitive dimension of images without surrendering their literary nature. But it must be supported by warrants that vouch for it. To the degree by which warrants establish plausibility, it can justifiably be concluded that the image has faithfully brought into conjunction the believer's existential posture with the impact of God. Admittedly the biblical authors did not enter into this kind of speculation, but we are constrained to undertake it in seeking to understand "the truth" they intended to express. But we can only infer, from the images themselves and what is generally known of the Bible's social milieu, what constituted plausibility for these ancient peoples. The warrants to be used fall into two general, closely related categories. The one is subjective and primarily individualistic in nature. It deals with what may reasonably be said about the way images are held by the self, cut off for the moment from social relations. The second category is concerned with objective consequences of images. In this instance the previous methodological isolation of the self is rectified as images work themselves out in the public domain. There are two public domains, the religious community itself and the world outside the community. Correspondingly different warrants may come into prominence as one passes from the individualistic level to that of the social. From an emphasis upon private intensity and aesthetic propriety, one moves to the widening influence of images upon social, moral, and religious behavior. However, as one approaches the public level, ideologically set apart from the religious community, warrants less closely linked with images are used. Existential engagement is reduced in importance in favor of more objective criteria.

Poets, mystics, and proponents of faith-knowledge have reminded us that images strike the imagination with a sense of intuitive certitude. The biblical images appear to have accomplished this. The image does not defend itself; no mediating interpretation stands between it and the mind. Spontaneously one is assured that what the image says of God is true. Certitude is the subjective assurance that one has met God, and that the image has correctly reflected this encounter. To be sure, certitude must be distinguished from the more objective criterion of certainty, with which it is sometimes confused. Certitude is the feeling of rightness one has at the deepest level of the reason, affections, and volitions, tinged by the tentativeness of faith.[50] In worship, if not in a philosophical frame of mind, faith clings to this assurance, not waiting for confirmation by some other means. Without the root of certitude, doubt itself would disappear, since nothing would bind the question that hovers on the lips of the doubter. Thus certitude is the first warrant for the plausibility of the images that bring it about.

This subjective assurance seems to have been accompanied by a conviction of truth. Obviously, that about which one feels certitude is true for the believer. Throughout the range of images, the Bible offers the conviction of truth as the accompaniment of this assurance. But again, this is truth that resonates with the inner nature of the believer. It is not truth subject to scientific or mathematical calculation. It has to do with truth as suggested "in the inner parts" in respect to both the receptivity of the self, without which truth could not be realized, and the sense that one's inner nature is being shaped by a truth from outside the self. The two coalesce in certitude, and the image is the successful evidence that this union has been realized.

At this point another warrant appears, that of the appropriateness of the image. To what degree did the image faithfully reflect the experience of God? Still in the realm of the subjective, the biblical images have about them an inevitability. Some may, upon reflection, seem clumsy or inept, and others have an aesthetic appropriateness that brooks no contradiction. The image of God as a rock, for example, signifying strength, protection, and stability, is appropriate in a way that the weight or size of a rock is not. God as heavy or of particular proportions would be discordant to what the believing author wishes to convey. Even with images of God as angry, deceitful, or cruel, the aesthetic element of appropriateness enhances the vigor of the image. But we should not use the term *aesthetic* as a synonym for beauty,[51] but rather in a sense closer to its Greek origin, wherein perception and sensitivity, even of the physical body as well as of the imagination, are involved. Some images, as of disease, pain, drought, and so on, which God causes, are directly dependent upon those kinesthetic sensations, and although appropriate, are neither beautiful nor morally uplifting. Yet the resultant literary forms give expression to the truth, which has been experienced by a sentient, imaginative being.[52] Aesthetic vividness does not once and for all certify truth or validity, but when truth is felt by means of an image, it nurtures intuitive certitude while drawing into intelligible clarity the otherwise formless and lifeless. In part this is what is meant by saying that an image "illuminates." It makes comprehensible the vagaries of human existence. In respect to the individual it clears the way to an understanding of sorrow, guilt, joy, and peace, but at the same time it enlightens the self as to what God is doing in producing these inner feelings. The illuminative power of an image brings into intimate connection the feeling of truth or certitude and the nature of God. But this liaison is not effected by rational inference from cause to effect or vice versa. The two foci are brought into unity in the immediacy of individual perception that the image makes possible.

It would be strange if another warrant of plausibility did not play a part. Subjective assurance includes commitment in the form of belief. Belief is not to be understood as a halfway step to complete knowledge.[53] It is a trusting of God. In one sense the image itself is trusted as being faithful in its representation of God, but in a deeper sense the image is only the instrumentality by which trust in God himself came to birth. The image says of those who accept it that they abide in and are loyal to the God of the image. This is one of the remarkable features of the biblical images, for even in the most deplorable circumstances some of the biblical writers held firmly to God. Their commitment brooked no evidence that would tear them away from the deity. He could slay, mercilessly punish, pour out the vials of his wrath, or be hidden in the torturous complexities of human experience, but he could not be denied as the determiner of destiny. How could it be otherwise? Unless the certitude brought by the images manifested itself in a conviction, the very existence of subjective assurance would be in doubt.

When we survey the images in both Testaments, we soon realize that they functioned in communities of faith and worship. They gained plausibility or communal validation as they entered into the texture of a social existence. What they suggest is caught up in the consequences they had for these believing fellowships. Religious acts of worship are carried out in their light, where awe, fear, supplication, and rejoicing are present. But these consequences, although important, less effectively serve the purposes of plausibility, since although they are observable, their inner meaning is hidden from the public, and even from those within the community. Somewhat more effective for being publicly observable are the moral acts engendered by the images. Motives are still concealed, but actions directly affecting others may better give a clue as to whether the behavior corresponds to the description of God. God's forgiveness is to be matched by human forgiveness. God's love is to be shared among those within the group. God's judgment does not relieve the prophet from judging the failures of his people, and when God's wrath is exposed, people are to repent of their evil ways. The operative principle is that of harmony or consistency between the affirmations made by the images and behavior. This is not to say that biblical folk always obeyed the dictates of the Lord. Far from it.[54] But the images showed what they were to do, and the standards by which their actions were to be judged within the religous group. In this sense the warrant of conduct applied only within the limited area of the in-group. An equally telling warrant is the capacity images had of being shared. The longevity of at least some of the images argues for the fact that across the span of years that the Bible covers, people continued to use images of God. Longevity of course does not establish continuing plausibility. The death of some images makes that clear. However, those which endured show that images once did communicate and were shared in widely differing situations. Like-minded persons found that images were not locked into individual privacy, but could be cross-checked by the witness of others. Thus a presumption of validity is to be seen in the near universal testimony to the plausibility of the images. In the same way, when an image no longer could be attested to by the words "That's what we experienced also," the image was corrected or finally lost its vigor and was set aside.

The power of images is not limited to the bounds of the religious community and its worship. Images have been used to understand not only individual lives and the life within the religious communities, but also to shed light on the universal meanings of nature and history. And this consequence brings the question of plausibility into a more expansive domain than that served by religious devotion. By so doing, warrants are sought that derive less directly from an inspection of the images themselves than from those held to be widely accepted by rational peosple. The temptation is great at this point to assume that warrants drawn from this wider public are the deliverances of some universal mentality possessed of definitive authority. But they too have arisen within the relativities of social and historical circumstances, motives, and intentions, by which philosophy and science have succeeded in setting the predominant tone of Western rationality. Once that caveat has been entered, we may accept certain variants that operate within this broader spectrum, where little or no religious intent is involved.

The first warrant in this category carries over from the realm of the religious community. The biblical authors of the divine images were speaking for the most part to the members of the religious community, but they often intended their words to be of wider significance. To claim that the Lord reigns forever, that he is Lord over all the earth, that he created the world, that he saves whom he will, are claims that could be easily understood by anyone. Communicability and the sharing of meaning were not to be limited to fellow believers. These affirmations are breakthroughs into a world of discourse where intelligibility ranges broadly. That such claims couched in images have been understood outside the religious orbit is established by the way in which world leaders have often appealed to them in guiding the fortunes of states. And poets have repeatedly laid them under tribute. "Outsiders" have understood the images even when they have bent them to their own ends. And if certain images of God have had meaning to those outside the religious community, then some further measure of plausibility is gained.

Additional evidence of the plausibility of images in the public domain is to be found in the act of conversion. Christianity was a missionizing religion from the outset, as was Judaism. Conversion depended in large part on a person's ability to understand the images used in the proselytizing process before he or she became a member of the religious group. These persons, whether their conversion was sudden or gradual, came to recognize that what the images say is "true" to what is transpiring within and around them prior to their explicit acceptance of the God whom the images portray. What was opaque or unintelligible became clear, and they were persuaded that they should live a life informed by these images. If the images had been incomprehensible at the outset, conversion could not have occurred. When conversion was complete, people knew even better how to use the images and internalize them as the language of the new communal life. Thus the images enter into the ambience of worship as well as moral conduct. As Bowker points out, plausibility is enhanced by "the degree of match between what they suggest and what is discovered when they are incorporated in the construction of a particular life."[55]

Images, or as often symbols, have engendered and controlled overt behavior of individuals and groups. When adherents of Judaism and Christianity acted in the public arena, however sure they were of the truth or validity of their commitments, they were open to the judgment of others. Members of a religious body that is not coterminous with the society are not immune from the strictures of that society. Nowadays freedom of religious belief and thought may be protected under the aegis of the law, but actions that disturb the peace of the "civitas," or fall below the standards of the secular society, are not allowed full sway or tolerated, even in a democracy. The rationale of a government may be deeply influenced by religious imagery, but in spite of this fact, religiously motivated persons cannot with impunity challenge the norms set by a society or a government. Religious insights may exceed these norms in ethical sensitivity, as the history of protests against oppressions makes clear, but a price is to be paid in suffering, often incommensurate with the measure of success these efforts produce. So in the cases of Jeremiah and Jesus. Sometimes religious accommodation is made to societal norms, and a conservative support of the prevailing ethos results. Occasionally religiously motivated persons are seen as falling below societal norms to such a degree that, in the United States at least, the state intervenes. However, even without governmental enforcement, local or wider publics exert effective pressures for minimal conformity to acceptable social norms. And, of course, when believers fail to adhere to the standards of their own faith, the familiar cry of hypocrisy may be heard from those who may have neither use nor respect for the religious traditions in question. In this case the norms are presumed to derive directly from the traditions themselves. The norms used in this country by society generally are notoriously difficult of precise definition. But among these the most obvious are faithful and equitable dealings with fellow human beings, truthful utterance, respect for persons, and a modicum of consistent and dependable conduct. Such criteria may have originated in religious convictions, but they maintain themselves apart from explicit religious sanction. They appear as independent emanations of some vague, common moral sense.

How then have these criteria served as warrants for the plausibility of biblical images? They are external in respect to the assessment of religious validity, yet they weigh in the balance. Consistency or correspondence between the picture of God given by the image and the appropriate human response is one warrant I have already mentioned, and it is soon picked up and used by the society where failure to reflect at least the nobler aspects of God is discovered. But appearing as a purely rational criterion, consistency extends itself into the moral realm, as it estimates the degree to which fidelity, honesty, justice, compassion, and truthfulness are correlated with the images. As already suggested, correlation of behavior with the view of God given in an image is not a one-to-one correspondence. Obviously, the biblical record does not show that when God is angry, people should imitate him by being angry, or when he is loving, people automatically love him and others. But correlation need not be understood as imitation. Correlation is most faithful to the biblical testimony when it is an appropriate response to the nature of the deity. When he is angry, human beings ought to cower or repent. When he is imaged as a transcendent king, lawgiver or judge, people are to obey. And when he is loving, love ought to be the proper response. To show that the image of God is faithful to the reality it portrays calls not for imitation in all cases, but for the appropriate response enjoined by the image. That the people in the Bible do not so conform is not proof of the inadequacy of the image, but rather of a human failure to live up to what is demanded. This line of inference between the God of the image and human behavior is tenuous, but it nevertheless lends plausibility to the validity of the image when people have repented, obeyed, and loved.

Another external warrant that played its part in the plausibility of images is that of their capacity to be universalized. Images, we have insisted, often do silently appeal for universal acceptance, but now the question of universalizing may be understood as a demand of moral philosophy. Can the conduct resulting from the image be universalized? Clearly some of it can be, while other behavior fails the test. All people in like circumstances, it would seem, should not slay defenseless enemies because God bids them to do so. But that conclusion is manifestly laden with moral insights drawn from other eras in which such behavior is considered inhumane. Universality, however, does not of itself forbid such actions. It only affirms that when confronted with similar situations, universalizing a proposed course of action, or one already carried out, could justify, that is, give warrant for that action. To the modern eye, the action may be reprehensible, but that does not cancel the operation of the universalizing principle. In modern warfare we continue to use it as revenge, and in popular morality it still has its place, in spite of the learned arguments that have recently been lodged against it as a moral principle. With a different emphasis it is contained in the "golden rule" as the summation of the law and the prophets (Matt. 7:12). Certainly, as a warrant of high morality, the principle of universalizing leaves much to be desired, but the intention is not to make biblical images palatable. Rather, when they are held up to the external warrant of the universalizing principle, sense is made of images, giving plausibility to what they affirm of God.

In the last analysis, image language was confessional language, and not scientific or philosophical language, but that does not mean that one was free to say whatever one pleased about God. The range of biblical images is extensive, but it is held within the scope of an underlying conviction of complete dependence upon God.[56] Antecedent to any knowledge claims about God is the relation pictured by the variety of images about him. Access to God was existentially prior to knowledge of him.[57] Without that relation, knowledge would not have been possible, and the question of truth or validity would never have arisen. Knowledge is itself only one kind of relation to the deity, and it is secondary to the experience of dependence upon which the images depend. This fact does not underplay the cognitive element essential to images, but is to be seen fused with the other functions of images. The emotional and volitional factors that the images express have their say in the total impact of the image. Those who wrote believed God, not simply propositions about him.[58] Consequently, although overemphasizing the peaceful outcome of that experience, more than does the Bible, one author is correct when he writes, "What is most striking in the total experience seems to me to be not its cognitive elements but its affective and conative elements. . . . What one comes to know from religious experience is chiefly how to live, how to be at peace with oneself and with the universe at large. Whatever power it is that enables men to achieve such serenity of mind, this they call God."[59] And this is to say that the existential dimension of both individual and social experience is a central locale from which plausibility derives its most persuasive authenticity.

No disinterested demonstration of the truth of images has resulted from this inquiry. Only the possible grounds upon which images may be held to be true have been explored. Whether the plausibility established on those grounds is taken for "truth" by modern people awaits the impact of God upon their lives. Then imaginative interpretation of that religious experience will find some resonance with the biblical images of God or will seek other literary vehicles consonant with their experience, time, and place, as the living God of the Bible still calls for fresh imagery.

NOTES

1. H. D. Lewis, "On Poetic Truth," *Philosophy, The Journal of the British Institute of Philosophy* 21 (July 1946): 160.
2. Dorothy M. Emmett, *The Nature of Metaphysical Thinking* (New York: MacMillan Co., Ltd., 1957), 4.
3. G. L. Prestige, *God in Patristic Thought* (London: S.P.C.K., 1952), xv.
4. James Barr, *Biblical Words for Time, Studies in Biblical Theology*, no. 33 (Naperville, Ill.: Alec R. Allenson, Inc., 1962), 161, 162. Philological research need not be held in disrepute, as Rodney Needham's *Belief, Language and Experience* shows (Oxford: Basil Blackwell, 1972), chaps. 2–4. Ironical evidence of the difficulty of distinguishing interpretation from "what the Bible says" can be found in a publicity "blurb" for the Anchor Bible, e.g., "Again and again, contemporary scholarship makes ancient Scripture more meaningful," yet "every contributor is concerned exclusively with what the Bible says, not with any one interpretation of 'what it means.'" *Christian Century*, September 13, 1978, 840.
5. E. D. Hirsch, *Validity in Interpretation* (New Haven and London: Yale University Press, 1967); see 8, 16–17, 38–42. Unlike Barr, Hirsch insists that knowledge of the original languages is necessary to construe a test.
6. Paul L. Holmer, *The Grammar of Faith* (New York, Hagerstown, San Francisco, London: Harper and Row, 1978), 134.
7. Cf. Wohlfahrt Pannenberg, *Faith and Reality*, trans. John Maxwell (London: Search Press; Philadelphia: The Westminster Press, 1977), 50. "Just because God in himself is indeterminate and transcendent, all we know of him is his created manifestation." Robert C. Neville, *God the Creator* (Chicago and London: University of Chicago Press, 1968), 119.
8. Cf. Earl R. MacCormac. *Metaphor and Myth in Science and Religion* (Durham, N. C.: Duke University Press, 1970), 120; "The revelatory sphere of special history cannot be wholly discontinuous either with the nature of the finite being who is to receive it or with the finite experience and language through which he must express and interpret it." John E. Smith, *The Analogy of Experience* (New York, Evanston: Harper and Row, 1973), 20.
9. James M. Gustafson, *Can Ethics Be Christian?* (Chicago: The University of Chicago Press, 1975), 127.
10. John Bowker, *The Religious Imagination and the Sense of God* (Oxford: Clarendon Press, 1978), 29.
11. Cf. Holmer, *Grammar of Faith*, 8, 9, 14–15, 25.
12. Ibid., 133.
13. David H. Kelsey, *The Uses of Scripture in Recent Theology* (Philadelphia: Fortress Press, 1975), 159, 205.
14. Ibid., 183.
15. Ibid., 175, 176.
16. Cf. Gordon D. Kaufman, "Attachment to God," *Andover-Newton Quarterly* 17, no. 4 (March 1977): 266, 269.
17. Cf. Holmer, *Grammar of Faith*, 10.
18. I omit from consideration "demonic" forms of mysticism.
19. The effort to maintain the independence of "knowledge of" from "knowledge about" has seldom been entirely successful. Cf. Ronald W. Hepburn, *Christianity and Paradox* (London: Watts, 1958), chaps. 3, 4; Henry N. Wieman, *Man's Ultimate Commitment* (Carbondale: Southern Illinois University Press, 1958), 135–43. The opposite view is assumed by Holmer. *Grammar of Faith*, 189.
20. Cf. Frederick C. Copleston, S.J., *Religion and Philosophy* (Dublin: Gill and Macmillan, 1974), 77.
21. Ninian Smart, *Reasons and Faith* (London: Routledge and Kegan Paul, 1958), 71.
22. Cf. Matthew Fox, O.P. "Spirituality for Protestants," *The Christian Century* 95, August 2, 1978, 734; John F. Teahon, "A Dark and Empty Way: Thomas Merton and the Apophatic Tradition," *Journal of Religion* 58, no. 3 (July 1978): 263ff.
23. Amos N. Wilder, *Theopoetic* (Philadelphia: Fortress Press, 1976), 17; cf. Friedrich Heiler, *Prayer*, trans. and ed. Samuel McComb (London, New York, Toronto: Oxford University Press, 1932), chaps. 7–10.

24. Norman Perrin, *Rediscovering the Teaching of Jesus* (London: S.C.M. Press, 1967), 238, 241, 244; cf. *The Myth of God Incarnate,* ed. John Hick (Philadelphia: The Westminster Press, 1977), 195ff.

25. Cf. Clyde A. Holbrook, *Faith and Community* (New York: Harper and Row, 1959), chap. 2.

26. Holmer, *Grammar of Faith,* 25.

27. Cf. ibid., 211; "The test of a sound moral and religious passion is whether it gives confidence and overcomes despair in the presence of the multitude of distractions that the world provides." 65.

28. Cf. D. Z. Phillips, *The Concept of Prayer* (New York: Schocken Books, 1966), 12; cf. 22, 38, 141, 143, 148.

29. Cf. Glyn Richards, "A Wittgensteinian Approach to the Philosophy of Religion: A Critical Evaluation of D. Z. Phillips," *The Journal of Religion* 58, no. 3, (July 1978): 289; Phillips, *Concept of Prayer,* 8.

30. Richards, "A Wittgensteinian Approach," 292.

31. Phillips, *Concept of Prayer,* 61, 83.

32. Ibid., 122; cf. 103, 105, 106.

33. Cf. D. Z. Phillips, *Religion Without Explanation* (Oxford: Basil Blackwell, 1976), 151. Phillips errs in confusing language-games and actual experience, as Dallas M. High points out. "Doubting and Groundless Believing," *Journal of the American Academy of Religion* 59, no. 2 (June 1981): 262.

34. Cf., e.g., Hilary Putnam, *Meaning and the Moral Sciences* (London: Routledge and Kegan Paul, 1978), on the need for a common language, rules of proof, and evidence within a particular community, by which truth or meaning may be determined.

35. H. Richard Niebuhr, *The Meaning of Revelation* (New York: The Macmillan Co., 1941), 94.

36. Ibid., 99.

37. Cf. ibid., 100.

38. Cf. ibid., 115–33.

39. John MacQuarrie, *Thinking About God* (New York and Evanston: Harper and Row, 1975), 119.

40. Niebuhr, *Meaning of Revelation,* 140.

41. Cf. H. H. Price, *Belief* (London: George Allen and Unwin Ltd.; New York: Humanities Press, 1969), 454.

42. Holmer, *Grammar of Faith,* 126.

43. James Bogen has dealt carefully with the question of truth and plausibility in metaphors. Cf. "Metaphor as Theory Fragments," *The Journal of Aesthetics and Art Criticism* 37, no. 2 (Winter 1978): 177–88.

44. Bowker, *Religious Imagination,* 12.

45. Cf. *Opus Posthumous,* ed. and introd. Samuel French Morse (New York: Alfred A. Knopf, 1977), 110.

46. H. D. Lewis, "On Poetic Truth," 160.

47. Owen Barfield, *Poetic Diction* (London: Faber and Gwyer, 1927), 74.

48. Cf. Amos Wilder, *Early Christian Rhetoric: The Language of the Gospel* (New York: Harper and Row, 1964), rev. ed. (Cambridge, Mass.: Harvard University Press, 1971), 84; Norman Perrin, *Jesus and the Language of the Kingdom* (Philadelphia: Fortress Press, 1976), 129.

49. "We may justly infer what God intends, by what he actually does. . . ." "Dissertation Concerning the End for Which God Created the World:, *The Works of President Edwards . . . .* Reprint of the Worcester Edition (New York: Leavitt and Allen, 1843) 2:204. "Instead of defining what God ought to do from some sweet anterior conception of divinity, it [Calvinism] defines what God is from what God actually does in the world that he has made and providentially governs." *Works of Jonathan Edwards,* vol. 1: *Freedom of the Will,* ed. Paul Ramsey (New Haven: Yale University Press; London: Oxford University Press, 1957), 1:107.

50. Douglas C. MacIntosh, as a philosopher of religion, distinguished certitude from certainty. "From certitude through tentativeness to certainty—that is the idea for our faith and theology, as for the rest of our thought." *The Problem of Religious Knowledge* (New York, London: Harper and Brothers, 1940), 374.

51. As the poet Archibald MacLeish pointed out in respect to distasteful images, the idea that images are "beautiful" does not make better poems. "Poems are not meant to be beauti-

ful." *Poetry and Experience* (Cambridge: The Riverside Press; Boston: Houghton Mifflin Co., 1961), 55.

52. Roger Hazelton has laid down norms for determining the validity of metaphors, which apply to biblical images: "adequacy to lived experience, of 'logical fit' and aesthetic immediacy taken together, and of fidelity to biblically grounded tradition as it stirs and shapes one's present faith." *Semeia* 13, no. 2 (Missoula, Mont. 1978): 175.

53. An intricately wrought denigration of the concept of belief may be found in Rodney Needham's *Belief, Language, and Experience.* See 66ff., 71ff., 131, 136, 191ff. For an opposing view see Ernest Gellner, *Legitimation of Belief* (Cambridge: University Press, 1974), who finds that the logicisms of the Wittgensteinians give only a skeletal world, blind to values, meaning, and history, and not the actual world we inhabit.

54. Speaking of the Old Testament, one author has correctly pointed out, "What these writings testify to *directly* is not the religion of Israel, but of different individuals and groups attempting, with varying degrees of success, to make their vision prevail in the wider society. What they tell us *indirectly* is that more often than not the 'religion of Israel' was something quite different." Joseph Blenkinsopp, *Prophecy and Canon* (South Bend and London: University of Notre Dame Press, 1977), 141.

55. Bowker, *Religious Imagination,* 184.

56. For a criticism of "absolute dependence," see Robert Roberts, "The Feeling of Absolute Dependence," *The Journal of Religion* 57 (July 1977): 3, 252ff., where he concludes that the association of the experience with the concept of God has been at best a confusion (266). And Holmer scorns Schleiermacher's notion of absolute dependence as trivial. *Grammar of Faith,* 94.

57. As David Pellauer points out, "The truth criterion of religious language is manifestation rather than verification or falsification which presupposes it." In "Paul Ricoeur on 'The Specificity of Religious Language,' " *The Journal of Religion* 61, no. 3, (July 1981): 280.

58. In respect to persons, H. H. Price held a contrary view that might apply to God: "Believing a proposition is primary and believing a person is derivative because it has to be defined in terms of believing a proposition." *Belief,* 39.

59. C. H. Whitely, "The Cognitive Factor in Religious Experience," *Religious Language and the Problem of Religious Knowledge,* ed. and introd. Ronald E. Santoni (Bloomington and London: Indiana University Press, 1975), 265.

Part II

6

An Interlude: Hermeneutics and the Second Naiveté

In earlier chapters various methods of interpreting biblical texts have been discussed and evaluated. However, in these days of burgeoning interest in hermeneutics, one can scarcely avoid invoking the names of such leading figures in hermeneutical theory as Hans-Georg Gadamer, Paul Ricoeur, Martin Heidegger, Claude Lévi-Strauss, and Ludwig Wittgenstein.[1] Diverse as the theories of these preeminent figures may be, in one way or another they have introduced a major revolution in methodology for biblical texts, as for literature generally. No attempt can be made here to survey the contributions of these scholars to the revolution, but as the biblical images of God to be dealt with in the following chapters come to us embedded in texts subject to hermeneutical analysis, it is appropriate to pay heed to at least two of the methods that have been propounded. The question is whether in these cases a critical reading of their hermeneutical techniques helps or hinders the phenomenological description of the diverse images.

In the broadest sense hermeneutics has been understood as the theory and practice of reading a text—in this case a biblical text. Except in the case of fundamentalism, the stock-in-trade of biblical hermeneutics has been a historical-critical methodology in which efforts have been made to reconstruct the historical and religious context of a passage, the author's intention, and the audience to which a passage was first addressed.[2] The ascertainment of the most probable original meaning of the text and its relation to the "presumed" author's other writings and similar literary deposits, as well as the most appropriate translation, when that is desired, are also part of this traditional hermeneutical practice. However, important as this type of hermeneutic practice has been, now the term *hermeneutic* is conceived in an even more specialized, technical fashion. The tendency in the two current hermeneutical programs under consideration is initiated by meeting a text as distanced (a distanciation) from both a presumed author's intention or its original reception. The text stands for itself and

89

should be treated as such, although the preliminary work of the historical-critical and literary is presupposed. But then to advance the hermeneutical exercise, a decision has to be made as to what direction the ensuing analysis will take. In what direction should the interpreter look? The structuralist interpretation begins with the assumption that the significance, as distinguished from the sense, of the text lies hidden "beneath" or "behind" the text. This interpretation of the hermeneutic task seeks a codelike, atemporal structure of thought that needs to be exhumed to better illuminate and make possible an understanding of what is at stake. Another hermeneutic, which we shall follow in greater detail, moves in another direction by positing a significance that lies "in front of" the text and is to be spelled out. Presumably, in this case the significance, again in distinction from the sense of a passage, lies somewhere "ahead" as a literary referent, potentially of theological import. Thus there is a future or anticipatory orientation of this hermeneutic.

Structuralism, in this case in its linguistic form, is described in relation to biblical stories, as not being "so much the description of the surface meaning of the narrative as it is the deciphering of the basic meaning or code which lies behind the individual stories."[3] From this analysis a system of entities (words, phrases, etc.) from the passage is sometimes developed, which then is arranged in diagrammatic form. These diagrams are intended to show the unconscious relations among what appear to be the diverse units or signs in a discourse, and thereby open the way to tease out the rational system of ideas underlying a complex text.[4] However, this superrationalism appears to fail in respect to theological significances, as David Tracy has pointed out.[5] The same charge holds even more strongly in respect to religious significance as distinguished from both intellective and theological meaning. Undoubtedly the configurational pattern of a text may be brought to light by structuralism, but it leaves a skeletal deposit and introduces one to an ahistorical, artificial world from which the vibrant, emotive tonalities have been stripped. Consequently, structuralism does little to advance the intuitive comprehension of the divine images, especially since they will be treated as independent units drawn from complex texts.

The hermeneutic that begins with the assumption that the significance of a text lies "in front of" it is traced out by David Tracy, who in turn leans heavily upon the writings of Paul Ricoeur, Gadamer, Heidegger, and Lonergan. This method appreciates the importance of the traditional methods of scriptural analysis, but finds that no combination of them coupled with structuralism can deliver theological significance. For that purpose, hermeneutics in a different style is necessary, which is then defined as "the discipline capable of explicating the *referent* as distinct from either the sense of the text or the historical reconstruction of the text."[6] The sense of the text refers to the internal structure and meaning of a text, and is opened to an interpreter by semantic and literary-critical techniques, whereas the historical reconstruction of the text includes an analysis of the religiocultural elements the text presents. The referent, which is the center of interest for this type of hermeneutic, can best be understood as that literary component to which the text points and which potentially bears theological significance. It is that meaning which lies, as it were, beyond or "in front of" the text, and is identified as a way of perceiving reality as a "mode of being-in-the-world"—an expression that links it to Heidegger's analysis of Being itself and his "fore-structure of understanding." The referent enables recognition of a new dimension of reality that does not appear on the surface of the text, but one, when appropriated imaginatively, that reorients one's life perspective. Referents are of two types. One is the "object-referent," which it is claimed has existential import as a perception of reality, hitherto hidden. The other is a "subject-referent," whereby the personal vision of the presumed author is uncovered. Thus there is captured both the intended purpose of the text as well as the intentionality of the presumably unknown writer. It is denied that this outcome results by "empathizing with the psychic state or cultural situation of the author" as some forms of traditional method might hold,[7] although how we come to understand the personal vision without something akin to empathy remains moot. The mode of being-in-the-world stands then awaiting the further theological explication that the hermeneutic has prepared.

The hermeneutical process to this point has been understood to depend upon the realization that a given text has undergone "distanciation," by which is meant that the text is distanced from or independent of both the original intention of the author and its reception by those to whom it was originally addressed.[8] As in the case of Jesus' parables, for example, "we do not understand the meaning of the parables by understanding either the author's intention or the community's or Jesus' life situation."[9] Thus at this point the text is reckoned with apart from its historical context, standing impervious to the traditional techniques of biblical scholarship. When the referent or referents are so achieved, it is claimed, the end product "is neither a psychic nor a physical event," but one that is "ideal or noematic."[10] With this terminology we are within the Hegelian milieu, where pure ideality and nonexistential notions pertain. This transposition into the Hegelian mode of thought is not unexpected, since Hans-Georg Gadamer, a major influence in this hermeneutical development, regards himself as "more in the tradition of Hegel, than of Schleiermacher."[11]

Although one seeks the referent "in front of" the text, a curious turn is made to the past when the ideal referent is now dubbed a "retrieval." This term has especial importance to the historical theologian, for it is supposed that what has been discovered or rediscovered are Christian meanings that once were meaningful and true in past cultural situations, and which in the present may be adjudged to be either equally meaningful and true or meaningless and untrue.[12] Among examples given of such retrievals are Bultmann's existential reinterpretation of Scripture, as well as those eschatological theologies which have recovered the "lost" political insights of Scripture and the left-wing Reformation.[13] However, whether these are in fact retrievals of lost, overlooked significances or are novel reconstructions oriented to contemporary cultural and religious interests appears questionable. Whatever may be the case, this discrimination of referents or retrievals allows for imaginative appropriation in two forms: in ethical terms, as when one asks whether the mode of being-in-the-world is valuable and adequate for moral insight or conduct, or in metaphysical terms, as when one asks whether this mode of being-in-the-world is internally coherent when properly explicated, and whether it is adequate to the rest of experience.[14]

The theological task proper begins at this point. A fundamental theology is developed in correlation with broader, more common experiences, whereby a systematic working-out of the criteria and methods of theological argument is achieved.[15] In turn a systematic theology will be built on fundamental theology, including both specific Christian doctrines and historical and practical theology.[16] Thus a hierarchical pattern emerges which, as in the traditional role of natural theology, moves from hermeneutics to fundamental theology and then to the various types of specialized theology, detailed in Tracy's *The Analogical Imagination* (56–58).

An example of how the hermeneutical procedure lays the foundation for Christian theology can be seen as one works out the meaning of the affirmation that in Christ, God's "true limit-representation of divine love" is displayed. The principal referent in what Tracy calls limit-language is the by now familiar "mode of being-in-the-world" as "an agapic, self-sacrificing righteousness willing to risk living at the limit where one seems in the presence of the righteous, gracious God re-presented in Jesus Christ." To make this confession is to respond to a summons to risk one's own life at the limits by commitment to living out one's life in a righteous and agapic fashion in the presence of the only God there is, manifested as the "Father" of the Lord Jesus Christ.[17] Upon this insight as one basis, theology in its several forms does its work, but I must admit that after so much laborious hermeneutic analysis, the outcome seems astonishingly meager and commonplace to one acquainted with Christian writings and life.

With this sketch of a hermeneutical method before us, it remains to ask in what ways it is relevant to the display of divine images in the following chapters. One presupposition that both structuralism and this hermeneutic share is the conviction that no biblical text, inclusive as it is of symbols, images, and parables, bears its essential meaning on the surface, easily understood by the reader. All texts crucial to theology are held to be by definition opaque and therefore subject to further analysis to realize their true significance.[18] Hence all literalism is put out of court at the outset, but also the immediacy with which, in this case, images speak to the reader. However, this observation should not be taken as a defense of literalism, but rather to point out the danger that overanalysis or overinterpretation may present to meeting images on their own ground. Distanciation, in fact, looks like an invitation to such overanalysis. However, another assumption colors this first rather trite one, namely, the fact of preunderstanding. This fact is acknowledged in Tracy's hermeneutic. Prior to entering on the hermeneutical analysis, the interpreter already possesses some idea, concept, or better, attitude that finds a given text worthy of attention.[19] The text is not a blank, nor is the mind of the interpreter. Preunderstanding may be likened to an intuitive perception of the meaning of a passage, grounded in one's previous theological or religious orientation, and which, as in the cases of Tracy and Ricoeur, decisively influences the final hermeneutical outcome.[20] To say this much is not to deny that preunderstanding is subject to correction and amplification by further experience, of which hermeneutics may take account,[21] but unless the preunderstanding is completely destroyed in the process, its import remains the fundamental directive of any interpretation that follows. In this light it is difficult to accept Tracy's claim that the theologian, if not the hermeneutist, must start his "inquiry without an assumption either for or against the meaning, meaningfulness, and truth of a symbol or doctrine under analysis."[22] Preunderstanding would seem to operate against any *tabula rasa* theory of biblical interpretation. And because of this fact it may be said, contrary to Tracy's position, that "the view of hermeneutics which begins with the assumption that the text requires interpretation . . . has the matter backward. It is not the text that requires interpretation, but . . . the interpreter."[23] Unless the text seizes upon the interpreter's frame of mind, there is presumably nothing worthy of explication in the text. The personal involvement is essential to the hermeneutical task as it is for the theologian. Thus the ground is laid for a frontal confrontation with the images of God, not simply as subjects for hermeneutical or theological operations, but as entities that incite preunderstanding of both a cognitive and existential type of appropriation. Although each image as preunderstood may be fertile in additional significance, it may also be observed that initial understandings are not necessarily false, even if they have not passed through the alembic of hermeneutical investigation. In fact, validation by consequences, as argued in chapter 5, may show that an image had validity prior to the processes of validation itself. It may be, even as Tracy's unfolding of Christ as the representative of God's agapic righteousness suggests, that an image is itself the referent for which hermeneutic has striven. Clearly, unless Tracy, as an intelligent, devout Christian with acquaintance with biblical and Christian teaching, had some perspective antecedent to the analysis of Christ, other interpretations of the referent he describes would have been possible, as the many examples in historical Christianity have shown. So in the case of the images of God, the first collision between the reader and the text may have uncovered the images as the unacknowledged referents for which Tracy has labored diligently. Or, to put the matter succinctly, if one does not have an inkling of a preunderstanding of Micah's question, "What does the Lord require of you, but to do justice, and to love kindness, and to walk humbly with your God?", one is not party to any further theological discussion of the significance of the question.

Hermeneutics as discussed by Tracy appears to be for the benefit of two audiences. The primary focus of his study lies in preparing a hermeneutical basis for what he called fundamental theology as distinguished from systematic theology. So in explaining his project, he makes it clear that no combination of historical, literary-critical, or structuralist methods can "give the theological meaning of the text."[24] The service that his hermeneutical exercise offers is for Christian theologians who, once having found the referents, can build a theology thereon. However, a broader audience is also to be taken into consideration, composed of "anyone who can read" or "any intelligent interpreter."[25] Whereas the former purpose relates to those concerned with the technicalities of theological construction, the latter lays open to any intelligent person the ideal meaning of a text. In the former case, but less obviously in the latter, nothing is said of the relevance of hermeneutics to the devotional spirit of the worshiper. To be sure, Tracy stressed the role of the imagination in the appropriation of textual referents by the theologian, yet, if it be true that images find their proper context in worship, there is something wooden and sterile about the manner in which the referents are dealt with.[26] But it is the aim of the deployment of images that follows to see them always in the light of worship as imaginative products retaining the resonance from which hermeneutical practice tends to strip them. However, agreement with Tracy's position does appear when it is noted that there is an existential import of the object-referent, that is, the perception of a reality that potentially transforms one's life orientation. Tracy cites with approbation what Ricoeur calls "existential verification,"[27] and in this respect the display of images, as well as what I have argued in chapter 5, comes into accord.

Two other terms operative in the hermeneutical enterprise also have bearing on the ensuing chapters. *Distanciation* has occurred, not in Tracy's sense, but in standing at a distance from the images themselves, so that they may sound their own notes uncluttered by complex commentary. In this respect, although the images are distanced from the technicalities of historical, literary, or hermeneutical methods, they may still retain the context of worship in which they first arose and functioned. *Retrieval*, the other word used in hermeneutics, has been presupposed. It is hoped that when the images stand on their own, their meaning constitutes, as far as

possible, a retrieval of their initial impact and significance. Thus the explication of images is to be understood in partial but not total agreement with
the outcome of hermeneutical effort. The images are self-referential in the
same way that a note of music with its overtones is grounded in the basic
key that is struck. The image as it stands is the key that is struck; the
overtones are the significances that spread from it. As units of thought and
imagination, their resonance comes from the "overtones." Or to change
the figure, as atoms and molecules carry with them a field of force, so also
images as nuclear units carry with them a field of illumination. Or again to
change the figure, we may say with Heinrich Ott's observation about history, "The pictures are primary; the facts are a secondary abstraction."[28]
The image is central in our context; the hermeneutics is secondary.

We come at last to the matter of "the second naiveté", which might even
be called an offshoot of distanciation. The second naiveté as employed in
the following chapters is not to be confused with literalism, the first
naiveté, for that naiveté robs images of their power and relevance to worship. Rather, secondary naiveté returns to the text, after the many forms of
interpretive work have been done, in order to offer a clear-cut sense of the
imaginative impact resident in the image.[29] It is not surprising that after the
torturous complexities of hermeneutics, even the practitioners of the art
find themselves returning with relief to the original texts.[30] We find Tracy
admitting on behalf of all hermeneutists that "even at the end of our most
rigorous critical endeavors, we all seem to find either that a second naiveté
has been restored to us to allow the symbols, now purified of literary
accretions, to speak again." Or, he continues, our criticisms may have
rendered these symbols, myths, fictions, "no longer meaningful for the
struggle to achieve authenticity."[31] It is in this fundamental sense that
hermeneutics ends in the second naiveté. Equally, the images of God to
follow, having survived centuries of hermeneutical interpretation, return
to us in the mode of second naiveté, capable of evoking our imaginative
and existential responses. Their impact, like that of the parables, lies once
more "in their realistic authenticity," not in the webs of interpretation the
theologian or preacher may have woven around them.[32] Thus the second
naiveté fulfills the hermeneutical purpose of providing an intelligible and
comprehensible datum for "anyone who can read." It is a call not for a
mind made blank, a *tabula rasa*, but for a fundamental honesty that refuses
to be endlessly entrapped in preliminary methodological practices. This, it
seems to me, is what Paul Ricoeur referred to when he wrote: "The
philosopher is not a preacher. He may listen to preaching, as I do; but
insofar as he is a professional and responsible thinker, he remains a begin-
ner, and his discourse always remains a preparatory discourse."[33]

As after the analysis of the structure, harmony, and orchestration of a
symphony all depends on its being played, so also after the critical work
has been done, the images, to be appreciated, must sound once more
through a second naiveté.

NOTES

1. Hans-Georg Gadamer found common ground with Wittgenstein's theory of "language games." *Truth and Method,* A Continuum Book (New York: The Seabury Press, 1975), 500, n. 12.

2. For a description of traditional hermeneutical methods, see John M'Clintock and James Strong, *Cyclopedia of Biblical, Theological and Ecclesiastical Literature* (New York: Arno Press, 1969), 3–4, 205–6.

3. Robert A. Spivey, "Structuralism and Biblical Studies: The Uninvited Guest," *Interpretation* 28, no. 2 (1974), 134.

4. Ibid. for examples of biblical structuralism, cf. Octavio Paz, *Claude Lévi-Strauss: An Introduction,* trans. J. S. and Maxine Bernstein (Ithaca, London: Cornell University Press, 1970), chap. 2.

5. Cf. David Tracy, *Blessed Rage for Order* (New York: The Seabury Press, 1978), 77.

6. Ibid., 52. In spite of the book's title, Gadamer, in repudiating scientific method, repeatedly insists that he is not dealing with methodology for the human sciences, e.g., "I do not wish to elaborate a system of rules to describe, let alone direct, the methodological procedure of the human sciences" (xvi). "The purpose of my investigation is not to offer a general theory of interpretation and a differential account of its methods" (xix). However, Tracy seems inclined to treat hermeneutics as a methodology for interpretation.

7. Tracy, *Blessed Rage,* 78.

8. Cf. ibid., 50–51.

9. Ibid., 77; cf. 76.

10. Ibid., 75.

11. Hans W. Frei, *The Eclipse of Biblical Narrative* (New Haven and London: Yale University Press, 1974), 342 n. 1; cf. Gadamer, xxiv.

12. Cf. Tracy, *Blessed Rage,* 239–40.

13. Cf. ibid., 251, n. 9.

14. Cf. ibid., 79. For criticisms of Tracy's reference to "common human experience" see Van A. Harvey, "The Pathos of Liberal Theology," *Journal of Religion* 56, no. 4 (1976): 382ff.

15. Cf. Tracy, *Blessed Rage,* 250 n. 1.

16. Cf. ibid., 239.

17. Cf. ibid., 221.

18. Cf. ibid., 50.

19. Cf. ibid., 251, n. 7. "A person who is trying to understand a text is always performing an act of projecting. He projects before himself a meaning for the text as a whole as soon as some initial meaning emerges in the text." Gadamer on Heidegger, 236; cf. 235–53.

20. E.g., cf. William James Lowe, "The Coherence of Paul Ricoeur," *Journal of Religion* 68, no. 4 (October 1981): 391.

21. Cf. Robert W. Funk, *Language, Hermeneutics, and Word of God* (New York, Evanston, London: Harper and Row, 1966), 52.

22. Tracy, *Blessed Rage,* 239.

23. Funk, *Language, Hermeneutics,* 12.

24. Tracy, *Blessed Rage,* 74, 77.

25. Ibid., 75.

26. Cf. ibid., 78.

27. Ibid., 211.

28. Funk, *Language, Hermeneutics,* 111, 113.

29. I regard Part I and the comments in this chapter as constituting the preliminary work for the second naiveté.

30. Cf. Tracy, *Blessed Rage,* 209–10; Cf. Gadamer, *Truth and Method,* 237.

31. Ibid.

32. Cf.Funk, *Language, Hermeneutics,* 204.

33. Lowe, "Coherence," 391.

7

Naturalistic Images of God

Theories about images now come to a halt before the images themselves. Here the phenomena must stand forth and speak for themselves without recourse to the "infinite regression" of scholarly commentary.[1] Here, as Charles Davis observed, "The critic must not dissolve them through commentary, supposing that only their meaning, as reformulated in his interpretation, is relevant, and not their impact."[2] Consequently, the amassing of examples of images found in the following chapters may not lend itself to elegance of literary expression, but a price must be paid to free the images from the clutches of a hermeneutical apparatus that veils as often as it reveals their import. Theological commentary also must be kept to a minimum, lest it jar with the worship setting where the images came to birth. After all, living experience precedes the theological scaffolding erected upon it. Both hermeneutical and theological niceties must wait upon bare description while "second naiveté" performs its function. Disputes over the dating of documents, the fictionalizing and synchronizing of events, the foreshortening of time sequences, the idealizing of biblical personages, as well as theological reflections, give way to the exposition of the images in their own right. Nor will images be arranged consistently with certain themes of biblical theology. The success of that approach is marred too often by its omission, reinterpretation, or depreciation of some images in order to bring them into conformity with theological presuppositions. When this happens, the full range of images of God is diminished, and the distinctiveness of the two Testaments is jeopardized.

Faced with a profusion of images of God, one may introduce order by reference to the worldly experiences that gave form to the images. The daily experiences of biblical folk are reflected in them. What they saw, heard, physically felt and believed went into the composition of images. Sense experience as well as cultural influences molded the forms the religious imagination took in elucidating the meaning of God.[3] Settled opinion has it that God cannot be "sensuously perceived, touched, seen or heard,"[4] but it is as often by the senses that God's impact is felt as by social experience.[5] And it is to the realm of sensed physical objects that investigation first turns.

As previously suggested (chap. 2), reference to what is natural bears two meanings. Human culture is natural. It is not an unnatural appendage to human experience, for it is the product of inventiveness and creativity common to all human beings. Supervening upon nature itself, it transmutes nature into tools and artifacts usable in daily life, while at its higher levels it creates the arts, sciences, and humane studies. It is one of the natural habitats of human existence. On the other hand, the "natural" refers in a more carefully limited sense to nature. Rocks, wind, light, fire, sky, water, storm, topography, and biological life are all uncreated by, and only subsequently subject to, human manipulation; these constitute nature. Nature is the given whence human life springs, and with which, as long as life lasts, people live intimately. It influences the destiny of empire as surely as does the human will, and its obdurate character does not easily bend to human intentions. Therefore it is not strange that it provides some of the most powerful images of God.

Some inanimate, physically sensed products of culture come to mind as the basis for images. The tools of warfare, an unfortunate feature of culture, are associated with God. To portray his protective power he uses a shield (Gen. 15:1; 2 Sam. 22:3; Ps. 84:11). As a warrior he uses the sword, shoots the arrow, and blows the martial trumpet as he marches into conflict (Zech. 9:14). Israel is his hammer and weapon (Jer. 51:20). He is also the fortress, stronghold, or tower of refuge in times of trouble (2 Sam. 22:2; Pss. 13:3; 61:3; 62:2, 67; 71:3; 91:2; Nah. 1:7) A house furnishes an image of security (Ps. 90:1), which God as a lamp illumines (2 Sam. 22:29). When Jeremiah identifies God as "the fountain of living waters,"[6] he contrasts the Lord with a broken cistern that fails to hold water (2:13). In a more elevated sense, God in his glory is depicted as a temple, another figure based on human ingenuity (Rev. 21:22).

In turning to images drawn from nature in its conventional sense, one must draw a distinction between its inanimate and animate features. Much of nature for the ancient Hebrews was not seen as the impersonal reality to which modern science introduces us. The Old Testament saw nature and mankind incorporated in a "psychic whole" in which nature is permeated by a diffused awareness.[7] Domestic animals were included in this psychic entity (Exod. 20:10; 23:12; Deut. 5:14; Lev. 20:22; Job 31:38, 40), and even heavenly bodies were counted as animate, as when the morning star sings (Job 38:7). The Psalmist calls upon the sun, moon, highest heavens, and waters above the heavens to praise the Lord (148:3). Surely poetic imagery is found in these passages, but as has been observed, "There is a realistic extension of anthropomorphism to nature as well as to God, and both types, the lower as well as the higher, are much more than arbitrary figures of speech or mere poetic licenses. Nature is alive through and through, and therefore the more capable of sympathy with man, and of response to the rule of its Creator and Upholder, on whom it directly depends."[8]

These remarks may be valid, but it is also true that the ancient Hebrews did distinguish between the domestic animals that were part of the psychical whole of "family"[9] and wild animals, as well as between animate and inert nature. In many cases it is the lack of animation or psychical infusion that gives peculiar strength to images of God. Nature in its entirety was not swallowed up in psychic energies. It has a "quasi-independence of its own," else nonsense is made of the Creation stories by an emanationist theory of origins.[10] The study of images based upon nature consequently has to proceed upon the assumption that God sustained an intimate relation to both animate and inanimate phenomena. Certainly the biblical authors did know the difference between rocks, wind, or light on the one hand, and the aliveness of nature on the other. They used nature's inertness to portray God and in some cases narrowly missed identifying him with it. However, the fear of idolatry defeated any tendency to go in that direction. "Nature," it has been said, "can never speak the word 'pardon,'" but "this perfectly valid discovery still leaves the further question open, whether God *through nature* may speak that word to those who sincerely seek Him through nature and have heard of no other way."[11] Apparently this was true for the people of the Bible.

Wind and its scarcely distinguishable cognate, breath, are prime examples of how a phenomenon of nature was pressed into the service of imagery. From its purely physical status and origin, it became "spirit," as in man, where it represented the ability to experience that which had no counterpart in the physical senses, and it came to stand for the higher faculties of a person.[12] Also it was understood to be a third personalized being distinct from both man and God, and at last it came to be regarded in Christian tradition as one of the highest images of deity, becoming the third member of the Trinity (chap. 9). But this evolution had its humble source in the sheer physical fact of wind.

The manifold physical characteristics of wind proved highly adaptable to expressing the diverse moods of God. Wind plays upon the human body; it is kinesthetically apprehended. The human body feels it in immediacy without intermediary, as part of the world about and the breath within. Its effects are directly perceived as it moves objects about in random fashion. It is tangible, yet invisible and formless. It has no perceptible shape. It is a nothingness with power, a vacuity that acts wordlessly. It is ever moving. When it howls, its uncaring noise is heard. It ranges freely and unpredictably, is transient and undependable. Its temperature may be cool or hot; in mood, it can be gentle as a zephyr or as turbulent and violent as a storm. It cleanses by sweeping away and destroying debris. It moves the passive and inert elements of the world, enlivening them to become animate, at least for a time. It is power.

These characteristics form the basis of many images wherein God is seen as using the wind for his purposes. It blights the land (Gen. 41:6). It causes Jonah to become faint (Jon. 4:8). In its beneficence it brings food to the Hebrews (Num. 11:31). In its destructive nature it rends mountains (1 Kings 19:11), carries off idols (Isa. 57:13; Dan. 2:35), and Job finds that it wipes away his honor (30:15). But it is also a messenger of God (Ps. 104:4), and he himself rides upon it (2 Sam. 22:11, Ps. 104:3). By it God eliminates the unworthy shepherds of Israel (Jer. 22:22). Their iniquities sweep men away like the wind (Isa. 64:61). God's breath is like an overflowing stream that reaches up to the rock (Isa. 30:28). By their apostasy the people of Israel have sown the wind and will reap the whirlwind (Hos. 8:7). The fruitlessness of Ephraim's political alliances is described as a herding of the wind and the pursuit of the east wind (Hos. 2:1), another figure of the vacuity of these efforts. God's glory is accompanied by a turbulent wind (Exod. 1:4). The fragility and impermanence of human life are depicted as wind that "passes and comes not again" (Pss. 78:39; 103:16). Life itself in the words of the Preacher is wind, having no intrinsic value (Eccles. 1:14, 17 et al.). The false prophets' words are as empty as the wind (Jer. 5:13), as are the lying utterances of the preachers (Mic. 2:11). Job's words are cast aside as the wind (6:26; 8:2). The distress of the people is likened to a woman in childbirth, who brings forth wind (Isa. 26:18). The man who troubles his household "will inherit the wind," destruction, and chaos (Prov. 11:29). The wind is free and unpredictable; "it blows where it will"; it is heard, but no one knows where it comes from or where it goes. It is mysterious (John 3:8). Its instability accounts for those Christians who are "tossed to and fro and carried about with every wind of doctrine" (Eph. 4:14). At Pentecost the gift of the spirit comes upon those gathered "like the rush of a mighty wind" (Acts 2:2), and its bodily effects cause them, in the estimation of onlookers, to act like drunken people. In these images it is the wind, in its variant forms, that expresses the power of the deity or, on the other hand, spells out the emptiness of human endeavor.

A not unfamiliar use of wind or breath as creative or the life principle is found in the creation stories. The Priestly account of Creation pictures the wind hovering over the chaos prior to God's commands that order the chaos (Gen. 1:2). (The word *wind* has sometimes been translated as "spirit," thus removing its more naturalistic connotation.) The earlier Creation story has God breathing into man his own breath, thereby making him a living being (Gen. 2:7). This act, as von Rad notes, "distinguishes not body and 'soul,' but more realistically body and life."[13] In his vision of the valley of dry bones, Ezekiel refers to the creative power of God, when God speaks to the bones, "I will cause breath to enter you, and you shall live" (Ezek. 37:5). The creatures of the sea are created when "thou sendest forth thy breath" (Ps. 104:30). Elihu announces that "the Spirit of God has made me and the breath of the Almighty gives me life" (Job 33:9). In a contrary way an idol is distinguished from the living God by the fact that "there is no breath at all in it" (Jer. 10:14). God is supreme by virtue of his inherent creative power as the sole source of life. But the transitory character of wind or breath sounds in Job's lament that his life is only breath (7:7). It is clear that breath is a gift not given in perpetuity. For a time it energizes, but when it ceases, death occurs. When God withdraws it, the human being dies, and God is the death-dealer (Ps. 104:29; Eccles. 12:7).

On the one hand God uses wind, and on the other he is intimately associated with it. But those characteristics of wind that bespeak transitoriness or the worthlessness of life do not pertain to him. Rather it is the freedom and power of the wind that is carried over into the nature of the deity. It is the creative and death-dealing powers associated with breath that characterize him. They are not simply devices that he uses as from a distance; they are part of God himself. His is the breath that enters into man and animals, thus giving life. His is the breath removed from them at death.

An even more direct connection between a natural phenomenon and the image of God is that of a rock. It is an image that did not carry over into the New Testament except as a reference to Christ (Mark 12:10; 1 Cor. 10:4; Eph. 2:20; 1 Pet. 2:4). But it is one of which the Old Testament writers were fond. The word *rock* conjures up ideas of massive stability, inert resistance to change, dependability, impermeability, enduringness, and protection from the elements. In contrast to the shifting fortunes suggested by wind, *rock* stands for a durability over long stretches of time. As Whitehead correctly said, "So far as survival value is concerned, a piece of rock, with its past history of some eight hundred millennia, far outstrips the short span attained by any nation."[14] Rock is something to hide behind or even within if it is understood, as it should be in some passages, as a cliff with openings (Isa. 2:10, 21). When seen as a formidable height of stone, rather than simply an errant boulder, it produces awe. The images of God as a rock make use of these qualities. Hence the emphasis placed upon God as a refuge, fortress, or stronghold. He is a place of safety from dangers both within and without. The Song of David recorded in 2 Samuel 22 and Psalm 18 sounds the pervasive theme: "The Lord is my rock, and my fortress and my deliverer, my God, my rock in whom I take refuge" (2 Sam. 22:2, 3; Ps. 18:2). Repeatedly the image appears in the Psalms (31:2; 62:2, 6, 7; 71:3; 94:22). Isaiah picks up the refrain in reminding his hearers that they "have not remembered the Rock of refuge" (17:10), and encourages them in the song to be sung in Judah to "Trust in the Lord for ever, for the Lord God is an everlasting rock" (26:7). He pictures a future in which with gladness of heart they will go "to the mountain of the Lord, the Rock of Israel" (30:29). The uniqueness of God contrasted with the other rocks (gods) is set forth by the Deuteronomist in the song of Moses: "For their rock is not as our Rock," presumably because their rock does not have the enduring hardness God possesses. Or as Hannah prays, "There is none holy like the Lord, there is none besides thee; there is no rock like our God" (1 Sam. 2:23; Ps. 18:31) Deutero-Isaiah has God asking "Is there a God besides me?" and answering the rhetorical question, "There is no Rock; I know not any" (44:8).

God is imaged not only in terms of the rugged passivity of a rock. Personal characteristics and communication are also attributed to it. Jacob sees God as the Rock of Israel, bearing the name of Shepherd (Gen. 49:24), while Moses criticizes Jeshrun for scoffing "at the Rock of his salvation" (Deut. 32:15). David exalts the rock of "his salvation" (2 Sam. 22:47) as do the Psalms (19:14; 78:35; 95:1). The Rock begat you (Deut. 32:18); the Rock speaks (2 Sam. 23:3); one pleads with it for answers (Ps. 28:1); in a strangely mixed figure "my rock and fortress" is asked to "lead me and guide me" (Ps. 31:3); in depression the Psalmist asks "my rock, why hast thou forgotten me?" (Ps. 42:9); and the Lord is blessed as "my rock who trains my hands for war and my fingers for battle; my rock and my deliverer" (Ps. 144:1, 2a). Among these animate aspects of the Rock, ethical qualities are found: "The Rock, his work is perfect; for all his days are justice" (Deut. 32:4). "He is my rock, and there is no unrighteousness in him" (Ps. 92:15). The coming of the Chaldeans, Habbakuk sees as having been ordained as a judgment by the Rock (1:2).

Thus on the one hand the physical characteristics of rock form the background for protection and refuge, while on the other the rock is personified. Whether the latter represents a Hebraic view of nature as animate, it is difficult to say with confidence. In any case, it is clear that the experience of rock was transferred by the imagination of the biblical authors into a personification and animation. The apparent unchangeability of rock showed the enduring trustworthiness of God as the one in whom alone complete confidence and assurance can be placed. And as a rocky promontory standing out from the surrounding countryside it pictures God as looming up above all "rocks" in a massive majesty, that induces breathless awe and humility in the worshiper. Wherever rock imagery occurs, power is involved. At times the power is latent, as seen in the enduring stability of rock when it affords protection; at others, power is active, bringing about change, as in saving Israel.

Among the most fertile naturalistic phenomena from which the imagery of God sprang is that of light. Repeatedly light is associated with God, although he is not identified with it in every instance. The characteristics of light in whatever condition it occurs make a readily adaptable foundation for spiritual truth. It is superpersonal and mysterious. It reveals itself, and it also reveals other objects. It is self-acting and spontaneous. It emanates from some source, yet does not diminish the power of its source. It can dazzle and blind when concentrated, and it opposes darkness, clarifying that which otherwise would be hidden. It is pleasant and beneficent and even beautiful. It appeals to the eye, rather than to the ear. All these characteristics are used in the various images of light. The figure of light is so impressive that Edgar P. Dickie used it as the focus of his book *God is Light*, although maintaining that God is "never identified with it" in the Old Testament.[15] In summarizing the uses to which it is put in the Scriptures, he sees it as expressing release from error, deliverance from wrong thoughts of God and fellowmen, release from anxiety and sin's power and guilt, granting of certainty in making moral choices, and providing peace in the midst of turmoil and disharmony. In the New Testament religious certainty, conviction, peace, and a confidence unshaken by argument are the gifts of light. Dickie concludes that "Light is a symbol of the self-communicating, self-authenticating goodness of God."[16]

However, Dickie appears to be in error in his judgment that God himself is never identified with light. He is the light-bringer (Pss. 18:28; 43:3; Isa. 10:17; 45:7), but also the light itself. The Song of David in 2 Samuel affirms that "thou art my lamp, O Lord" (22:29). The Psalmist speaks of the "light of his countenance" (4:6, 44:3; 89:15). The Lord is "my light and my salvation" (Ps. 26:1), and the use of nature is explicit when God is called the sun (Ps. 84:11) and flame (Isa. 10:17). Light is most appropriate as an image of the divine glory as found in the visions of Ezekiel and in the late Isaiah: "Arise, shine; for your light has come, and the glory of the Lord has risen upon you" (60:1). "The Lord will be your everlasting light and your God will be your glory" (Isa. 60:19, 20). And Micah says, "When I sit in darkness, the Lord will be a light to me" (7:8).

As in the Judaic Scriptures light disperses darkness, seen as evil, death, ignorance, and distress, the figure is carried over into Christian Scriptures. John's Gospel is rich in its exposition of the contrasts between light and darkness, life and death, where Christ is viewed as the true light (1:9, 12:46). Light and life become virtually interchangeable: "In him was life and the life was the light of men" (1:4). Light animates and guides those who believe in Christ. Christ himself announces that "I am the light of the world; he who follows me will not walk in darkness, but will have the light of life" (8:12; 9:5). Much depends in these passages on whether the reader identifies Christ with God or leans to the view that Christ is an emissary of God. If the former alternative is accepted, it is God in Christ who is the light of the world, whereas the second alternative subordinates Christ to God (chap. 11). Paul associates the light God has commanded to shine out of darkness with "the light of true knowledge of the glory of God in the face of Christ" (2 Cor. 4:6). The opening passage of Hebrews, where the Son is said to reflect the glory of God (1:3), bears the sense of light, since the Greek word for effulgence or radiance lies behind the English translation of the word "reflection." The first Johannine epistle states that "God is light" (1:5), and Revelation ecstatically proclaims the glory of God as the light of the New Jerusalem, where there is no need for the light of the lamp or sun, "for the Lord God will be the light of its inhabitants" (21:23; 22:5). The dazzling brightness of God's glory, if not God himself, sets him apart from all that is worldly, for he "dwells in unapproachable light" (1 Tim. 6:16).

The manner in which God's glory is figured by light expresses the splendor of his manifestation. Yet the world *glory* itself is one whose meaning baffles interpreters. It bespeaks the goal of the devout life. It summons human beings to an objective worship that begets both humility and an exaltation of spirit virtually unanalyzable, since it breaks through the limits of human discourse. It is no wonder that Bevan has to conclude that the image of God in his glory as light is best understood "when no attempt is made to explain it," and one comes almost to feel it as a "literal statement of recognized truth."[17]

Light and fire are closely related natural phenomena. It might be argued that fire was the product of human invention rather than of nature. No matter how it entered the human scene, it is also a part of nature, as in lightning and volcanic action. As such it became the basis of a limited number of images of God. Its natural properties are given full play in both Testaments. Fire is irresistible energy, tangible, visible, multiform, and potentially dangerous, provoking fear. When set loose, its unpredictable power destroys all before it. It melts metallic objects and burns up organic matter. Yet it also cleanses and purifies, and serves as a test where impurity is detectable (see Num. 31:23).

Fire is a favorite instrument of God's judgment and wrath. Sodom and Gomorrah are destroyed by it as a punishment for the evil they have practiced (Gen. 19:24). The men of Korah with all their goods are consumed by the fire that comes forth from the Lord (Num. 16:35; 26:10), although as the second passage has it, "The sons of Korah did not die"! (v.11). The wrath of God is turned against the idol worshipers: "for a fire is kindled by my anger, and it burns to the depths of Sheol" (Deut. 32:22). The disobedience of the sons of Aaron incites fire to come forth from the presence of the Lord to devour them (Lev. 10:2), whereas the fire "from before the Lord" consumed the properly offered sacrifice (Lev. 9:24). Elijah's contest with the priests of Baal finds God to be the true God because he answers by fire (1 Kings 18:24; 38). Elijah, again, proves that he is a man of God when fire burns up the troops sent by the King of Samaria (2 Kings 1:12, 14). The Psalmist sees the power of God exercised as "fire goes before him, and burns up his adversaries round about" (97:3). With wind, fire and flame are God's messengers (104:4). If men fail to return to the Lord, God's wrath in the form of fire will descend upon them (Jer. 4:4; 17:4; 21:22; Nah. 1:6; Zeph. 3:8). If the Sabbath is not kept holy, even Jerusalem will be destroyed by the fire of God's wrath (Jer. 17:27). The third "Isaiah" has the Lord coming himself in fire to execute the unrighteous (Isa. 66:15, 16). Another use of fire is found in Zechariah's writings. The angel of God proclaims a future in which Jerusalem will be protected from her foes. "For I will be to her a wall of fire round about and I will be the glory within her" (2:5). As with the fire chariots ready to protect Elisha, so here the fire has lost none of its destructive capacity against Israel's foes. Its deterrent power is substituted for the man-made walls, which might fall, whereas the fire of God's defense cannot be breached.

Fire is the accompaniment and sign of the divine presence. The flaming bush miraculously outlines holy space where God is present and from which he speaks (Exod. 3:2–5). By a pillar of fire, as well as the cloud, God's concern for his people is exhibited as he guides their wanderings (Exod. 13:21, 22; 14:24; Num. 14:14). At Sinai the Lord's might and awe-inspiring presence is accompanied by "thunders and lightning," and he himself descends upon the mountain in fire (Exod. 19:16, 18). At various times he speaks out of fire (Deut. 4:12, 33, 36; 5:4, 22, 26; 18:16; Ps. 29:7). Even as with the images of light, so fire represents the overwhelming majesty of the deity (Isa. 10:16). So Ezekiel fuses light, lightning, and fire in his vision of God's glory. Fire flashes continually, something appears as burning coals of fire, and out of the fire lightning emanates (1:4, 13). As some commentators would have it, the vision is that of the sun chariot, overwhelmingly impressive as the presence of the great God.

The ways in which God employs or is associated with fire show him to be the fire-bringer, but there are very few references that show him to *be* fire. The Deuteronomist pronounces the Lord God "a devouring fire, a jealous God" (4:24; 9:3). A doubtful identification might be inferred from David's song in Second Samuel, where smoke comes from the Lord's nostrils and "devouring fire from his mouth" (22:9), or again when Isaiah says of the light of Israel, that is, God, he will become a fire (10:17). But no doubt is left of the intent of the writer of Hebrews when he calls God a "consuming fire" (12:29).

Other aspects of nature are used to represent God. Water, which in various forms portrays cleansing, fertilizing, healing, or danger (2 Sam. 22:17; Ps. 18:16; Isa. 43:2), is also unstable (Gen. 49:4). Its vitalizing power appears when God is imaged as "the fountain of living waters" (Jer. 2:13; 17:13). But its instability is used when Jeremiah asks, "Wilt thou be to me like a deceitful brook, like waters that fail?" (15:18). Earth never is pressed into service to provide an image of God, for repeatedly God is the Creator of and Lord over earth. It is his footstool as king (Isa. 66:1; Acts 7:49), whereas heaven (sky) is his dwelling place and throne. From heaven he looks down upon all the earth (Ps. 102:19), and humans are reminded that he is in heaven and they are on earth (Eccles. 5:2). He fills both heaven and earth (Jer. 23:24), yet is elevated above all. Sometimes the word *heaven* is used as a circumlocution for God, but he is never identified explicitly with it. Mountains are also used to express his transcendent authority, as at Mount Sinai, Mount Carmel, and Zion. Jesus' sermon on the Mount, the

Transfiguration scene, and his appearance to the disciples after the Resurrection employ high places to signify divine illumination. Many references in the Old Testament refer to God's holy mountain (Pss. 48:2; 87:1; Isa. 11:9), and a few speak of a mountain as the abode of God (Ps. 68:16, 18). But he is never pictured as a mountain.

Animate features of nature become images of God as living creatures best express his wrath or protection. God is the fierce lion roaring so that the rest of nature trembles (Amos 1:2; Jer. 4:7; 25:30). When Hosea spells out God's judgment upon Ephraim, he likens God to a lion, a leopard, or a bear: "I will tear open their breast and there I will devour them like a lion, as a wild beast would rend them" (13:7–8). Isaiah takes up the image of the lion that is not diverted from its prey by the futile shouting of shepherds, but then in an abrupt change of imagery, he adds, "Like birds hovering, so the Lord of hosts will protect Jerusalem" (31:4, 5). Here both the savagery and beneficence of God are depicted.

The images drawn from nature all bespeak power, devastating or benign. If God were not powerful, he would be like the idols Isaiah scorned and satirized. Power draws attention to itself. It makes itself felt, heard, and seen. Power lets mankind know that reality is present. It demands to be respected. One is humbled by it and stands in awe of it. God's goodness is ineffective without it, wandering off into a realm of ideal possibilities without the embodiment that power gives.[18] The ethical attributes of God, his justice and righteousness, his concern and love for Israel and Christians are acts carried out by his power. Or to speak philosophically for the moment, axiology, which incorporates moral values, is founded upon ontology, that is, power or reality. So stark nature provided many of the images in which God's reality was manifested. But it was incapable of satisfying other aspects of God's nature. Personal imagery also displayed power and, what was even more important, the purposiveness of the deity.

NOTES

1. Cf. Walter J. Ong, S.J., "Maranatha: Death and Life in the Text of the Book," *Journal of the American Academy of Religion* 45, no. 4 (December 1977): 443. "We cannot everlastingly repair to one more piece to state the meaning of the last one, one more book to give the meaning of previous, one more commentary upon a commentary upon a text." Paul Holmer, *The Grammar of Faith*, (New York, Hagerstown, San Francisco, London: Harper and Row, 1978), 28.

2. Charles Davis, *Body as Spirit* (New York: The Seabury Press, 1976), 154.

3. "However deeply moving and profoundly convincing religious experiences may be, their actual content and their explicit meaning is always found in terms of conceptions derived from culture and beliefs of the individual involved." Gordon Kaufmann, "Attachment to God," *Andover-Newton Quarterly* 17, no. 4 (March 1977): 267.

4. Cf. John E. Smith, *The Analogy of Experience* (New York, Evanston, San Francisco, London: Harper and Row, 1973), 44. "God cannot be sensuously perceived," Lewis S. Ford, *The*

Lure of God (Philadelphia: Fortress Press, 1978), 72. "God is not present to be touched and seen and heard. . . ." Kaufmann, "Attachment," 266.

5. Augustine saw the connection between the senses and images. "And I enter the fields and roomy chambers of memory, where are the treasures of countless images, imported into it from all manner of things by the senses. And yet the things themselves do not enter it, but only the images of the things perceived are there ready at hand for thought to recall. And who can tell how those images are formed, notwithstanding that it is evident by which of the senses each has been fetched in and treasured up." *Confessions*, bk. 10. chap. 8. 12, 13.

6. Augustine was fond of the image of fountain, e.g. God as a fountain of mercies. *Confessions*, Bk. 4. chap. 5.7; Bk. 5. chap. 1. 16, 26; Letter 148, sec. 5, *Nicene and Post-Nicene Fathers of the Christian Church*, ed. Philip Schaff (New York: The Christian Literature Co., 1892), vol. 1.

7. Thus E. C. Rust, *Nature and Man in Biblical Thought* (London: Lutterworth Press, 1953), chaps. 3 and 4. Also Johannes P. E. Pedersen, *Israel*, trans. Aslang Møller (Oxford: H. Milford, Oxford University Press, 1925), vols. 1 and 2.

8. H. W. Robinson, *Revelation and Inspiration in the Old Testament*, (Oxford: Oxford University Press, 1946), 16.

9. Cf. Rust, *Nature and Man*, 54.

10. Ibid., 66.

11. Edgar P. Dickie, *God Is Light* (New York: Charles Scribner's Sons, 1954), 3.

12. Bevan argues that *ruach* (wind) represents a higher dignity than *nephesh*. "It is used for the stronger and higher activities of man's inner life, for which *nephesh* would not be appropriate." Edwyn Bevan, *Symbolism and Belief* (New York: The Macmillan Co., 1938), 162, 170.

13. Gerhard von Rad, *Genesis*, trans. John H. Marks (Philadelphia: The Westminster Press, 1961), 75.

14. Alfred N. Whitehead, *Symbolism, Its Meaning and Effect* (Cambridge: The University Press, 1928), 76.

15. Dickie, *God Is Light*, 34.

16. Ibid., 39, 40. Cf. also Bevan, *Symbolism and Belief*, chap. 6 on Light.

17. Bevan, *Symbolism and Belief*, 141.

18. "There may be beings we can adore for their goodness which are as powerless as the self-subsistent values and the eternal objects of modern philosophy. But what is powerless cannot have the character of deity; it cannot be counted upon, trusted in; to it no prayers ascend." H. R. Niebuhr, *The Meaning of Revelation* (New York: The Macmillan Co., 1941), 185.

8

Anthropomorphic Images of God

Mankind is immersed in nature. The physical body, with its aches and pains and sensations of well-being, attests to its inescapable grounding in nature. One's place in history is dictated by the physical sexual acts of parents, and at last the failure of the physical organism spells death. Physical joys and pains are transmuted into psychological joys and pains, as also the joys and pains of the spirit exhibit themselves in physical manifestations. This intricate and intimate association of flesh with the psychical aspects of human beings seems clearly to have been dominant in the Old Testament, where man is obviously a part of nature, and yet has mental features that lift him above sheer brute existence.[1] So intimate, indeed, is the relation between these two aspects of human beings that the idea of a survival of the individual as a disembodied soul after death is virtually unknown in the Hebrew Scriptures. Nothing survived death in Israelite anthropology: "Man was made of dust, and into him was breathed the breath of God. When he died, the body returned to dust (that observably was the case) and the breath returned to air. What was there that could survive death? Nothing."[2] The New Testament, on the other hand, tends to see the psychical or spiritual aspect of human beings as distinguishable from the physical, and thereby makes place for the continued existence of the soul after death. But in neither case is there a detailed examination of the relation between the physical and spiritual attributes of human beings. The dual interplay between the two is simply accepted.

Consequently, in respect to images of God, some lean heavily upon the physical elements of human beings, while others are dependent upon the mental features. Those of the first type are properly anthropomorphic images, and those of the second anthropopathic. The term *anthropomorphism* should be retained for those images of God which picture him as having bodily human form and exercizing the physical functions essential to a body, while *anthropopathism* is appropriate to those human aspects that make up the subjectivity of the self, such as emotion, volition, memory, knowledge, wisdom, and moral character. When this distinction is made, however, anthropomorphism and anthropopathism are not totally sundered from each other. Behind some anthropopathism there lurks an anthropomorphism, as in the cases of God's speaking or hearing. These acts are grounded in anthropomorphic realities, although both imply that God enjoys the capacities of intelligence, an anthropopathic attribute. Yet many anthropopathic images are essentially "disembodied" representations of God. They refer to invisible capacities of the human self, transferred to God.

Anthropomorphic images have usually been placed at a lower level of religious sophistication than anthropopathisms. The latter are held to be associated with the loftier character of the deity, whereas the former make God too limited and concrete, or even debase him. So Edwyn Bevan argued that "all modes of speaking of God which represent Him as having material form or a local habitation—all those familiar phrases about the hand of God or the eyes of God or the throne of God—are symbolical." They are merely poetical metaphors. On the other hand, he continued, "the modes of speech which attribute to God characteristics of the human mind and spirit are, if not literally true, at any rate much nearer the reality." But even among what have been called the anthropopathic images, Bevan admits that "there are grades of resemblance to the reality," and he illustrates the differentiation by contrasting God as wise, just, or loving with God as angry.[3] This tendency to downgrade anthropomorphic images, and to approve some anthropopathic ones in preference to others, reveals how criteria from sensibilities developed in independence of the Bible are introduced as means of evaluation. The Bible, however, makes no such distinctions. Anthropomorphic images lie side by side with anthropopathic ones, and anger or vindictiveness is as much a part of the composite picture of God as are love, justice, or wisdom. Preferences drawn from experiences of another period force invidious distinctions between these images, each of which presumably had equal value in its day. This practice of selectively reading the record, common as it is, may be justifiable today in the light of sharpened ethical and religious awareness, but it should not be used to eliminate from consideration or reduce in significance those images which do not accord with these sensibilities. Nor should the fact that scholarly opinion often relegates anthropomorphisms to the earliest strata of literary and historical deposit be determinative of the role that these images play in the total biblical panorama. Even the Priestly account of creation, usually considered to be the product of a relatively advanced period of Jewish religious thought, has its anthropomorphic features, and the New Testament unblushingly included passages in which God assumes the human form of Jesus.

One of the dominant interests of the Priestly authors and editors was to make clear that God in his holiness stood at a great distance from mankind. However, their account of the creation of humanity did not avoid anthropomorphism. The original parents were made in the image of God (Gen. 1:26, 27; 5:1, 2; 9:6); male and female he created them. It is usually pointed out that these passages do not state that God is in the image of mankind, yet it is all but impossible to avoid the conclusion that the writers have merely reversed the order of the imagery whereby the nature and, if one will, the form of male and female is the ruling source of the imagery. It has even been suggested that the words of Genesis 1:26 refer to a "physical resemblance between God and man," or at least that God has visible form, if not a physical body. It is not denied that mankind is like God in moral and spiritual qualities, but one author, Ryder Smith, claims that this is not the truth that the passage teaches.[4]

In the New Testament Paul makes use of the notion of man (male) as bearing resemblance to God. Since he stresses the distinction between male and female in the passage, it seems probable that the Apostle intends the resemblance in some degree to include a physical resemblance to God. A man, he counsels, should not worship with his head covered, "since he is the image and glory of God" (1 Cor. 11:7). But in emphasizing the maleness of both man and God, Paul has not faithfully reproduced the meaning of the Genesis passage (1:27), which includes the female. If only males bear the image of God, then the universalism of Genesis is restricted. Theologically it is even more restricted when Pannenberg can deny the natural affiliation between mankind in general and God, in his assertion: "Man is not an image of God simply by nature if we understand by that what human beings just are in any case."[5] Apparently influenced by his Christian convictions, Pannenberg wants to express the idea that the true image of God in man is found in Christ, and in those of a Christlike nature. But in doing so, he has narrowed the circle of those who bear the image of God to the faithful, in contradiction to the meaning of the creation story.

By the inversion of man's being the image of God, rather than God's being in the image of man, it could be said that we have a case of theomorphism rather than anthropomorphism. Yet it is through the anthropomorphism that one clue is given to the nature of God. With the passage of time the slightest hint of a physical resemblance of God to man was to be eradicated. Physical matter, in Christian thought, became a sign of debasement, and spirit was exalted. So Tatian could write, "The perfect God is without flesh; but man is flesh. The bond of the flesh is the soul; that which encloses the soul is flesh."[6] The soul, which bears the image of God, is no longer, as in early Hebraic anthropology, inseparable from the physical body. It is caged by physical matter, which in no way bears the image of God. In modern times Paul Tillich accentuated the difference from the Old Testament view by identifying the image of God with the rational element in human beings. "Man is the image of God," he wrote, "because his *logos* is analogous to the divine *logos*, so that the divine *logos* can appear as man without destroying the humanity of man."[7] In spite of sophisticated attempts to interpret the anthropomorphic images of God in man, we do well first of all to allow for the naive realism of the biblical record. Later views in Scripture and those produced by exegetes certainly move beyond anthropomorphism, but they cannot eliminate from the pages of the Bible these more starkly realistic images. It may be, as one critic puts it, that "the incorporeality of God was too abstract a thought for an Israelite even of the fifth century," but we are not in the business of offering excuses for ancient peoples who do not share a perspective yet to be developed.[8] The anthropomorphisms remain as vigorous, impressive images that prevent the religious imagination from rendering God as a formless, cloudy being visited only intermittently by spiritual virtuosi. The Bible is not so delicate in respect to modern tastes, and it retains the earthy anthropomorphic relics as testimony to the lively impress God makes on human nature and history.

Foremost among the anthropomorphic images of God stands the earliest story of God's creation of man (Gen. 2:4ff.). God works up or molds from the dust an inert human figure, as though by physical exertion. He breathes his own breath (wind, air) into this passive entity, which then comes alive. He physically places him in the Garden and gives orders as to his behavior in respect to the trees planted there. On second thought he realizes that the man needs a helper, so out of the same material of which man is made, beasts and herds are created. This experiment fails, so God by extracting a rib from the man makes a woman. After the disobedience, the Lord walks in the Garden to enjoy its coolness, but the human couple shrink from his presence and hide. But God cannot see them and is forced to ask "Where are you?" (Gen. 3:9). The man recognizes the Lord's presence either by his steps or his garments brushing against the vegetation, and at last the couple stands self-condemned when they admit their nakedness. The curses then follow.

The emergent image of God is clearly anthropomorphic. Here God is no intangible, all-knowing, all-powerful, eternal spirit. He is limited in knowledge and, as the walk in the Garden implies, he occupies space. He is a being shaped upon the lines of a finite, physical figure with capacities scarcely exceeding those of his creation. He even fears them (Gen. 3:22). But God is also anthropopathically imaged. His creative attempts may have revealed lack of foresight, but this God has intelligence. He sees the man's needs. He issues commands; he immediately perceives that the man has convicted himself by admitting his nakedness (Gen. 3:11). And the curses he utters are entirely understandable, although severe. He exhibits power both by his words and in driving the man and woman from the Garden (Gen. 3:24).

One need hardly be reminded that such imagery occurs in the form of a myth that should be taken seriously, not literally, as we have been repeatedly told. Various profound truths about the facts of human life are found here. Humans come from the dust and will return to it. Life is fragile and transient, beset with toil and difficulty. A disjunction has occurred between the animal world and man. The earth, which ideally would not have to be labored over to produce food, has turned against mankind. Disobedience is indigenous to humans. Sexual differentiation brings shame with it. Woman is subordinate to man, and because of her part in the disobedience, childbirth will be painful. To recount these observations or others about human life is to show forth in mythical terms the very substance of that life. There is a realism, naive though it is, that cuts to the heart of experience, and by the vivacity of the images found in the story one sees by sober insight the nature of human existence as some ancient Hebrews understood it. It may be counted as less exalted in tone and more primitive in conception than the resonant lines of the Priestly account of creation, but its anthropomorphic and anthropopathic imagery carry a weight and depth lacking in the sophisticated, Priestly statements. The imagery illuminates as it interprets, and without it the force of these passages would be lost. But as suggested, the Priestly account also contains anthropomorphic elements. God creates by speaking, naming, and commanding; he sees that parts of his creation are good (Gen. 1:12, 18, 25). And perhaps most clearly, anthropomorphism shows in his resting on the seventh day (Gen. 2:22). Some critics have interpreted God's resting as merely a cessation of his work, thereby relaxing the impact of the anthropomorphism, which suggests that the Lord was exhausted and needed to recoup energies exerted in creation. Anthropomorphisms may limit the deity, but they also intensify his reality for the religious imagination. In another early piece of Scripture, the story of the Tower of Babel, a similar literary and religious effect is achieved. Because he cannot see what men are doing on earth, God descends through space to see the city they are building (Gen. 11:5). The limitation of the deity's knowledge is apparent, but even more significant is the fact that he has location, presumably in heaven. He occupies space himself and passes through space in his descent. He moves as a human body would move, not occupying all space at once, but going from one point to another. The same figure is used when after finishing his conversation with Abraham, God "went up" (Gen. 17:22). In both cases God is presumed to have a body. The Babel story goes on to show that the dispersal of the people and the confusion of their languages (an etiological myth) is due to his fear and that of his court, that man will threaten his authority (Gen. 11:6). So anthropopathism also enters the picture, revealing the insecurity felt by the deity.

Many acts and physical functions common to human bodies are attributed to God. He physically shuts up Noah and his family in the ark (Gen. 7:16). He touches objects. By his finger he writes on tablets of stone (Exod. 31:18). He has hands by which he exercises his power (Exod. 3:19, 20; 15:6; 1 Sam. 5:6; Job 12:9, 10; Ps. 31:5; Rom. 10:21; John 10:29). This image of God is often used to express the Lord's control over mankind and the security to be found in his keeping. As Bevan said of this figure, it makes us feel God's action more vividly and realize a truth more adequately than some "concatenation of more abstract intellectual notions."[9] Such is the impact of anthropomorphic imagery. And when the hand of God is modified by the word *right*, it stands in the New Testament for the exaltation of Christ to the status of royal authority. This is the form in which Christ is portrayed in Stephen's speech in Acts (2:33), and again in Hebrews (1:3, 10:12). The arm of God is another favorite image. It expresses the absolute support, dependence, and comfort to be found in the deity, for "underneath are the everlasting arms" (Deut. 33:27). On the other hand, by his arm his power in creation is exhibited (Jer. 27:51). By it he redeems his people (Ps. 77:15), and wreaks destruction and punishment. Whether by his hand or arm he throws down great stones upon the Amorites "and they died" (Josh. 10:11), and Isaiah foresees the "descending blow of his arm" bringing punishment on the Assyrians (30:30). God has the features of a man. By the breath of his nostrils he piled up the waters at the Red Sea (Exod. 15:8), and from his nostrils, in scenes of earthly catastrophe, smoke goes up (2 Sam. 22:9, 16; Ps. 18:8). In one case he saves by the power of breath. In the other, smoke associated with the devouring fire from his mouth signifies destructive power. His face or countenance will shine upon his people (Num. 6:25, 26). If his people will return to him, he will not "turn away his face" (2 Chron. 30:9), for if his face is averted, pain and sorrow follow (Ps. 13:1). To see the face of the Lord is to realize blessedness (Matt. 18:10; Rev. 22:4). God's face would not be complete without a mouth. He speaks to Moses "mouth to mouth" (Num. 12:8), and man lives "by everything that proceeds out of the mouth of the Lord" (Deut. 8:3). A mouth, of course, is a vehicle to express God's communication with the world. He creates by speech, and directs Moses and the Patriarchs. The prophets feel the burden of responsibility to speak his words. "Thus says the Lord," precedes their oracles. The notion of God's voice is repeatedly used. He speaks the commandments (Exod. 20:1). He talks confidentially with Moses, face to face as a man speaks to a friend (Exod. 33:11). A conversation is held with the prophet Balaam, who at last answers Balak with the words "what the Lord speaks that I will speak" (Num. 22:7ff; 24:13), words repeated by Micaiah (1 Kings 22:14). The children of Israel are often castigated for failing to obey his voice (Deut. 8:20; 9:23; Josh. 22:2 Judg. 2:20; 1 Sam. 12:15; Jer. 3:13; 7:23, 24). The impression made by his voice is so strong that the boy Samuel mistakes it for the actual words of Eli (1 Sam. 3:4ff). Great and majestic power is associated with his voice and speech. Elihu says his voice thunders wondrously (Job 37:4, 5), and the Psalms bear witness to the power of his voice, for it thunders, breaks cedars, flashes flames of fire, shakes the wilderness, and like a tornado whirls the oaks (29:3ff.). It melts the earth

(Ps. 46:6). When God speaks, the waters above the heavens are put in tumult (Jer. 10:13). His roaring and shouting shake the whole creation (Amos 1:2; Jer. 25:30, 31; Joel 3:16). Whatever he speaks surely will be performed (Ezek. 12:25, 28). At times his words are words of peace (Isa. 40:1, 2; Ps. 85:8); at others he speaks in jealousy and anger (Ezek. 36:5). In the New Testament his voice from heaven identifies Jesus at his baptism as his son (Mark 1:11; Luke 3:22; cf. also Matt. 17:5; John 12:28). And John's gospel claims him to be the Word of God (John 1:1, 14).

If the image of "mouth" stands for God's voice and speech, so also the anthropomorphic image of "ear" expresses the conviction that God hears. Prayer presupposes that God hears both the supplications of those who seek him, and also their praises of him. Even as God speaks and man hears, so also man speaks and God hears; hence the vivacity that the image of God's ear gives. Hezekiah prays, asking God to "incline thine ear" (2 Kings 19:16; Isa. 37:17). The Psalms repeatedly use the image. "Give ear to my words, O Lord," followed by the Hebraic parallelism, "Hearken to the sound of my cry" (5:1, 2). And the figure is repeated throughout the Psalms (e.g., 4:1; 6:8, 9; 10:27; 17:1, 6; 31:2; 39:12; 55:1, 19, etc.). Even as God created the ear in man, "does he not hear?" the Psalmist asks (94:9). God's solicitude is expressed in this auditory image. The groanings of the Israelites in Egyptian bondage and their cries for help are heard by God, who sets in motion their redemption (Deut. 26:7; Exod. 2:24). Their murmurings against the Lord in the wilderness (Exod. 16:7) excite him to action. If widows and orphans are afflicted, the Lord promises to hear their cry and in anger to kill those who oppress them (Exod. 22:23, 24). His anger is kindled with dread consequences when people complain in his hearing (Num. 11:1ff.; 14:27; Deut. 1:34). Joshua's command for the sun to stand still succeeds because the Lord "hearkened to the voice of a man" (Josh. 10:14). Solomon beseeches God to have regard to his prayer and hearken to his supplication and that of the people (1 Kings 8:28ff.). Jeremiah foresees a time when the people will call upon the Lord and God promises "I will hear you" (29:12). Jonah's prayer in the belly of the fish is heard, and he is rescued (2:2ff.). Nehemiah recounts the history of his forefathers, who in spite of their evil, sought the Lord and "thou didst hear from heaven" (9:28).

In the references to prayer in the New Testament, the assumption of God's hearing is maintained. Without it, as also in the Old Testament, one of the most essential parts of worship would be excised. So Jesus tells his followers to pray (Matt. 9:38), and instructs them how to do so (Matt. 6:5, 9ff.). Children are brought to him so that he can lay hands on them and pray for them (Matt. 19:13). And the scene in Gethsemane is climaxed by the agony of Jesus in prayer (Mark 14:32ff.). In the Gospel of John it would seem that Jesus had no need to pray. His life is completely under God's will, and he virtually directs events about him. Nevertheless he does pray.

At the raising of Lazarus, he thanks the heavenly Father for hearing him, and adds with complete assurance, "I know that thou hearest me always, but I have said this on account of the people standing by . . ." (11:41, 42). The passage sounds as though he really had not prayed, but had spoken for the benefit of those near by "that they may believe that thou didst send me" (v. 42). In another instance he promises to pray to the Father so that he will send another counselor, although at that point he does not pray (14:16). In what purports to be a prayer, although its content has a didactic ring to it, Jesus asks that he be glorified. Those persons to whom he has given the words that the Father had given to him know that he has come from God. "I am praying for them; I am not praying for the world." But he also prays for those yet to be converted. "I do not pray for these only, but also for those who believe in me" through the disciples' words. He asks that those "whom thou has given me, may be with me where I am" so they may behold his glory (17:1, 6–9; 20, 24). The difference between this "prayer" and the prayer he taught in the Sermon on the Mount suggests that the Johannine passage is less a prayer to God than a series of teachings reworked by the author of the Gospel, with theological interests in mind. Prayer to God was certainly an essential part of the life of the early Christians. They attend the temple and in their homes eat together and praise God (Acts 2:46, 47). The Ephesian letter urges them to pray at all times (6:18). The Thessalonians are exhorted to pray constantly, giving thanks in all circumstances (1 Thess. 5:16), and the author of 1 Timothy asks his readers to pray in every place (2:8). Clearly, unless God is believed to hear, in whatever sense that is possible, these admonitions would be pointless. And if his "ear" is open to human supplication and praise, the communication from God to man in speech is paralleled by man's words to God. A reciprocal relation is established, but there is no doubt that the deity has the last word.

God speaks and hears, and also has "eyes" to see. To be in the eyes of the Lord is to be favored, approved, cared for, and safe. Noah enjoyed favor in the eyes of the Lord (Gen. 6:8). The land into which the Israelites will enter is always under the eyes of God, that is, under his care (Deut. 11:12). He keeps Jacob as "the apple of his eye" (Deut. 32:10; Ps. 17:8; Zech. 2:8). The Danites are sent on their way in safety, for the eye of the Lord is on them (Judges 18:6). Those who fear him are under his eye, that they may be saved from death and famine (Ps. 33:18, 19; 34:15). Israel is to be saved because it is "precious in my eyes" and "I love you" (Isa. 43:4). The servant of God is honored in the eyes of the Lord (Isa. 49:5). The Babylonian captives are promised return, for "I will set my eyes upon them for good" (Jer. 24:6). Ezra recounts how the builders of the temple were not hindered from their work when challenged because the eye of their God was on them (5:5). However, if God hides his eyes, favor is lost (Isa. 1:15). In the author's evaluation of various kings, the formula of doing right or not doing right in the eyes of the Lord is monotonously employed (1 Kings 15:5, 11; 2 Kings 12:2; 14:3; 15:3, 34; 16:2, etc.). The note of God's judgment echoes in these passages with favor for some and disapproval for others, according to the historian's estimate of their fidelity to the Lord. It is by his eye that punishment will come upon sinners. Amos proclaims, "I will set my eyes upon them for evil and not for good" (9:4). The boastful cannot stand before his eyes (Ps. 5:5). His eyes search out truth (Jer. 5:3), but do not find it among his wayward people, according to Ezekiel. Consequently his eye will not spare or pity them (Ezek. 5:11; 7:4, 9; 8:18; 9:10). In prayer to God, Samuel is humbled in God's sight (2 Sam. 7:8), and in seeking God's help in his sickness, Hezekiah pleads for God's attention by asking him to open his eyes to him (2 Kings 19:16; Isa. 37:17). The oversight of the Lord on all that happens is expressed in figures that are eventually to be turned into the doctrine of omniscience. Elihu warns that God sees everywhere; his eyes are always upon the ways of man (Job 34:21, 22; Prov. 5:21; 15:3). As the Chronicler puts it, "the eyes of the Lord run to and fro throughout the whole earth" (2 Chron. 16:9). But in foreseeing his own death, Job affirms that "the eye of him who sees me will behold me no more; while thy eyes are upon me, I shall be gone" (7:8). He will go down to Sheol where God does not see.

One last anthropomorphic image of God is his "feet," a figure seldom used. In a description of God's power over nature, 2 Samuel speaks of God's bowing the heavens and "thick darkness was under his feet" (2 Sam. 22:10; Ps. 18:9), thus suggesting his domination. The place of his sanctuary will be beautiful, and there he makes "the place of my feet glorious" (Isa. 60:13). In his temple vision, Ezekiel uses the kingly image. The Lord says "the soles of my feet will be placed there" as a sign that he will dwell in the midst of his people for ever (43:7). Feet seem to stand for God's firmness and abiding nature, even as they also bespeak his kingly radiant presence and domination.

Anthropomorphic images may be discounted as unworthy of the exalted God, but they convey a sharpness of delineation of the divine nature scarcely bettered by the anthropopathisms with which they are intimately connected. They strike the mind with the force of God's presence that has outlived the querulous criticisms of theological sophistication. They may not do justice to all aspects of God, but those who wrote and used them were aware of the sensible impact that the deity makes upon human life, for which no more lucid images have been formed.

NOTES

1. Rust claims that man "may not be immersed in nature and treated as a part of it." However, he also maintains, with many other biblical scholars, that the Old Testament views man as an animated body in which "the physiological and the psychical were closely intertwined." E. C. Rust, *Nature and Man in Biblical Thought* (London: Lutterworth Press, 1953), 49, 104.

2. John Bowker, *The Religious Imagination and the Sense of God* (Oxford: Clarendon Press, 1978), 42.

3. Edwyn Bevan, *Symbolism and Faith* (New York, The Macmillan Co., 1938), 206.

4. Cf. David Cairns, *The Image of God in Man* (New York: Philosophical Library, 1953), 22.

5. Wohlfahrt Pannenberg, *Faith and Reality,* trans. John Maxwell (London: Search Press; Philadelphia: The Westminster Press, 1977), 49.

6. *The Ante-Nicene Fathers,* American Reprint of the Edinburgh ed. (Grand Rapids, Mich.: Wm. B. Eerdman's Publishing Co., 1951), 2:71.

7. Paul Tillich, *Systematic Theology* (Chicago: The University of Chicago Press, 1951), 1:259.

8. *The Interpreter's Bible* (Nashville, New York: Abingdon-Cokesbury Press, 1952), 1:484.

9. Bevan, *Symbolism and Faith,* 259, 260.

9

Anthropopathic Images of God

Whereas anthropomorphic images are based upon the physical aspects of human beings, the anthropopathic images depend upon those capabilities with which human self-transcendence is associated. While anthropomorphisms may be scoffed at as leading to the image of the "old man in the sky," anthropopathisms are stoutly defended on the grounds of their moral and spiritual superiority. Presumably they reflect the higher powers of God as they do of man, lifting both above the realm of nature. Should not God be imaged by the noblest elements of humankind, such as rational endowment, self-consciousness, and self-determination? However, many of these anthropopathisms can only be exercised on the basis of their anthropomorphism. Hating, choosing, or loving are often manifested by images drawn from the "cruder" level of a physical agency. In fact, this intimate association of the bodily images with those of an anthropopathic type has led to the unfortunate tendency to collapse anthropopathism into the all-inclusive category of the anthropomorphic.

Yet the two types are distinguishable. When God is imaged as choosing, remembering, knowing, being jealous or angry, loving and forgiving, it is not physical reality that supplies the material for the image. It is rather, if I may use the word, the "psyche" of God that is given expression. If anthropomorphisms depict God as active and dynamic in bodily terms, the anthropopathisms do so in terms of His personal attributes. The God depicted by the biblical authors is not an impersonal Absolute, which as William James said, "neither acts nor suffers, nor loves nor hates," a being that "has no needs, desires or aspiration, no failures or successes, friends or enemies, victories or defeats."[1] The biblical texts themselves seem to vibrate with dynamism as though they partook of God's own energy as he goes about his manifold works. And so freighted is the Bible with these anthropopathic manifestations that it becomes necessary, difficult as it may be, to make a judicious selection among them according to some coherent plan. Consequently, those of a broadly psychological type, including the intellectual and emotional aspects of deity, are discussed first here, followed by ethical images, and concluding with those which in some manner represent the less attractive features of the deity.

High among the psychologically based images are those which portray God as knowing, having understanding or wisdom. To be sure, a few references suggest that he is limited in this respect. In the Garden he has to ask, "Where are you?" (Gen. 3:9), and "Who told you that you were naked?" (Gen. 3:11) The anthropomorphic tales of God's coming down to see what was going on at the Tower of Babel and in Sodom and Gomorrah (Gen. 11:5, 7; 18:21) suggest that without on-site inspection he would be ignorant of what man was doing. Hosea has God criticizing Israel for having established kings "without my knowledge" (8:4), although the context may imply "without divine authority." Some wicked persons act as though God could not see them, and they say "How can God know? Is there knowledge in the Most High?" (Ps. 73:11) The lament of the Psalmist is that the wrongdoers prosper, while he has kept himself clean and innocent and he only has endured chastisement. His comfort lies in the future punishment that will befall the evildoers, and God's eventually bringing him to glory (vv. 13, 14, 18–20, 23, 24). After all, God does know him, and the boast of the wicked that God is ignorant of their ways is an illusion. Job suggests that there is a place where he is beyond God's knowledge in Sheol: "The eye of him who sees me will behold me no more: while thy eyes are upon me, I shall be gone, like those whom thou dost remember no more, for they are cut off from thy hand" (7:8; Ps. 88:5).

The dominant theme of God's knowledge and wisdom sounds throughout the Old Testament texts. God sees, that is, he knows that his creation is good (Gen. 1:31). He knows both good and evil (Gen. 3:5). Hannah's prayer of exultation sings of the Lord as "a God of knowledge" (1 Sam. 2:3). The author of Joshua announces "the Mighty One, God the Lord, He knows; and let Israel itself know" (22:22). Job allies strength and knowledge when he says "With God are wisdom and might; he has counsel and understanding . . . with him are strength and wisdom" (12:13, 16; 36:5). He mockingly asks, "Will any teach God knowledge, seeing he judges those that are on high?" (21:22). Isaiah sees the punishment of Assyria coming about "by my [God's] wisdom, for I have understanding" (10:13). In praise of God's power, he claims God's understanding to be unsearchable, beyond anything man may imagine (40:28). The vision of the valley of dead bones finds the prophet humbly answering God's question as to whether the bones can live with the words "O Lord God, thou knowest" (Ezek. 37:3). Paul in a mystifying passage contrasts the wisdom of the world with "a secret and hidden wisdom of God," which apparently refers to the salvation God has planned through Jesus Christ (1 Cor. 2:7), for Christ himself is "the power and wisdom of God" (1 Cor. 1:24).

God's knowledge is not confined to a generalized understanding; it enters into the intimate details of human life. When Abimilech takes Sarah, believing her to be Abraham's sister and not his wife, God confronts Abimilech with the words, "Yes, I know that you have done this in the integrity of your heart" and prevents him from touching her (Gen. 20:6. The Psalmist repeatedly refers to God's penetration even into "the secrets of the heart" (44:21; 94:11; 103:4). The folly and wickedness of the Psalmist comes within the orbit of divine knowledge (69:5). When he is in distress of spirit, "Thou knowest my way" (142:3), a refrain heard again in Job's anguish (23:10). The 139th Psalm attests to God's overseeing knowledge. When the Psalmist sits down or arises, when thoughts and words are held within before they are formed, God "knowest me right well" (vv. 2, 4, 14). God knows Job's integrity (31:6). He knows the soul of man: "Does not he who keeps watch over your soul know it?" the writer asks (Prov. 24:12). The transgressions of Israel are an open book to God, "for I know how many are your transgressions and how great are your sins," Amos claims (5:12). Deutero-Isaiah pictures God as knowing the obstinacy of his people (48:4). The prophet Jeremiah's life is spread before God's knowledge: "Thou, O Lord, knowest me; thou seest me, and triest my mind toward thee" (12:3; 15:15). God announces "I the Lord search the mind and try the heart" (Jer. 17:10). The insolence of Moab does not escape God's attention (Jer. 48:30). The same knowledge of the intimate details of human life is rehearsed in the New Testament. Jesus' words on prayer attest that the Father knows what one needs before the asking (Matt. 6:8, 32). In the selection of a replacement for Judas, the followers of Jesus pray the Lord "who knowest the hearts of all men" to show who is to be chosen (Acts 1:24; 15:8). Paul downgrades the wise of the world because God knows their innermost thoughts to be futile (1 Cor. 3:20).

God's incisive comprehension of human life was so inclusive that the ways of human beings had been chosen and decided for them before ever they knew them. The destinies of nations and individuals are subject to his foreknowledge. Pharaoh's dream as interpreted by Joseph means "that the thing is fixed by God," and he will bring it to pass (Gen. 41:32). In directions to Moses the Lord knows in advance that unless his power is exerted, Pharaoh will not let the Hebrew people go (Exod. 3:19). The whole Exodus episode is suffused with God's prevenient actions and foreknowledge. He chooses the Hebrew people in advance of their recognition of him as their only Lord. And this fundamental fact of their existence is sounded in Amos's dire warning of future punishment: "You only have I known of all the families of the earth; therefore I will punish you for all your iniquities" (3:2). When Sennacherib comes against Judah, Isaiah prophesies of him that the destruction he carries out has been determined long ago, as is his retreat, because God has known all along "your sitting down and your going out and coming in" (2 Kings 2:25; 27–28; Isa. 37:26, 28). In a more individualistic view, Jeremiah finds himself chosen to be a prophet by God's foreknowledge. So the Lord speaks to him: "Before I formed you in the womb I knew you, and before you were born I consecrated you; I appointed you a prophet to the nations" (1:5). Jeremiah is thus caught in a profession that brings nothing but suffering. His life has been laid out for him. In the prophet's mouth God places the promise of the return from Babylonia, "For I know the plans I have for you, says the Lord, plans for welfare and not for evil, to give you a future and a hope" (29:11). Job's despair is heightened by his realization that one's length of life is limited: "his days are determined and the number of his months is with thee, and thou hast appointed his bounds that he cannot pass" (14:5).

A strong emphasis in the New Testament is placed upon God's fore-knowledge, by which he has decided what is to happen to Jesus and the new sect. Stephen is represented as making clear that Jesus' death is no mere accident of history, for this Jesus was "delivered up according to the definite plan and foreknowledge of God" (Acts 2:23). Those who were witnesses to all these things were themselves chosen by God to be witnesses (10:41), so that they could testify that Jesus was "the one ordained by God to be judge of the living and dead" (10:42). The life the Christians are to live has been assigned to them (1 Cor. 7:17). Even though their numbers are made up of the foolish and weak, lowly and despised in the world's eyes, God chose them (1 Cor. 1:27, 28; James 2:5). From the beginning they had been chosen to be saved (2 Thess. 2:13), and they have become a chosen race (1 Pet. 1:2, 2:9), even as Christ "was destined before the foundation of the world" and made manifest to them at the end of time (1:20). Paul boasts in Romans that he is an Israelite, a member of a people "whom he [God] foreknew" (11:2). In the same letter the apostle reads the purposes of God as carried out by predestination and foreknowledge. "For these whom he foreknew he also predestined to be conformed to the image of his son . . . and those whom he predestined he also called"; these in turn are to be justified and glorified (8:29, 30). In this way God's knowledge is linked with salvation. The Psalmist puts it, "the righteous are known to God" (1:6). "The Lord knows the days of the blameless and the heritage will abide forever" (37:18). Cast in Christian terms, "The Lord knows those who are his" (2 Tim. 2:19), and "the Lord knows how to rescue the godly from trial" (2 Pet. 2:9). The Ephesian letter finds the author proclaiming that God's plan of the mystery, hidden for ages, is now being manifested by the church as "the manifold wisdom of God." The entire plan of salvation, in accordance with God's eternal purpose, is realized in Jesus Christ (3:9–11).

Not less impressive testimony of God's wisdom and understanding are the images of God's knowledge as playing a decisive role in his creation of the world. In cataloguing the manifold works of God, the Psalmist says "In wisdom hast thou made them all (104:24), and Jeremiah repeats the re-frain. "It is he who made the earth by his power, who established the world by his wisdom, and by his understanding stretched out the heavens" (10:12; 51:15). The wise adviser of Proverbs attests that "The Lord by wisdom founded the earth; by understanding he established the heavens" (3:19). So God's knowledge and wisdom are firmly knit into the awe-inspiring vision of the natural world. If one is to take the meaning of the "Word" used in the Prologue of John's Gospel to signify the wisdom of God and the principle of intelligibility woven into creation, the clause that reads "all things were made through him, and without him was not anything made that was made" also bespeaks the divine wisdom as the creative agent of the world.

It is clear that these images of God's knowledge, wisdom, and understanding come close to affirming the omniscience of God, although there are exceptions. That attribute of God will be discussed later, but it is of interest at this point to see how Christ is pictured as possessing this power. As might be expected, the high Christology of the Johannine literature makes this claim in several places (John 16:30). The scene in the garden where Jesus is captured describes him as "knowing all that was to befall him," thus making Judas's betrayal of no effect (John 18:4). In his resurrection appearance, Peter says of him, "Lord, you know everything" (John 21:17). But in the first epistle of John omniscience is attributed to God alone—for "God is greater than our hearts, and he knows everything" (3:30).

God not only knows, plans, chooses, and elects in advance, but he possesses among other psychological powers that of memory, a capacity related to knowledge. Some images of God's remembering are merely ways of expressing the fact that he paid attention to certain persons, as to Noah and the beasts in the ark (Gen. 8:1) and to Rachel (Gen. 30:22). More important, God's memory is a way of describing his fidelity to the covenant, the Patriarchs, and other important persons. The rainbow reminds him of the covenant between himself and earth, and every living creature (Gen. 9:15, 16). The groaning of his people in slavery brings to mind the covenant with Abraham, Isaac, and Jacob (Exod. 2:24; 6:5; Lev. 26:42). The Psalmist rehearses the same theme in respect to his "steadfast love and faithfulness," His promise to Abraham and to his servant and to "us" (98:3; 105:42; 106:45; 119:49; 136:23). Ezekiel returns to the theme in contrasting Israel's breaking the covenant and God's own faithfulness in keeping it. "Yet I will remember my covenant with you in the days of your youth" (16:60). God remembers Ephraim with love, although "as often as I speak against him, I do remember him still. Therefore my heart yearns for him" (Jer 31:20).

Frequently prayers are offered in which appeals are made to God to remember persons for their virtues. Hezekiah's prayer for health asks God to "remember now, O Lord, my faithfulness" (2 Kings 20:3; Isa. 38:3). Nehemiah repeatedly asks God to remember him for his good (5:19; 13:14, 22, 31). God remembers Jeremiah's devotion (2:2; 18:20). God is asked to remember the afflictions, the weakness, and the frailty of human beings, and to take pity on them (Ps. 78:39; 87:50; 103:14; Job 7:7; 10:9). Sins are not to be remembered, and transgressions are to be blotted out. "I, I am he who blots out your transgressions for my own sake, and I will not remember your sins" (Isa. 43:25; Jer. 31:34). And the Psalmist beseeches God not to remember the sins of his youth and his transgressions (25:7). Yet even with these comforting thoughts of forgiveness, God is seen as one who does not forget the evils men do. The corruption of Ephraim he holds in mind, "But they do not consider that I remember all their evil wishes" (Hos. 7:2). Because of their infidelity Jeremiah says "therefore the Lord does not accept them, now he will remember their iniquity and punish their sins" (14:10). The memory of God in this way stands for his endurance. Human beings cannot escape him, for he retains tenaciously all they have done of good or evil.

Some scholars cannot bear the thought that God is a God of emotional or passionate turns of mind. Schooled in the theology that magnifies the metaphysical attributes of God, they hold to the impassibility of the deity. So F. H. Brabant can assert, "We are all ready enough to admit that, when in the Old Testament we read of God repenting, being appeased of His anger, His sorrow, His weariness, it does not mean a real alteration of mood. He may seem to change His plans, but He never changes His mind. . . . "[2] The images, however, tell a different story. He does not *seem* to change his plans; he actually does so. He is sorry he ever created man, and is grieved to his heart by having done so (Gen. 6:6). He repents of having made Saul a king (1 Sam. 15:11). While Joel advises his hearers to return to God who is gracious, merciful, slow to anger, and abounding in steadfast love, he also describes him as one "who repents of evil" (2:13). This is a God who does change his mind. His will is turned in different directions by the circumstances that take place in time, and this fact, like others of an emotional nature, clearly shows anthropopathism at work.

It is a matter of embarrassment that the Bible does not scruple to present God as a highly passionate being. He loses equanimity and sheds immutability, often with no respect to moral discrimination or accountability. The wrath or anger of God is strewn across the pages, even if they signify to modern minds the notion that such a passion is a sign of divine weakness as well as of unethical behavior. The tendency is strong, therefore, to downplay the passages wherein God exercises his wrath as being incompatible with his more loving and forgiving nature. Apparently God's anger is to be seen as a holdover from a more primitive stage of religious development. But if we accept the fact that the biblical authors and those upon whom they report actually experienced God in these terms, we had better understand these images of anger in their original sense. The reality of God as wrath so impinged upon them that when pain, physical or mental, frustration, and disaster struck, the most appropriate image which formed in their minds was modeled on what they themselves felt in these circumstances.

From beginning to end the people of the Bible inhabit a perilous and hazardous world. Nature and nations threaten to destroy them. Rulers oppress them or lead them astray. Tribes linked by a common heritage fall to squabbling among themselves. Treason and deception mark political fortunes. Wars are fought, accompanied by rape and slaughter. Storms, earthquakes, drought, and flood ravage the land, endangering their livelihood. Death is an ever-present possibility when disease and plague strike the innocent and guilty alike, without rhyme or reason. Individuals succumb to depression and seek comfort and peace from whatever source is at hand. Yet amid all this, there are those who cling to God and attempt to make sense of the misfortunes that incessantly befall them. And one way of doing so is to image God as angry and wrathful.

In many passages of the Jewish Scriptures God is imaged as a mighty, volatile being, easily provoked to anger and ever ready to let loose his terrible wrath. He is an irritable personage who does not lightly accept man's insubordination. He will not allow his implacable purposes to be crossed without pouring out in concrete acts his awful anger. Moses beseeches the Lord that he be permitted to see the good land beyond the Jordan, but God in his anger shuts off Moses' plea, saying "Let it suffice you. Speak no more to me of this matter" (Deut. 3:25, 26). God is easily provoked to anger by the idolatries of the Israelites (Jer. 7:18; 8:19; 25:6; Zech. 8:14), and even relatively minor matters, such as the complaints of the Hebrews, set him off in a fit of anger (Num. 11:1).

However, one interpretation of God's anger is that it is a means of discipline or deterrence. It is held over people as a threat to be averted. The Israelites are warned against marriage with the tribes they will meet in the promised land because of the possibility of apostasy, which incurs the Lord's anger to the point of their destruction (Deut. 7:4). If they are disobedient and idolatrous, in his anger he will "shut up the heavens, so that there be no rain, and the earth yield no fruit," and they will quickly perish (Deut. 11:17). When they sack cities, the sacred emblems found there are not to be retained, so that the Lord "may turn from the fierceness of his anger," and show mercy (Deut. 13:17). For failure to keep to the covenant no pardon can be expected; only massive destruction and death will follow (Deut. 29:20, 23, 24, 27), and they will be uprooted "from their land in anger and fiery and great wrath" (v. 28). If those appointed to give judgment for the Lord fail to do so with faithfulness and a whole heart, they will incur wrath upon themselves and their brothers (2 Chron. 19:10). The rulers of the earth are warned to "serve the Lord with fear and trembling, to kiss his feet lest he be angry and you perish in the way, for his wrath is quickly kindled" (Ps. 2:11). The Psalmist sees God's anger as a chastisement to be averted. "O Lord, rebuke me not in thy anger, nor chasten me in thy wrath" (Pss. 6:1, 38:1). Life is to be lived under the constant threat of God's power manifested in anger (Ps. 90:11).

The theme of God's anger as a deterrent continues in the New Testament. Of Jesus, Bevan states, "There is never a word in any saying attributed to Jesus in any of our four Gospels to suggest that he repudiated as too severe the Old Testament conception of God".[3] The woes heaped upon the Scribes and Pharisees by Matthew foretell a punishment to follow (chap. 23). Although the words *anger* and *wrath* are not used by Jesus when he warns people to fear, the idea of God's wrath is implicit. "Fear him who, after he has killed, has power to cast into hell" [Gehenna] (Luke 12:5). John's Gospel announces that anyone who does not obey the Son shall not see life, but the wrath of God will rest upon him (3:36). Paul sees the sinfulness of man as storing up wrath for the day of wrath "when God's righteous judgment will be revealed" (Rom. 2:5, 8). Christ's sacrifice will prevent the wrath of God from being exercised upon those who are saved (Rom. 5:9). And a ruler is not to be resisted, since he is a servant of God, whose wrath he executes. "Therefore one must be subject, not only to avoid God's wrath, but also for the sake of conscience" (13:4, 5). There is a wrath of God yet to come upon evildoers, so beware (Col. 3:6). The most savage prospects of the wrath to come are found in the book of Revelation. Those who worship the beast will be treated to the "wine of God's wrath" and shall be tormented with fire and brimstone forever (14:10, 11). The angel of the Lord, sweeping the earth with his deadly sickle, will throw the vintage of the earth into "the great press of the wrath of God," whereupon "blood will flow as high as a horse's bridle, for one thousand six hundred stadia" (14:19, 20; 16:1). Christ, as the Lamb of God, will be the avenging one from whom men will seek shelter. "Fall on us and hide us from the faces of him who is seated on the throne and from the wrath of the Lamb; for the great day of their wrath has come, and who can stand before it?" (6:16, 17) The exercise of God's anger is not always deferred to the future. It has already been felt in all its savage intensity. Upon hearing the complaints of the children of Israel, God is incited to anger, and he burns among them and consumes some outlying parts of the camp (Num. 11:1). The incipient revolt of Miriam and Aaron against Moses angers God, so he departs from his people (Num. 12:9). The idolatry with the gods of Moab sets off the wrath of God, and he orders the chiefs of the people to be hanged before him so that his "fierce anger" may be turned away (Num. 25:3–5). Moses blames the people for having provoked God's anger against him so that he could not cross the Jordan (Deut. 4:21). The people disobeyed in respect to the sacred objects of Jericho, and "the anger of the Lord burned against the people of Israel" (Josh. 7:1). Because they went after the heathen gods, serving the Baals and Ashtaroth, God punished them in his anger by allowing them to be plundered, and giving them over to their enemies: "the hand of the Lord was against them for evil" (Judg.

2:12–18). Uzzah, having touched the ark, is struck dead (2 Sam. 6:7). A dreary litany of God's angry actions rolls on. The Psalmist prays for God's punishment upon evildoers. "Pour out thy indignation upon them, and let thy burning anger overtake them" (69:24; 78:21). So "full of wrath" is God that "he utterly rejected Israel" and "vented his wrath on his heritage" (78:58, 62). All of life is lived under the Lord's anger "for we are consumed by thy anger; by thy wrath we are overwhelmed" (90:7, 11). The prophet Hosea saw that kings have been both given and taken away from Israel in the Lord's anger (13:11). Isaiah offers a dreadful image of God's continuing wrath in which mountains quake and corpses are refuse in the streets, "for all this his anger is not turned away, and his hand is stretched out still" (5:25, 9:12, 17, 21, 10:4). God's wrath is as a whirling tempest, breaking over the heads of the wicked (Jer. 30:23, 24). Habakkuk cries, "Thou didst bestride the earth in fury, thou didst trample the nations in anger" (3:12). Yet it is by wrath that God will protect Jerusalem. "I am jealous for Zion with great jealousy, and I am jealous for her with great wrath" (Zech. 8:2). The New Testament is no less relentless. Paul finds that God's wrath is being exhibited in his punishment of those who, having seen the plain evidence of God's power and deity in the creation, nevertheless suppress this knowledge. "The wrath of God is revealed from heaven against all ungodliness and wickedness of men who by their wickedness suppress the truth" (Rom. 1:18ff.). Nor does it seem to the apostle that there is the least injustice in God's visiting his anger upon his people. Their very wickedness brings into effect his justice. How then can they say that God is unjust to inflict wrath on us? How else can he judge the world? (Rom. 3:5, 6). The writer of Hebrews likewise resorts to the Old Testament references to God's wrath to emphasize that disobedience and failure to believe in Christ brings down God's fury in fire. "It is a fearful thing to fall into the hands of the living God" (10:26, 31), for our God is a consuming fire." (12:29).

This easily provoked, berserker God has little part to play in modern worship or the thought world of our time. His wrath is discounted by both the devout and the unbeliever as the childish, fearful imaginings of an era long past. However, many of the experiences that prompted the images of a wrathful God are still present: war, drought, famine, poverty, volcanic eruptions, tornadoes, and all manner of inexplicable physical and mental suffering. Events have changed little, but interpretations, if any, have changed considerably. In a cultural scene where belief in or denial of God's rule is merely a private option, and secular interests are dominant, these harsh aspects of life are relegated to the inscrutable will of God or used to support belief in his nonexistence—or more often left without explanation. Not so the biblical authors. Although they dared not claim to be privy to the deep purposes of the deity, they found disaster comprehensible when viewed from the standpoint of an angry God. There was an intelligible purpose in it all.

Images of an angry God express the power of God, but moral considerations also enter the picture. Psychological features merge into ethical images. True, divine power is not always associated with images of God as a moral being. In a nature Psalm that exalts his power and glory, there is scarcely a note of the ethical except in a closing stanza in which strength and peace are besought for his people (Ps. 29). It is not for any ethical reason that Ezekiel sees God as acting for his people's salvation. It is for his own holy name and power that he is to rescue them. Holiness transcends morality. "It is not for your sake, O house of Israel, that I am about to act, but for the sake of my holy name, which you have profaned among the nations to which you came" (Ezek. 36:22). The Lord's crushing answers to Job's complaints give no inkling that his power is colored by compassion. The attempt to salvage God's moral character in respect to Job was undertaken by one scholar who maintained, "Whatever the Lord will tell him, the fact which counts and which overwhelms his consciousness is that there is indeed a God who cares for him. This God loves his creature to such a measure and in such a way that he intervenes directly in an I-Thou encounter."[4] But in all this there is not a word in the text that suggests love or care. It is Job's ignorance that is overcome by the display of God's wisdom and power, not the torment of his body and soul.

God is a moral being, and under the rubric of his righteousness a variety of images come into their own. God is impartial and equitable in judgment. When Abraham bargains with the Lord over the fate of Sodom, he scores a major point by asking, "Shall not the Judge of all the earth do right?" (Gen. 18:25) When Laban and Jacob quarrel, appeal is made to God to pass judgment on their respective claims, since he will be fair (Gen. 31:53). Peter proclaims the impartiality of God: "Truly I perceive that God shows no partiality" (Acts 10:34), and Paul echoes it (Rom. 2:11; 10:12; Gal. 2:6). Impartiality is essential to divine judgment and justice. Deutero-Isaiah has God establishing the norm of conduct, for "I, the Lord, speak the truth, I declare what is right" (45:19). And the righteousness that God declares will be implacably executed. Thus "The Lord tests the righteous and the wicked and his soul hates him that loves violence. On the wicked he will rain coals of fire and brimstone; a scorching wind shall be the portion of their cup. For the Lord is righteous, he loves righteous deeds, the upright shall behold his face" (Ps. 11:5–7). The Lord is good, Nahum says, but punishment will befall his adversaries (1:7–8). Nor is God's implacable righteousness set aside in the Christian dispensation. The writer of 2 Thessalonians relishes the evidence of the righteous judgment of God, which has been with the church during its persecutions and will fall upon those who have effected them (1:5–9). The book of Revelation assumes that the righteousness of God will vindicate and save believers and punish the enemies of the Christians. "Just thou art in these thy judgments" (Rev. 16:4).

If God in his righteousness is unyielding, he also is patient and merciful even in respect to his just anger. The expression "God merciful and gracious, slow to anger" is used plentifully (Exod. 34:6; Num. 14:18; Nah. 1:3; Jon. 4:2; Joel 2:13; Pss. 103:8; 145:8). His anger is but for the moment, and his favor is for a lifetime (Ps. 30:5). He has often restrained his anger and not stirred up his wrath (Ps. 78:35). "Thou, O Lord, art a God merciful and gracious, slow to anger and abounding in steadfast love and faithfulness" (Ps. 86:15). In his song of the vineyard, Isaiah has God say "I have no wrath" (27:4), and in the face of Jacob's rebelliousness "I defer my anger" (48:9). God proclaims to faithless Israel, "I will not look on you in anger, for I am merciful" (Jer. 3:12). Hosea finds God reaching out in compassion to Ephraim: "I will not execute my fierce anger, I will not destroy Ephraim . . . I will not come to destroy" (11:9); instead he will love Israel "for my anger has turned from them" (14:4). And for Paul, God has endured with patience those who would otherwise be destroyed, for the sake of making known the riches of his glory for those to be saved (Rom. 9:22, 23). So the righteousness of God in judgment is alleviated by the images of his gracious mercy.

The righteous God is "the faithful God" (Deut. 7:8–9), and the Psalms never tire of rehearsing the image (48:8; 51:1; 63:3; 89:1–2, etc.). His abiding strength can be relied on "for it endures to all generations and stands fast as does the earth" (Ps. 119:90). Because of his love for Israel, "I have continued my faithfulness to you" (Jer. 31:3). In wrestling with the fate of his Jewish brethren, Paul asks if the faithlessness of some of them nullifies the faithfulness of God. Not at all, he answers, because God's truth and faithfulness are left unscathed by human infidelity (Rom. 3:3–4). The Corinthians in their time of trouble are reminded that "God is faithful" (1 Cor. 1:9; 10:13), and the church at Thessalonica is called to depend upon God's faithfulness (2 Thess. 3:3). The letter to Titus expresses with admirable bluntness the dependability of God when it says that God never lies (1:2). Those Christians who suffer persecution are encouraged to entrust their souls to their faithful Creator (1 Pet. 4:19). A faithful God is one in whom to deposit one's total trust. In the midst of social and political turbulence, when the accepted patterns of human life are wrenched apart, there is one who gives stability. The moral integrity of the world, God himself, stands firm.

Nowhere is the image of God as the faithful one more tellingly or repetitiously expressed than in the phrase "steadfast love." It is so often repeated that it assumes the monotonous rhythm of a well-learned incantation. But the important feature of the phrase lies in its yoking of fidelity with love and all the attendant virtues that flow from the latter. The servant sent to find a wife for Isaac is grateful for the Lord's steadfast love (Gen. 24:12, 27). Joseph in Egypt is the recipient of it (Gen. 39:21). The Hebrew people are led out of slavery by God's steadfast love, which he will continue to show to faithful generations (Exod. 20:6; 34:6, 7; Deut. 5:10; 7:9). The Lord is not niggardly with his steadfast love; he abounds in it (Num. 14:18, 19). And the pages of Chronicles 1 and 2, as well as of Ezra and Nehemiah, are inundated with grateful references to it. One curious passage raises a question about the "steadfastness" of his love, when God swears he will not take away his steadfast love from the descendants of David, "as I took it from Saul" (2 Sam. 7:15)! Maybe a scribe nodded! The Psalms rejoice in the God whose paths are steadfast love and faithfulness (25:8–10). The Psalmist himself is saved by steadfast love (31:7, 16, 21), and those who trust the Lord are surrounded by it (32:10). It soars to the heavens and the clouds, transcending all bounds except those of the world itself (36:5). Psalm 136 provides a climax of worship when each episode of the creation and Israelite history elicits the chant, "for his steadfast love endures for ever." He loves the Hebrew people and will continue to do so in the future, multiplying their numbers and giving prosperity (Deut. 7:7, 8, 13; 10:15). In his tender love he says, "When Israel was a child, I loved him, and out of Egypt I called my son." "It was I who taught Ephraim to walk . . . I led them with cords of compassion, with the hands of love . . ." (Hos. 11:1–4). He takes the initiative in healing their faithlessness. "I will love them freely, for my anger has turned from them" (Hos. 14:4). Israel will be saved "because you are precious in my eyes, and honored, and I love you" (Isa. 43:4), "with everlasting love I will have compassion on you" (Isa. 54:8; 63:9). "I have loved you with an everlasting love; therefore I have continued my faithfulness to you" (Jer. 31:3). And Zephaniah exults over Jerusalem where "he will renew you in his love" (3:10, 15, 17).

The phrase "steadfast love" does not find a place in the New Testament vocabulary, although other expressions of the dependability of God's love continue. With the coming of Christ and the Holy Spirit, Paul claims, "God's love has been poured into our hearts" even as Christ's death manifests God's "love for us" (Rom. 5:5, 8). Paul shouts that believers are more than conquerors over all manner of tribulations through Christ's love, since no earthly or transcendent reality can "separate us from the love of God in Christ Jesus our Lord" (8:35–39). At a more mundane level, by way of paving the way for a contribution for the "saints," he adds the incentive that "God loves a cheerful giver" (2 Cor. 9:7). The Ephesian letter reminds its readers that even while they were dead in their trespasses, God in his love took the initiative in Christ to save them (21:4, 5). The Johannine literature is rich in images of God as the lover. Countless generations have recited the famous passage of John 3:16, "For God so loved the world that he gave his only son, that whoever believes in him should not perish, but have eternal life." In this Gospel Jesus comforts his disciples with the words "the Father himself loves you, because you have loved me . . ." (16:27). The epistles of John revel in the use of the word *love*, especially in respect to the divine initiative. "See what love the Father has given us" (1

John 3:1). "He who does not love does not know God, for God is love" (1 John 4:9, 10). "God is love, and he who abides in love abides in God, and God abides in him (1 John 4:16). "We love, because he first loved us" (1 John 4:19). It is noteworthy that the author does not say, "God is like love," but rather, unlike some passages in which God is imaged as likened to the attributes of human beings, God is here identified without remainder with love itself: "God *is* love." To experience this unique kind of love is to experience God himself in an immanent manner.

It is remarkable that after all the images of anger, wrath, punishment, and overwhelming displays of God's power, the Hebrews and Christians should ever have associated the deity with love. The daily experience of both groups looked more like one of never-ending hardship, brought on by natural disasters, intertribal bickerings, cheating, lying, in-group quarreling, warfare, and persecution by powerful nations and mobs. Yet in the face of this harried existence, the biblical authors rehearse the theme of a God who loves, showing mercy and compassion, and wondrously forgiving them their shortcomings. Both Hebrews and Christians were convinced that God exercised a solicitude for their ultimate welfare in a way that no merely just or vengeful deity could do.

The accompaniments of love are found in the images of God as merciful and compassionate. "The Lord your God is a merciful God" (Deut. 4:31; 2 Chron. 30:9; Pss. 26:6; 111:4, etc.). In Luke's rendering of the sermon on the level place Jesus says, "Be merciful even as your Father is merciful" (6:36). In Paul's writings God's mercy is coupled with the arbitrary will of God and his punishment. Reflecting upon God's word to Moses (Exod. 33:19), the apostle reminds his readers that it is God's mercy to be depended on for salvation, since "he has mercy upon whomever he wills, and he hardens the heart of whomever he wills" (Rom. 4:15–18). Toward those "who have fallen," God will show severity, but he is kind to those who continue to live in his kindness (Rom. 11:22). The letter of James counsels patience and steadfastness, since "the Lord is compassionate and merciful" (5:11). With mercy and compassion comes forgiveness: "Thou dost forgive the iniquity of thy people; thou dost pardon all their sin" (Ps. 85:2; 86:5; 103:3). The swelling tones of Deutero-Isaiah's opening oracle proclaimed comfort to Jerusalem, since her warfare is ended, and "her iniquity pardoned" (40:1–2). The wicked person is to forsake his ways and "return to the Lord, that he may have mercy on him, and to our God, for he will abundantly pardon" (55:7). Jeremiah, in announcing the new covenant as the basis of a fresh beginning for Israel, has God saying "I will forgive their iniquity, and I will remember their sin no more" (31:34). After Ezekiel has traced Israel's apostasies extensively in vivid sexual imagery, he has God's returning to the covenant theme. At that time, "I will forgive you all that you have done" (16:62, 63). In rehearsing the story of the Hebrew people, Nehemiah puts in brief compass the nature of God: "Thou art a God ready to forgive, gracious and merciful, slow to anger and abounding in steadfast love, and didst not forsake them" (9:17). One can scarcely overlook the image of God as a universally pitying and forgiving God, found in the book of Jonah. The petulant, narrow-minded Jonah, in his anger at Nineveh's repentance and God's change of mind about punishing the city, actually chides God by describing the Lord's virtues in such a way as to make them sound like weaknesses. A God who repents of the evil that Jonah had hoped to see poured out on the wicked city lacks the sense of just punishment that properly should have destroyed Nineveh. But God in the face of Jonah's sulky anger asks, "And should I not pity Nineveh, that great city, in which there are more than a hundred and twenty thousand persons who do not know their right hand from their left, and also much cattle" (3:10–4:11). Here God is the forgiver, since the city of Nineveh was associated both in fact and figuratively with the ruthless destruction of the Northern Kingdom, and the exile, if not the obliteration, of its people. The Lord's prayer includes the petition for God's forgiveness (Matt. 6:12; Luke 11:4), and Luke portrays Jesus on the cross as praying God to "forgive them," since his crucifiers are ignorant of the import of their actions (22:34). The church at Ephesus is to cease its wrangling, "forgiving one another, as God in Christ forgave you" (4:31–32). Forgiveness by God brings life out of death for those dead in their trespasses (Col. 2:13), and this forgiveness by God is to be a model for mutual forgiveness (Col. 3:13).

Forgiveness is but a sign of God's gracious generosity in blessing his people. The Deuteronomist claims that the Hebrew people's obedience to God's commandments will elicit blessings from the Lord on all their undertakings and on their property. "Blessed shall you be when you come in, and blessed shall you be when you go out," promises the Lord (28:1–6). He rewards the righteous (Ps. 18:20), and the Davidic king has been given his heart's desire and has met with "goodly blessings" (Ps. 21:2, 3). "Bless the Lord, O my soul, and forget not all his benefits," for he forgives and redeems, and "satisfies you with good as long as you live" (Ps. 103:2–5). The Lord is gracious, righteous, and merciful, and when the Psalmist was "brought low," he was saved. "Return, O my soul, to your rest; for the Lord has dealt bountifully with you" (116:5–7). The generosity of God, who gives good things to those who ask, is contrasted by Jesus with the good gifts that even evil parents give their children (Matt. 7:11). In his gracious generosity God gave his son for all, and will he not then "give us all things with him?" (Rom. 8:22). In fact, he is "able to provide you with every blessing in abundance, so that you may always have enough of everything and may provide in abundance for every good work" (2 Cor. 9:8). The epistle of James underlines God's liberality: "If any of you lacks wisdom, let him ask God, who gives to all men generously and without reproaching, and it will be given him" (1:5). And again, "Every good endowment and every perfect gift is from above, coming down from the Father of lights with whom there is no variation or shadow due to change" (1:17). An almost hedonistic note is struck in First Timothy, where rich people are reminded not to put their hopes in uncertain riches, but "on God who richly furnishes us with every thing to enjoy" (6:17). The salutations of several epistles also emphasize the graciousness of God the Father, and the Lord Jesus Christ (cf. Rom. 1:7; 1 Tim. 1:2; 2 Tim. 1:2; Titus 1:4; 2 Pet. 1:2).

Not least among the generous gifts of God is that of comfort (Isa. 40:1). In spite of the enmity of men, the Lord proclaims "I, I am he that comforts you; who are you that you are afraid of man who dies?" (Isa. 51:12). Like the tenderness of a mother, "so I will comfort you" (Isa. 66:13). Although he chastens, he also binds up and heals (Job 5:17, 18). Paul movingly plays upon the image of God as the great comforter when he writes to the suffering church at Corinth. God is the "God of all comfort, who comforts us in all our affliction." Even as Christ suffered, "so through Christ we share abundantly in comfort too" (2 Cor. 1:3–5). Also in Second Thessalonians a benediction is offered in which "eternal comfort and good hope through grace" will be a "comfort to your hearts" (2:16, 17). In the descent of the New Jerusalem, God assuages the pain and sorrow of the faithful. "He will wipe away every tear from their eyes, and death shall be no more, neither shall there be mourning nor crying nor pain any more, for the former things have passed away" (Rev. 21:4).

God may often be imaged as a warrior, but he is also the god of peace (Num. 25:12). Gideon is confronted by the peace that God gives him, whereupon he builds an altar that he calls "The Lord is peace" (Judg. 6:23, 24). Bildad affirms that "he makes peace in his high heaven" (Job 25:2). The Psalmist is sure that when the Lord speaks "he will speak peace to his people" (85:8). It is God "who makes peace in your borders" (147:14). The words of Isaiah bring comfort. "Thou dost keep him in perfect peace, whose mind is stayed on thee, because he trusts in thee" (26:3), and the prophet looks forward to it because "thou wilt ordain peace for us" (26:12). Again, the prophet Zechariah sees a future when war will be brought to an end, and "he shall command peace to the nations" (9:10). In the midst of their turmoil-filled existence the assurance of God as the giver of peace repeatedly resounds in the salutations and benedictions of numerous epistles. The Lord is named "the God of peace" with other expressions of similar meaning (e.g., Rom. 1:7; 15:33; 16:20; 1 Cor. 1:3; 2 Cor. 1:2; 13:11; 1 Thess. 5:23; 2 Thess. 3:16; 1 Tim. 1:2; 2 Tim. 1:2). Paul rebukes the quarrelsome members of the Corinthian church by reminding them that "God is not a God of confusion, but of peace" (1 Cor. 14:33). And the Philippian letter tells of the peace that God gives that passes beyond human understanding. If its readers follow what they have learned from Paul, then "the God of peace will be with you" (4:7, 9). Near the conclusion of Hebrews God is exalted as the God of peace "who brought again from the dead our Lord Jesus" (13:20, 21). In Revelation John salutes his readers with the words, "Grace to you and peace from him who is and who was and who is to come" (1:4, 5).

The image of God as the giver of peace also portrays his essential nature as peaceable. Even as human beings at times make peace, as in the case of physical warfare, or are themselves peaceable in disposition, so also is God. Human beings may make peace out of weakness or fall into a peaceful temper of mind that suggests the exhaustion of physical or psychological powers, but mere cessation of external or internal warfare is not the model for the peace God manifests or gives. The image is not built on weakness. Rather God has power to bring harmony out of disharmony, serenity out of upset, jangled emotions, and an abiding strength not to be subverted by fear, afflictions, or temptations. The peace he gives, and which is attributed to his very nature, resides in the empowerment to be a self in entirety and unity. When it applies to peace following warfare, the tribe or people is brought back into a psychic as well as a physical unity. Peace once achieved draws into a harmonious whole the parties hitherto at odds with each other. The peace God enjoys, and therefore is able to bestow upon humanity, is that of a unity of being in which there are no dissonances. As peace given brings integrity and poise to human selves grounded in God, so also God possesses total and unique integrity of being. His peaceableness, like that of humanity, reflects emotional and psychic stability and strength. Whatever else the great affirmation of Jewish faith meant, it was a proclamation of the God whose uniqueness lay less in his numerical identity compared to other deities than in his complete integrity and unity of being. "Hear, O Israel: The Lord our God is one Lord" (Deut. 6:4). He could rage, love, or change his mind, and so on, but he was also the peaceable one.

A number of anthropopathic images, sadly out of joint with those of a gentler kind, have yet to be accounted for. From the standpoint of later Jewish and Christian evaluations, these are considered to be amoral, immoral, even disgusting, and as a whole demeaning to God's nature. Some of them are vividly impressive as literary figures, but at the same time offensive or tasteless to aesthetic and religious sensibilities. Yet they are drawn from the ordinary feelings and attitudes of human beings, and they furnish the forms in which to read God's nature, either as actually experienced or as envisioned. The biblical writers were not squeamish about recording passages that were an essential part of the tradition. Without apology and seemingly without any sense of their incompatibility with other images in the same body of material, the authors set them down. It remained for later commentators to sort out the acceptable from the unacceptable, or to explain that in some instances such expressions were "symbolic" of deeper truths.

Before God rescues the Israelites, Moses in Egypt plaintively asks God, "O Lord, why hast thou done evil to this people" (Exod. 5:22), and later God warns that if they are unfaithful to the covenant he "will bring upon you all the evil things", until you are destroyed "from off this good land" (Josh. 23:15, 16). Without compromise, God announces "I form light and create darkness, I make weal and woe, I am the Lord, who do all these things" (Isa. 45:7). The King James Version even more bluntly has God saying, "I make peace and create evil." Jeremiah asks, "For behold, I begin to work evil at the city which is called by my name, and shall you go unpunished?" (25:29) Some commentators attempt to evade the force of such passages by suggesting that the evil God creates is not moral evil, but more like physical disaster.[5] However, if God is the sole God, the determiner of destiny, as the passages clearly imply, it matters little whether evil is moral or physical. Human beings suffer in both cases. For their apostasy "whenever they marched out, the hand of the Lord was against them for evil" (Judg. 2:15). Second Samuel recorded, when enough people had died of pestilence, that the threat to destroy Jerusalem was turned aside because "the Lord repented of the evil" (24:16). Amos linked catastrophic events to God's actions when he asked, "Does evil befall a city, unless the Lord has done it?" (3:66). Zechariah pictures God as changing his mind, he having once "purposed to do evil to you" (8:14), even as with the repentance of Nineveh God also repented of the evil that he had said he would do to them (Jon. 3:10).

The notion of evil itself becomes clearer as various images of God are pursued. Warfare and the warlike tendencies of a deity are not necessarily to be considered as immoral or unusual. War gods have been common stock in other religions. However, what casts the images of a warring God in the present category is not his warlike tendencies, but the merciless slaughter and genocide he commands, that go beyond any canons of warfare. Even after battles when blood-lust was high, the killings continue. The ferocity of the images represents the Israelites' conviction that they have actually experienced him in the role of an ally unrestrained in his treatment of their enemies and sometimes of themselves. In the warfare against Midian, commanded by God, every male is to be slain, thus cutting off further generations of that tribe (Num. 31:7). The Deuteronomist prophesies that God will vanquish the tribes that have hindered Israel's entrance into Canaan. When they are subdued, the Lord commands, "You must utterly destroy them . . . and show no mercy to them" (7:2). In their cities "you shall save alive nothing that breathes, but you shall utterly destroy them" (20:16, 17). The scenes in the book of Joshua spell out these prophecies. The capture of Ai led to the slaughter of the population of that city (8:22). "For Joshua did not draw back his hand, with which he stretched out the javelin, until he had utterly destroyed all the inhabitants of Ai" (8:26). The commandment of God that had passed through Moses to

Joshua justified unlimited bloodshed. "As the Lord commanded Moses his servant, so Moses commanded Joshua, and so Joshua did" (11:15). City after city was destroyed, tribe after tribe exterminated, as Joshua went on his bloody, savage way, all under the auspices of divine guidance and assistance (10:40). The Lord goes as far as to harden the hearts of Israel's enemies, the better to lure them into battle, where they were "utterly destroyed," a frequently used term, and in which they "should receive no mercy but be exterminated, as the Lord commanded Moses" (11:20). True, the book of Joshua editorially embellishes the story of the conquest of Canaan, making it read like a steadily victorious procession, but the book of Judges, yielding nothing as to God's ferocity, tells in a more realistic vein a less triumphant tale.

When the authors and editors of 1 Samuel take up the story of Samuel and Saul, we have Samuel, under the Lord's influence, directing Saul to "Go utterly destroy the sinners, the Amalekites, and fight against them until they are consumed" (15:18). Unfortunately for Saul, he fails to obey Samuel's command, with the melancholy result that he is stripped of his kingship, and having spared Agag, left it to Samuel to hew that king to pieces "before the Lord in Gilgal," a deed presumably pleasing to the deity (15:33b). Scenes of bloodshed engineered by God occur in the Psalms, where the Lord will shatter the heads of his enemies and allow his faithful ones to bathe their feet in their blood (68:21, 23). The wicked will be wiped out (94:23). In one of Jeremiah's poems, the man who brought news of the prophet's birth is cursed. "Let that man be like the cities which the Lord overthrew without pity" (20:16). The dirge of Lamentations over the sack of Jerusalem as a destruction done without mercy pictures God as having destroyed Israel (2:2, 5, 10). Ezekiel is commanded by God to say against Jerusalem, "Behold, I am against you, and will draw forth my sword out of its sheath, and will cut off from you both righteous and wicked (21:3). Habakkuk sees God in his fury trampling the nations in anger, and for the salvation of his people the prophet proclaims, "Thou didst crush the head of the wicked" (3:12, 13).

As an aftermath of war, the treatment of women prisoners, when there were any left, also casts an ominous light upon God's nature. When a beautiful woman is captured, the Lord, through Moses, advises that she may be taken in marriage after a period of mourning for her parents. If the marriage does not work out, or as the text puts it, "If you have no delight in her, you shall let her go where she will." However, she is not to be sold or treated as a slave, "since you have humiliated her," whether by having married her or by casting her out is not clear (Deut. 21:14). Whatever element of compassion may be detected in these lines is marred by the fact that the woman is finally to be left unprotected by any male or family group. Her fate will be degradation.

The genocidal tendencies of the deity are often associated with the image of his jealousy. As in the images of wrath, jealousy is associated with punishment, for apostasy and idolatry, but it also suggests a God whose very character is that of jealousy. The announcement by God that he alone is to be worshiped because he is a jealous God (Exod. 20:5; Deut. 5:9) is repeated not least of all by Moses, when he says that the Lord's name is "Jealous" (Exod. 34:14). One can understand the image of God's jealousy in the context of monotheism or henotheism, where it functions as an anthropopathic image, insuring the absolute rejection of gods who are no gods at all. Jealousy draws the line against polytheism, idolatry, and apostasy by establishing the deity's intolerance in respect to these presumptive deities. Expressions of this jealousy and intolerance in their original historical settings, however, do not clearly provide proof of monotheistic belief. In some cases God appears too closely linked to the fortunes of Israel alone to be accepted as a universal deity.

In this latter context jealousy, seldom counted a moral virtue, is taken by the biblical writers to be a characteristic of the God who attempts to keep the ever-wavering Israelites in strict obedience to himself. Phinehas is praised for his jealousy "in that he was jealous with my jealousy" and so prevented the people of Israel from being consumed "in my jealousy" (Num. 25:11). The God in the midst of Israel is a "jealous God" (Deut. 6:15; Josh. 24:18). His jealousy is provoked by strange gods—"with what is no god" (Deut. 32:16, 21; 1 Kings 14:22). The prophet Ezekiel connects the Lord's jealousy with the threat of anger and fury (5:13; 16:42; 36:5, 6; 38:19). It is a jealousy for his holy name, not simply for his people (39:25). The Psalmist asks "Will thy jealous wrath burn like fire?" (79:5). So also Joel 2:18, where God is jealous for his land but has pity on his people (also Zech. 1:14; 8:2). Vengeance is coupled with God's jealousy (Nah. 1:2), and Zephaniah pictures the whole earth as consumed in the Lord's jealous wrath (1:18; 3:8). In the New Testament, Paul criticizes the participation of the Corinthians in idol worship by asking a question echoing the Old Testament, "Shall we provoke the Lord to jealousy?" (1 Cor. 10:22). Clearly jealousy, although emanating from the dark side of the human psyche, was not thought to be an inappropriate designation of the divine nature.

The images of God as jealous intertwine with those of his wrath, and both play an important role in the images of a vengeful deity. In striking contrast to the images of divine forgiveness and reconciliation and even righteous punishment, the biblical God in the images of vengeance often appears as merely petty and vindictive. The people of Israel are called upon by God to execute his vengeance on the Midianites (Num. 31:3). In Moses' song, the Lord claims for himself the act of vengeance in words later used by Paul: "Vengeance is mine, and recompense for the time when their foot shall slip" (Deut. 32:35; Rom. 12:19). The song glories in this vengeance as the Lord is seen carrying out his vindictive judgment on his enemies (Deut. 32:41). He is to be praised, for "he avenges the blood of his servants and takes vengeance on his adversaries" (Deut. 32:43). David also praises God "who gave me vengeance" (2 Sam. 22:48; Ps. 18:47). The Psalmist calls for the Lord to show himself with the cry, "O Lord, thou God of vengeance, thou God of vengeance shine forth!" (Ps. 94:1) The prophets see God as one who takes vengeance, especially upon nations that have oppressed Israel. There is a day of vengeance (Isa. 34:8) when Israel is called to look forward to his coming. "Behold your God will come with vengeance, with the recompense of God. He will come to save you" (Isa. 35:4). The chants against Babylon resound with images of God's vengeance, yet to come (Isa. 47:3; Jer. 50:15, 28; 51:6, 11), as does the chant against the Philistines (Ezek. 25:17). The stirring announcement of the year of the Lord's favor also contains the words that make of it "the day of vengeance of our God," words not included in the famous passage that Jesus cites (Isa. 61:2ff.; cf. Luke 4:18).[6] All nations that fail to obey God will fall under his anger, and the execution of his vengeance (Mic. 5:15).

Although the New Testament does not glory in the images of a vengeful deity, as does the Old, God is not altogether lacking in vindictiveness. The apocalyptic vision of the destruction of Jerusalem, credited to Jesus, is described as "days of vengeance" (Luke 21:22). Paul, as we have seen, calls up the words of Deuteronomy, "Vengeance is mine, I will repay" (Rom. 12:19). Again a future is summoned up in which the Lord Jesus as the agent of God will inflict vengeance upon those who do not know God (2 Thess. 1:8). And the writer of Hebrews returns to the words of Paul and Deuteronomy which are directly attributed to him whom we know [God?], "Vengeance is mine, I will repay" (Heb. 10:30). It is entirely in keeping with the vengeful tenor of the book of Revelation that the martyrs cry, "O sovereign Lord, holy and true, how long before thou wilt judge and avenge our blood on those who dwell upon the earth?" (6:10).

Vengeance may occasionally be interpreted as a sign that no one gets away with wrongdoing in God's world. As such, in spite of the brutality associated with it, it may voice a respect for a moral universe where justice at last wins out. What is less easy to accept are those images of God who acts or commands actions that fall below this minimal level of justice. When the Lord torments or persecutes without apparent reason, senseless cruelty is evident. However grave Saul's disobedience to the Lord's commands, did it justify God in sending "an evil spirit" to torment him (1 Sam. 16:14; 18:10)? The righteous Job dares to speak of God as one who "hast turned cruel to me; with the might of thy hand thou dost persecute me" (30:21). Even in instances where punishment in some form might be justified, the punishment threatened or executed is out of proportion to the evil done. The images are of a God who so far exceeds the boundaries of fairness as to lose all semblance of an ethical character or rational control. Death is decreed for a series of wranglings that seem worthy of far less severe measures. The unspecified wickedness of Er, Judah's firstborn, is punished by death (Gen. 38:7). The innocent Egyptian firstborn are killed (Exod. 12:29–30). The affliction of widows and orphans will bring death by the sword, wives will become widows, and children fatherless (Exod. 22:24). Profanation of the Sabbath calls for death (Exod. 21:14). In discussing the events covered in Exodus, Deuteronomy shows no more leniency than the former accounts. Apostasy will beget complete destruction of the whole Israelite population (Deut. 6:15). Or as Jeremiah has it: "Behold, I will feed this people with wormwood, and give them poisonous water to drink" (9:15; 23:15). If a close relative attempts to lure away an Israelite from devotion to God, God commands that he is not to be listened to, pitied, or concealed. "You shall kill him . . . you shall stone him to death . . ." (Deut. 13:8–10). A rebellious son is to receive the same punishment (Deut. 21:21). The sons of Aaron, having lighted an unholy fire, are killed (Lev. 10:1, 2; 16:1, 2). A woman suspected of adultery must undergo a ritual of drinking water that causes her pain if she is guilty. Her body will swell up and her thigh will fall away (Num. 5:16–22). Plagues and assorted evils befall the people (Num. 11:33; 16:41–49). Similarly, because David had taken a census ordered by God, a pestilence falls upon his people by which innocent multitudes died (2 Sam. 24:1, 10, 15). The authors of Leviticus insure obedience by having God promise plague, infertility of the land, the ravaging of wild beasts, and subjugation to enemies (Lev. 26:14–33; cf. Deut. 28:58–61). The prophet Jeremiah hears the Lord saying "I will consume them by the sword, by famine and by pestilence" (14:11, 12; 29:17, 18).

Some of the punishments are peculiarly repulsive, as in the scene where a delicate woman, having given birth in a time of famine, eats the afterbirth and the children she has produced (Deut. 28:56, 57). Or again, "You shall eat the flesh of your sons, and you shall eat the flesh of your daughters" (Lev. 26:28). It is little wonder in circumstances like these and many others that God is imaged as filled with hate (Deut. 1:27). In his agony Job also sees God as one who "has torn me in his wrath and hated me" (16:9). And the God and Christ of Revelation often move in the same atmosphere of vengeful hatred toward all who have persecuted the Christians.

Among the least attractive images of God are those which disclose him as untrustworthy, deceitful, and treacherous. The writers of Exodus and Deuteronomy were not above attributing to the Lord "hardening of heart" for the enemies of Israel, the better to bring about his purposes. Thus Pharaoh is reduced to stubbornness and ignorance in a game that he can neither prevent nor win, as the series of miraculous plagues unfolds before him (Exod. 7:3ff.) The king of Heshbon is delivered into the hands of the Israelites by the same device (Deut. 2:30ff.). It was not only the enemies of Israel who were misled by the deity. Jeremiah cries, "O Lord God, surely Thou hast utterly deceived this people and Jerusalem" (4:10). To Jeremiah himself God has been like a deceitful brook, "like waters that fail" (15:18). "Lord, thou hast deceived me and I was deceived" (20:7). The Third Isaiah asks, "O Lord, why dost thou make us err from thy ways and harden our heart, so that we fear thee not?" (63:17).[7] When Stephen recites the history of the Israelites, stressing their apostasy, he credits the Lord with having given them over to the worship of the host of heaven (Acts 7:42). In a like fashion Paul speaks of God's giving over idolaters to "the lusts of their hearts to impurity" (Rom. 1:24). In these pictures of God it is noteworthy that mere abandonment by him is insufficient to account for human shortcomings. He does not simply leave human beings to themselves; rather he initiates actions to bring about these results. He deludes them into false worship. One of the most explicit images of God as untrustworthy is found in connection with "followers of Satan." "Therefore God sends upon them a strong delusion, to make them believe what is false, so that all may be condemned who did not believe the truth, but had pleasure in unrighteousness" (2 Thess. 2:11).

The whole collection of divine images that makes up this last category of "immoral" characteristics contradicts those which emphasize the Lord's steadfast love and righteousness. They sadly mar those of a more beneficent nature, and in many cases shrink the dimensions of the deity to the proportions of a god whose sole interest is in a select group of people, Israelites or Christians. However, they do also arise from genuine experiences interpreted in a theistic framework, where the vicissitudes of human life can find no explanation other than that God has either caused astonishing victories for his people by unethical means, or on the other hand, has disastrously let people down. If God is sovereign, all must finally be attributed to him, whether it be for good or ill fortune. One does not deny God in these circumstances, but one sees him as governing all, even when evil and misfortune result. Dependability remains, even in moments when it appears that God deceives or misleads man. Even the cry of tragic disappointment of Jesus on the cross, "My God, my God, why has thou forsaken me" is no denial of God. It is addressed to a God who exists and is there. As with a Jeremiah or a Job, an argument with God is set in motion, but it is not one in which atheism has any standing.

Later generations have held the demeaning images of God to be unworthy of God, or mistaken. As such, as earlier suggested, they are relegated to an earlier, cruder period of religious and ethical development. Apologies or mediating interpretations may often be offered for them. However, unfortunately the biblical texts themselves reveal these uncomplimentary images not only in the earliest strata of biblical material, but in later passages as well. The noblest as well as the most debasing anthropopathic images stand side by side, as the images reviewed above demonstrate. Why then are we tempted to accept only those which express God's beneficence and righteousness, and discard those that seem to us to besmirch his name? Certainly not on the basis of biblical authority itself. If the less attractive features of the divine nature are to be cast aside as coming from an "early" period, why not the most exalted ones that accompany them? Somewhere in past human experience these images rang true, and when irrational rage overcomes us, or life turns against us and the foundational securities of life shake beneath us, and it seems that God himself is vengeful or has turned his back upon his creation, they may continue to express that of which we scarcely dare to speak. God the void has turned into God the enemy, in Whitehead's striking words, as well as into the companion and friend. Life is touched at its depths by the power over against mankind, even as the same power at other times shows itself as loving, gentle, and forgiving.

NOTES

1. Quoted by G. Van Der Leeuw, *Religion in Essence and Manifestation*, trans. J. E. Turner, (London: George Allen and Unwin Ltd., 1938), 177.

2. Frank Herbert Brabant, *Time and Eternity in Christian Thought* (London, New York, Toronto: Longmans, Green and Co., 1937), 272.

3. Edwyn Bevan, *Symbolism and Belief* (New York: The Macmillan Co., 1938), 213.

4. Samuel Terrien in *The Interpreter's Bible* (New York, Nashville: Abingdon Press, 1954), 3:1173.

5. So James Muilenburg, *The Interpreter's Bible*, 5:524. Cf. André Lacocque, "Evil is no negation of God," *The Chicago Theological Seminary Register* 68, no. 3 (Fall 1978): 27.

6. The rendering of the Hebrew word *vengeance* is questioned by some scholars. "Requital" or "rescue" is sometimes preferred. Cf. *Interpreter's Bible*, 5:710, 711.

7. One commentator attempts to soften the impact of the Isaiah passage by asserting that "God is not blamed for injustice here." The mystery of divine providence and sovereignty alone is expressed. The Jeremiah passage in 4:10 "expresses the viewpoint of false prophets rather than that of Jeremiah." In 15:18 "he accuses God of disappointing him," not deceiving him! *Interpreter's Bible*, 5:737, 835, 943.

10

An Interlude: Is "Spirit" an Image?

"Spirit" is one of the central ideas of the Bible. It is also one of the most confusing, and therefore calls for independent, albeit brief attention. On the one hand, its origin obviously lies in the naturalistic realm of wind or breath (chap. 7).[1] However, its humble origin is discounted by one who states, "God is not to be depicted by a mixture of metaphors drawn from nature . . . he cannot be apprehended primarily by means of an undefined analogy, drawn from wind or breath (hence 'spirit')."[2] This judgment is premature in the light of innumerable passages where the spirit of God does act as an impersonal force like wind or breath.[3] On the other hand, "spirit," as an essential element of human life and consciousness, takes on anthropopathic qualities. Emotions, thoughts, desires, volitions, and awareness, as in humans, take their place in the concept. Thus the notion of spirit assumes a position superior to its naturalistic grounding, if not independent of it.

Whether as an impersonal or personal entity, the spirit of God is powerful. As impersonal, it drives Othniel to war (Judg. 3:10), and Samson performs incredible feats of strength under its influence (Judg. 13:25; 14:6, 19; 15:14). Caught up in the ecstatic prophesying of a band of prophets, Saul is turned into "another man" when the spirit of the Lord comes "mightily" upon him (1 Sam. 10:5–7, 10). Ezekiel envisions God's spirit as an elemental physical force, standing him on his feet (2:2) and moving him about (3:12, 14; 11:1, 5, 24; 37:1, 14; 43:5). Physical life and death in the animal kingdom directly depends upon God's giving or withdrawing his spirit (Ps. 104:30).

The impersonality of God's spirit persists in parts of the New Testament. It drives Jesus into the wilderness (Matt. 4:1; Mark 1:12; Luke 4:1). It is the power by which he casts out demons (Matt. 12:28). The Gospel of John has Jesus telling Nicodemus that the spirit, like the wind, "blows where it wills" (3:6, 7). In the same gospel, reference is made to the spirit, which believers will receive when Jesus is glorified, apparently a superhuman power (7:30; cf. 4:26). And it is by breathing upon the disciples that Jesus gives them the Holy Spirit (20:22). The similarity to the earlier creation story can scarcely be missed. The empowering of the Christian group comes "like the rush of a mighty wind," whereat tongues "as of fire" come upon each member present. So overcome are these people that their physical behavior prompts outsiders to regard them as drunk! And Peter's defense of this eccentric conduct is pitifully weak: "it is only the third hour of the day"—as though if the hour were later, the charge might have been justified. His stronger defense lay in quoting Joel's prophecy (Joel 2:28) as pointing to the "new age" then being inaugurated (Acts 2:2–21). Physical effects of the spirit are felt, including life itself, but the spirit also grants "new life" for the Christian. The God-given spirit dwells within the believer as in a temple (1 Cor. 3:16). It emancipates from the burden of the law, giving "life" (2 Cor. 3:6; Gal. 5:16–18). The spirit exhibits its powers in an anthropopathic way. Balaam prophesies when the spirit of God comes upon him (Num. 24:2), as does David (2 Sam. 23:2). All the prophets are given extraordinary insight and authority by the spirit (Neh. 9:30). Craftsmanship and technical skills are the gifts of the spirit of God (Exod. 31:3ff; 35:31ff). Understanding and intelligence are due to the spirit (Job 32:8). It directs, teaches, guides, and opens new perceptions, quite beyond ordinary comprehension. The Holy Spirit reveals to Simeon that he will not die before he has seen the Lord's Christ, and inspired by that spirit, he goes to the temple where he meets Jesus and his parents (Luke 2:25–28). The Holy Spirit knew beforehand that Judas would betray Jesus (Acts 1:16). Stephen speaks with "wisdom and the Spirit" (Acts 6:10), and filled with the Holy Spirit, he is enabled to see into heaven (Acts 7:55). Paul depends upon the spirit in going to Jerusalem, although he does not know what will happen to him (Acts 20:22–23). Through the spirit, God reveals hidden truth, but "no one comprehends the thoughts of God except the Spirit of God" (1 Cor. 2:7, 10–11). Those who have been taught by the spirit, which is from God, understand God's gifts and are enabled to interpret "spiritual truth" (1 Cor. 2:12–13). Human wisdom is incapable of understanding these higher truths; the spirit alone makes it possible. Or as the Gospel of John claims, the counselor and Holy Spirit will "teach you all things" (14:26). He (she, it) knows the future, expressly saying "in later times some will depart from the faith" (1 Tim. 4:1).

Not only insight and wisdom are given by the spirit of God, but also moral virtues. Isaiah's ideal king, invested with the spirit of the Lord, shall have wisdom and understanding (11:2), and Deutero-Isaiah has God proclaiming of his servant, "I have put my spirit upon him, he will bring forth justice to the nations" (42:1). Third Isaiah exults, "The Spirit of the Lord is upon me, because the Lord has anointed me to bring good tidings to the afflicted" (61:1). And Paul points out the fruits of the spirit as love, joy, peace, kindness, goodness, faithfulness, gentleness, and self-control (Gal. 5:22–23).

As with the prophets, authority is the gift of the spirit. At his baptism the descent of the spirit of God confers a new authoritative status upon Jesus (Matt. 3:16), although the book of Acts refers to his receiving "the power of the Holy Spirit" at his exaltation (Acts 2:33). The disciples are told that they shall receive power, that is, authority, "when the Holy Spirit has come upon you . . ." (Acts 1:8). And Paul sees himself as having been commissioned by God, since the spirit had been given to him as a guarantee (2 Cor. 1:21, 22).

It appears that at times early Christian communities were seized by the power of the Holy Spirit, although it is wrong to imagine that they were in a permanent state of rapture. Sometimes it appears as "joy in the Holy Spirit" (Rom. 14:17), or "inspired by the Holy Spirit" (1 Thess. 1:6). Or in the face of hardship, Paul and Barnabas go their way "filled with joy and with the Holy Spirit" (Acts 13:52). Sometimes personal weakness is overcome "through his [God's] Spirit in the inner man" (Eph. 3:16), or he [Spirit] intercedes on behalf of a believer, who scarcely knows how to pray (Rom. 8:26, 27). By means of the Holy Spirit God has poured love into the hearts of Christians (Rom. 5:5) and by faith they received the spirit (Gal. 3:2). With confidence the writer of 1 John assures his readers that they abide in God and he in them "because he has given us of his own Spirit" (4:13). Of particular importance, at least to the Corinthian church and for Paul, was the evidence of the spirit in the practice of prophesying or talking in tongues. Here the resemblance to the ecstatic mouthings of the band of seers, referred to in 1 Samuel, is clear. The spirit erupts like a fountain and is not to be quenched; "do not despise prophesying." But it, like "everything," is to be tested (1 Thess. 5:19–21). Although Paul boasts that he can speak in "tongues more than you all" (1 Cor. 14:18), and approves of the practice, he places these charismatic utterances on a lower level than love (1 Cor. 13) and intelligible discourse (1 Cor. 14), since "God is not a God of confusion but of peace" (1 Cor. 14:33).

In the main Paul held to the idea of the spirit as a free, spontaneous activity of God through Christ, but there is also evidence that the gift of spirit was in some degree under the control of human beings, as the reference to quenching the spirit indicates. It is an "object" that can be transmitted by certain endowed persons. Elisha, in the Old Testament, refers to it in these terms when he asks of Elijah "a double share of your spirit," and it is granted (2 Kings 2:9–12). Presumably, it was the spirit of God invested in Elijah. In the New Testament the granting of the Holy Spirit was distinguished from baptism. So Peter and John pray at Samaria that the newly baptized converts should also receive the Holy Spirit, for "it had not yet fallen on any of them, but they had only been baptized in the name of the Lord Jesus." Whereupon, the apostles laid hands upon them "and they received the Holy Spirit." Little wonder that Simon, observing what seemed to him a magical act, asked to be given this extraordinary power and was then virtually cursed by Peter, and called to repentance (Acts 8:15–23). At Ephesus the disciples of John said that they had never heard that there was a Holy Spirit, and after they were baptized Paul "laid his hands upon them" and "the Holy Spirit came upon them." Then they broke out in tongues and prophesied. The author of 2 Timothy reminds his readers "to rekindle the gift of God within you through the laying on of my hands" (1:6). Thus there was set in motion the idea that certain individuals had been given the authority to control the coming of the spirit, notably the apostles appointed by God as of first rank in authority (1 Cor. 12:28). If, on the one hand, the spirit acted freely and mysteriously, on the other it appears as a power strictly to be controlled by ecclesiastical structure lest anarchy break out. The conflict between these two views has lasted to the present, and the Bible does not resolve the issue. The problem is closely connected with the question as to whether God's spirit is to be regarded as an impersonal force or substance or as an independent being possessed of personal attributes.[5] Or is the spirit God himself? Lampe answers, " 'Spirit' seems to be the most adequate [word] to convey the truth that in his personal contact with personal beings it is God himself, and not an inter- mediary created agent or an impersonal energy, who engages with them . . . when we speak of 'the Holy Spirit' we are referring to God - himself. . . ." But exception to this conclusion might be based on Galatians 4:6.

The evidence for spirit anthropopathically conceived is strong, although it does not eliminate entirely the impersonalistic sense. The concept, apart from the Holy Spirit or God's spirit, is rooted in personal imagery. God uses personal spirits to achieve his ends (Judg. 9:23), and when his spirit departs from Saul, he sends an evil one (1 Sam. 16:14ff.). In these contexts spirit refers to independent, presumably created agents. But the spirit is also identified with God in personal terms, thus supporting Lampe's po- sition in respect to the Old Testament. The Psalmist asks the Lord to "let thy good spirit lead me on a level path" (143:10). Israel will be gathered by his spirit (Isa. 43:16). The Holy Spirit can be grieved (Isa. 63:10; cf. Eph. 4:30), or become impatient (Mic. 2:7). In the New Testament, as in the Old, the spirit speaks through people (cf. Matt. 10:20). As already de- scribed, the spirit teaches (John 14:26), bears witness (John 15:26; Rom. 8:16), and speaks to persons (Acts 10:19; 16:6; 20:23).

The personalistic attributes of the spirit, fitting with other an- thropopathic images of God, would seem to weigh heavily in the direction of God's identity with spirit. If so, the wind is not an image of God, but a flat description of him. But scholars disagree. One states, "The spirit of God is not to be identified with God himself," thus drawing a sharp line between deity and all images, personal or impersonal.[7] But no less emphat- ically Lampe maintains "that the being to whom the term 'the Holy Spirit' refers is God—no less."[8] But is there a difference between "the spirit of

God," used in the first citation, and "the Holy Spirit" in the second? If there is, it is of too slight importance to be obvious. However, passages that identify the spirit with God are relatively sparse. God may be identified with spirit when the parallelism of Hebrew poetry is taken account of in this passage, "The Egyptians are men, and not God; and their horses are flesh, and not spirit" (Isa. 31:3). The Lord encourages Zerubbabel by saying, "I am with you . . . my spirit abides among you"—again a possible parallelism (Hag. 2:4, 5). The Gospel is preached so that though judged in the flesh like men, "they might live in the spirit like God" (1 Pet. 4:6). But the only unequivocal statement in which God and spirit are united is in John's gospel: "God is a spirit, and those who worship him must worship in spirit and truth" (4:24).

In spite of theological reasons for identifying God and spirit, the paucity of biblical references in support of that view argues strongly, if silently, for the idea of spirit as an image of God. God is "like" a breath, a wind, an invisible power, or a person with psychic attributes. In the Old Testament the spirit of God stood for vital energy, which is "the creative and vitalizing force of the world" and is "the source, in men, of abnormal skill or strength or wisdom, of prophetic ecstasy or inspiration, and of moral purity." In the New Testament this energy was "ascribed to the continuous living activity of Jesus" and called "holy spirit."[9] But it should be noted that it was the spirit of God in and through Christ that the early Christians cherished and of which they felt themselves possessed. Yet so strong is the bond between Christ and God that often God as spirit and the presence of Christ are virtually interchangeable terms (chap. 12). Christ personalizes God as spirit, and without that fact "it is hard to imagine how the New Testament could have come to be written."[10] The image of "spirit" is irreplaceable for both.

NOTES

1. Cf., e.g., Edwyn Bevan, *Symbolism and Belief* (New York: The Macmillan Co., 1938), Lecture 7; G. W. H. Lampe, *God as Spirit* (Oxford: Clarendon Press, 1977), 45ff.; E. C. Rust, *Nature and Man in Biblical Thought* (London: Lutterworth Press, 1953), 101–16.

2. So G. Ernest Wright, *The Interpreter's Bible* (New York, Nashville: Abingdon Press, 1952), 1:363.

3. Cf. Lampe, *God as Spirit*, 50, 219.

4. The problem of legitimizing charismatic authority led to the institutionalizing of authority. Judaism and Christianity provide examples of "lineage-charismata and office-charismata resulting from the routinization of the original charismatic impulse." Joseph Blenkinsopp, *Prophecy and Canon* (South Bend, London: University of Notre Dame Press, 1977), 149.

5. Bultmann drew the distinction between the two views by the use of the terms *dynamistic* and *animistic*, and provides New Testament references to both. Rudolf Bultmann, *The Theology of the New Testament*, trans. Kendrick Grobel (New York: Charles Scribner's Sons, 1951), 1:155–56.

6. Lampe, *God as Spirit*, 61, 95. Lampe has surveyed the evidence about the spirit in the New Testament: Luke, in the Gospel and Acts, sees spirit eschatalogically (64–73); Paul, although sometimes using the word as an impersonal power (91), sees it as new life (73–91), and the Johannine literature, as with Paul's view of a new life, emphasizes spirit as God's personal outreach to his creation in the mode of Christ's presence, released from historical and cultural context (91–94).

7. *Interpreter's Bible*, 1:362.

8. Lampe, *God as Spirit*, 219. Bevan found the personifications of the "ruach" of God in Proverbs and Philo to be mere political metaphors. "It is an image which the mind entertains for a moment as a pictorial symbol: there is no assertion in sober prose that a personal Being exists distinguishable from God, who has the functions of the Spirit of God or of Wisdom or of the Logos. The new thing in the Christian Church was that the distinct existence of a personal Holy Spirit was taken seriously as a truth about the Divine Being." 187.

9. *Interpreter's Bible*, 9:36.

10. Lampe, *God as Spirit*, 62, 63.

11

Images of God and Christ in Social and Historical Context

The ancient Hebrews perceived nothing irreverent or demeaning in model-ing images of God upon nature. It bore the indelible impress of God's power and wisdom, and it served his purposes. But, as far as one can speak of beginnings, from the first, anthropomorphic and anthropopathic images also flourished. And it was these that helped to account for the heavy emphasis placed upon images drawn from social experience. Each Testament indicates that its authors were deeply aware that they were telling of a "people" with a unique destiny. And to recite that story, social, political, and military fortunes were given full play to express God's deal-ings with a "people." The realm of history was to take precedence over that of nature. Some modern scholars would go as far as to assert, "Nature and history are mutually exclusive,"[1] while another claims that Hebrew religion destroyed the ancient bond between man and nature.[2] The understanding of reality, it is said, can be compressed into the single word *history*.[3]

Yet it is odd that the Hebrews deposited so much of their religious faith in the historical realm. For Christianity, on the other hand, it is under-standable, since Jesus was a historical figure, believed to reveal the nature of God, as no figure in the Old Testament did. We have been incessantly reminded that for Israel "history came first in the order of knowledge," rather than the idea of God as creator of heaven and earth,[4] although how we know this to be true is not clear. Weight is also given to the contention that the word *nature* has no equivalent in Scripture, in spite of the obvious use made of nature in some images of God. Nor should it be overlooked that human beings participate in nature, thus broadening its meaning be-yond the sense of "nonhuman reality."[5] And if, in the end, God is counted as sovereign, nature as well as history must be under his control. It would seem that nature offered advantages as a vehicle for imaging God that outstripped anything history could provide. Conceived as it was, indepen-dent of scientific thought, it is kinesthetically experienced in the human body, as in birth, pain, disease, and health. Its effects do not await the intervention of thought. They are immediate, thus denying the distinction drawn by some, that God acts indirectly with nature and directly with human beings.[6] When fertility, plague, wind, and fire occur, God is seen as directly present in and through these phenomena, as he is in bringing health, prosperity, or peace to human beings. The distinction does not work, especially if the Holy Spirit is regarded, as it is in some passages, as an agent distinct from God, by which God indirectly affects human beings! Nature situated the biblical peoples in a particular time in history, and thereby limited the range of their experiences, and interpretations of them, as it does ours. And this also was a work of God. The permanence and stability of nature impressed them. There were the "eternal hills" and rocks, the sun and moon. As Jeremiah told it, "Thus says the Lord, who gives the sun for light by day and the fixed order of the moon and the stars for light by night. . . ." It is the Lord of hosts who says, "If this fixed order departs from before me . . . then shall the descendants of Israel cease from being a nation before me for ever" (31:35, 36). Compared to human history, nature endures far beyond any measurable span of time yet known to man. Whitehead, as we have seen before, once commented, "So far as survival value is concerned, a piece of rock, with its past history of some eight hundred millions of years, far outstrips the short span attained by any nation."[7] The biblical writers did not have geological knowledge, but they saw in nature a permanence that far exceeded their history, and they laid hold of that fact to image God. History, in any recognizable sense as human, no longer exists when the last person dies; nature may not. But as long as there was history, nature inescapably affected its transactions. Natural resources, "a land of milk and honey," water holes and springs, deserts and fertile fields shaped history. Geographical location made the Hebrew nation subject to the military adventures of Assyria, Babylonia, Egypt, Persia, Greece, and Rome. And mountains "round about" were places where God's "aweful" presence was felt in revelation: Sinai, Carmel, Golgotha. Or one looked to them for help (Ps. 121:1), and refuge (Luke 21:21). Yet nature went on its way, unmindful of human desires and purposes. Human beings lived and died by it, finding nature in themselves perishable (1 Cor. 15:53), without the enduringness of nature apart from them. It could provide images of a merciless God as well as a beneficent one. Endlessly variable, yet ever the constant companion of history, it had no denouement of its own apart from the history it sustained. So Isaiah envisioned a reconciliation within nature itself, and nature with redeemed Israel, as the fulfillment of both nature and history. "the wolf shall dwell with the lamb, and the leopard shall lie down with the kid, and the calf and the lion and the fatling together, and a little child shall lead them . . . the suckling child shall play over the hole of the asp, and the weaned child shall put his hand in the adder's den" (11:6–8; 65:25). Paul saw the creation waiting to be set free from its bondage to decay (Rom. 8:19–21).[8] But no fulfillment by salvation of nature is seen by the writer of Revelation: "Then I saw a new heaven and a new earth: for the first heaven and the first earth had passed away and the sea was no more" (21:1; cf. Isa. 65:17). The nature hitherto known is totally displaced by a new order in the apocalypse. As long as there was a nature, history went on, but without nature, history was to come to an end. History was dependent on nature, not nature on history.

In view of the reservoir of images that nature provided, why then did history bulk so large in building the religious structure of Jews and Christians? To some extent, in adopting the centrality of history and its social dimensions, both groups shrank the broader vistas of nature into the story of two peoples over whose destiny God presided. They put themselves and their God in the center of the drama and increasingly reduced nature to a subordinate position. Yet the domain of God was not limited only to the fortunes of one or the other of the two groups. Amos could challenge his people with the question put by God: "Are you not like the Ethiopians to me. . . . Did I not bring Israel from the land of Egypt, and the Philistines from Caphtor and the Syrians from Kir?" (9:7) As the God of history, he disposed of Assyria and Babylonia as he was to do with Rome. Still, it is strange that history, with its irregularities, its ever-changing meanings, its transience and frustrating unpredictability should have been accepted as the medium by which God was pictured. If nature is ambiguous as to its meaning, so even more is history. Its meaning no more rests upon its surface than does that of nature. Even the faithful cannot always descry its significance. "Thy footsteps were unseen," as the Psalmist puts it (77:10). It is a scene, as the Bible portrays it, of a series of crises in which God only here and there seems to put in his appearance. As one theologian wrote, "There is no Biblical evidence whatsoever for the view that God is revealing His providential purpose all the time. . . . God's providence seems to be more closely related to some events in history than to others."[9] There is indeed a spasmodic character to history where God intervenes only occasionally, that has led some modern theologians to speak of him as "breaking into history," an undoubtedly imaginative and dramatic way of interpreting God's action, but one that assumes a form of transcendence that leaves much of history inexplicable. Even the meaning of the word *history* is itself filled with difficulties, ranging from signifying all that happened in the past, the records and study of the past, the total field of human responsibility, to that favored by some biblical scholars as indicating "the totality of human events, past, present and future, as governed by God and directed towards his goal."[10]

In spite of the vagaries that the word *history* encompasses, there are several reasons for the Bible's stress upon history as its people lived it. First of all, to the Hebrew writers God was already the Lord of history because he rescued the Jews from Egypt. He had chosen them to be his own without an obvious reason (Deut. 7:7, 8; 26:5), and in spite of their way-wardness had brought them through and would continue to do so even if only a remnant survived. He had proved to be the God not only of the desert or the mountain. He was not limited to some one piece of land. He moved with them in their exploits and was with them in the promised land, as Lord of history, who also took over the realm of the Baals, lodging his vigorous protests against his people when they succumbed to the Canaanite fertility rites associated with nature. Another reason lies in the fact that the answer to the question of salvation was not to be found in nature. To be saved as a nation or as individuals depended, as they saw it, upon God's operation in historical events. To the question of redemption nature had no answer, but history with all its complications seemed to provide the arena in which God most meaningfully acted. Thus Christianity, with its historical figure of Jesus, strengthened the already prevalent importance of the historical dimension of the Old Testament. And the tendency to anthropomorphism and anthropopathism seen in the social, political, judicial, and familial images of God was the product of this historical orientation. At last history in which God was active was the lens through which nature itself was to be seen and interpreted.

Whether in later respects the choice of history as the preeminent domain in which God was believed to be present was wise remains a question. The relative lack of interest in nature, and even its degradation in Christian thought and the preoccupation with history and the God of history left behind it a legacy in which nature became a step-child of theology. For a long time no theology of nature developed, and in its place at times so sharp a division between nature and history existed as to deny the sovereignty of God over both. It was left to the natural sciences to tell us about nature, with God left out of consideration, and in that view nature as fully experienced became abstract, skeletonized, or even unrecognizable. The full impact of nature upon human life, both within and without, was largely lost in a scientific age, and even the biblical sense of nature's vigorous immediacy shriveled. But writing at a time far distant from the biblical period, Hegel was not too far off the mark in respect to the importance of history *vis à vis* nature in the Bible. "It was indeed fashionable," he said, "at one time to admire the wisdom of God as manifested in animals and plants. . . . If we admit that providence reveals itself in such objects and materials, why should we not do the same in world history? . . . The [divine wisdom] is one and the same in great things and in small."[11]

History is the context in which the social images arise and to which, in turn, they give shape. To understand history, to the degree it permits of understanding, is to recognize God in it under a variety of guises, which the biblical authors created out of their social experience. These images often overlapped in their meanings, and to some extent to treat them in a serial manner threatens their mutual involvement. The difficulty is compounded if in treating them in distinction from each other, the impression is given that a chronological development is intended. Except for the changes introduced in the New Testament, these images are for the most part considered without any attempt to assign them to definite historical periods. However, for the purposes of clarity it is desirable to begin with one image that draws within its orbit several others.

The image that best accomplishes this task is that of King, Lord, or in a general sense, Sovereign. This political image derives its form from the concrete experience of the Hebrew people with earthly kings, and it penetrates both Testaments.[12] In contrast to the idea of kingship found in the surrounding cultures where kings were often divinized, the Hebrews gave a distinctive meaning to their kings. The Hebrews had been singled out by God in Egypt for freedom, and as his chosen people in the desert they lived without a king. It was Moses, not a king, who led this people into a covenant relation with God, and it was as covenant-maker that God appeared in the narrative. In fact, "Kingship never achieved a standing equal to that of institutions which were claimed—rightly or wrongly—to have originated during the Exodus and the desert wanderings."[13] The establishment of Saul's kingship was clouded by divine displeasure and considered by God to be a sign that his people "have rejected me from being king over them" (1 Sam. 8:7; also 10:19, 25, 12:13–25). David could refrain from killing Saul because "he is the Lord's anointed" (1 Sam. 24:10), but divine approval did not deter him from the extermination of Saul's house, with the exception of Jonathan's son (2 Sam. 21:1–9). David's kingship and his dynasty had the sanction of God (2 Sam. 7:16), but his determination to build a temple to God in Jerusalem brought down upon him the criticism of Nathan, who spoke for the old tradition of the God of the desert. "Thus says the Lord: Would you build me a house to dwell in? I have not dwelt in a house since the day I brought up the people of Israel from Egypt to this day, but I have been moving about in a tent for my dwelling" (2 Sam. 7:5–6). When the fateful split occurred between the northern and southern kingdoms, the followers of Jeroboam cried, "What portion have we in David? . . . to your tents, O Israel! Now see to your own house, David" (1 Kings 12:16). Thus the Davidic kingship approved by God was broken in its continuity, which previously held the tribes together under David, Solomon, and briefly under Rehoboam. Both in Saul's case and in that of Rehoboam, divine approval proved to be only a temporary protection to the office and the individuals occupying it, although the Davidic line continued in Judah.[14] In general, the king seems to have been primarily a secular functionary, having little place in religious matters, although responsible for his people and the conditions of their worship.[15] His was not a sacred office, although one Psalm has been interpreted as addressed to him as God (45:6, 7).[16] Oversight of things holy was reserved to priests.

The king's authority was exercised under that of God, and as such he could be called to account in the Lord's name by the prophets. Moreover, the time came when it was believed that it was the kings of Judah who had led the people astray and brought on the exile in Babylon.[17] Frankfort concluded that it was the transcendence of God that "prevented kingship from assuming the profound significance which it possessed in Egypt and Mesopotamia, "not least because he failed to be instrumental in the integration of society and nature."[18]

In spite of these comparatively low estimates of kingship, kings were often in fact held in high esteem. Their enthronement was the occasion of joyful acclaim (2 Sam. 15:10; 2 Kings 9:13; 11:12). In the minds of the authors David became the ideal king who ruled with justice and was loyal to God, and Solomon in the full flush of prosperity and peace became the model king, blessed by wisdom from God greater than that possessed by any other man (1 Kings 4:29). Neither David nor Solomon was above reproach in personal morals, but David clung to his faith in God, whereas Solomon in his old age turned away after other gods "and his heart was not wholly true to the Lord his God, as was the heart of David his father" (1 Kings 11:4). The marriage of some unidentified king called forth the highest praise of him as a person and a warrior, and his virtues were extolled as one anointed by the Lord (Ps. 45). In another outpouring of praise, God was asked to "give the king thy justice, O God, and righteousness to the royal son." Only then may there be prosperity, protection of the poor and needy, peace, and a long life for the king, during which he will triumph over his foes (Ps. 72). Without fear of contradiction, Elihu could ask, "who says to a king, 'worthless one?' " (Job 34:18). So kings could be elevated to the highest position in Israel, while at the same time they never were beyond the harshest criticism. We are left with a paradoxical view of earthly kings that runs throughout the Old Testament. Kings under God exercised authority and power. They enjoyed, sometimes briefly, the glorious accoutrements of the office, yet their moral and religious conduct redounded to the welfare or misfortune of their people. Perhaps one scholar brings out best the unique status of kingship when he points out that in the civilizations surrounding Israel, the king was "usually regarded as representing God before the people," whereas in Israel "the king was regarded as representing the people before God."[19] Yet kings were closely associated with God, since the cursing of the king could be viewed as also a cursing of God (1 Kings 21:10, 13), and worship of one was connected with worship of the other (1 Chron. 29:20).

From the contradictory estimates of kingship, only the highest ones survived in the images of God. It was understood that God had cared for his people long before ever there were earthly kings (Gen. 36:31), and as late as the prophet Hosea that period had become idealized. The prophet portrayed a future in terms of it when the children of Israel "shall dwell many days without king or prince" (3:4). The brutality, disunity, and anarchy when Israel was without a king and "every man did what was right in his own eyes" (Jud. 17:6; 18:1; 19:1; 21:25) demonstrated the need for a leader. In a military and political sense, kingship was to be the salvation of the nation. It brought some measure of unity to the tribes; it provided a military leader and became a symbol that would engage and focus the patriotic and religious sentiments of the people. For those who wrote in the Davidic tradition, the formula for survival and success was clear: one earthly king, one God, one unified nation. Little wonder when kingship flourished that God should be designated as king. In the blessing of Moses, abruptly inserted into the narrative, the very circumstances under which God became king are described: "Thus the Lord became king in Jeshurun when the heads of the people were gathered, all the tribes together" (Deut. 33:5).[20] The passage is anachronistic, apparently an attempt to trace the origin of God's kingship to the earliest events of Israel's history.

When God came to be called king is likely to remain a puzzle, but there is overwhelming testimony that kingship was a favorite image of God. With that exalted term went all the attendant attributes ascribed to the noblest of earthly rulers: power, majesty, and glory, and from subjects came respect and obedience. "Thine, O Lord, is the greatness and the power, and the glory, and the victory and the majesty . . . thine is the kingdom, O Lord, and thou art exalted as head above all . . . " (1 Chron. 29:11). The term *Lord,* often used with that of "king," appears not only as a substitute for God's personal name, but also as a sign of ownership and mastery over subordinates. In other contexts, however, *Lord* was also used as a form of address applied to men and angels (Gen. 19:2; 27:29), and it found its way into the Christian vocabulary applied to Jesus.[21] However, attention will be focused only on those passages where Lordship and Kingship are obviously interchangeable.

The temple experience of Isaiah knits together Lordship and Kingship, when the prophet claims to have seen the Lord sitting upon a throne, high and lifted up. And the words "for my eyes have seen the King, the Lord of hosts" (6:5) make the meaning explicit. The phrase *Lord of Hosts* or *Lord God of Hosts* suggests the military leadership expected of a king as well as his being surrounded by multitudes of those obedient to his orders, such as angels and courtiers (Isa. 22:5, 12, 15).[22] The condescension and generosity of the king after victory is also stressed (25:6–8). Second Isaiah broadens the meaning of God's kingship by adding creatorship: "I am the Lord, your Holy One, the Creator of Israel, your King" (43:15, 44:6, 21).

The grief of a Jeremiah over his people's apostasy moves him to cry, "Is the Lord not in Zion? Is her King not in her?" (8:19). "Graven images" and "foreign idols" have replaced the king, who now is provoked to anger. This is the king who in his wisdom rules over nations, who makes the earth quake, and whose indignation the nations cannot withstand (10:7, 10). In spite of their rebelliousness God announces his sovereignty over the scattered peoples and announces the judgment they must pass through. "As I live, says the Lord God, surely with a mighty hand and an out-stretched arm, and with wrath poured out, I will be king over you" (Ezek. 20:33ff.). As the source of strength and the victor over Israel's enemies, "the King of Israel, the Lord" is in the midst of his people (Zeph. 3:15), while Zechariah, looking forward to the day of the Lord, puts off to that time God's entering fully into his universal kingship. "And the Lord will become king over all the earth; on that day the Lord will be one and his name one" (14:9). Malachi excoriates those whose blemished sacrifices, brought before God, are an indignity to one who announces, "I am a great King . . . and my name is feared among the nations" (1:14).

But it is the Psalms in which God as king is most fully expressed. He is prayed to (5:2); he is King for ever (10:16), and as the King of glory he enters the temple (24:7–10). By his might he ordains victories for Jacob, for he is "my King and my God," sings the Psalmist (44:4). He subjugates nations under Israel as "a great king over all the earth" (47:2), and Mount Zion is defended by him as "the city of the great King" (48:2, 3). The processions "of my God, my King" enter into the sanctuary (68:24). His gentleness is reflected by the fact that sparrows and swallows find a home at his altars, "O Lord of Hosts, my King and my God" (84:3).[23] He reigns over all the so-called gods (85:3). Then the great enthronement passages come, which depend clearly upon the idealized pictures of the installation of earthly kings (93:96–99). He reigns and the people tremble before him. His holiness sets him apart as the "Mighty King," the lover of justice, and the founder of equity (99:1, 4). It is fitting to extol and bless his name (145:11), and to rejoice with dancing and music in his worship (149:2, 3).

The New Testament presents a different problem. Whereas in the Old Testament the references to God as king or lord are clear, in the Christian Scriptures the references to God as king and lord recede, giving place to Jesus Christ as Lord. God is clearly depicted as Lord in some passages (e.g., Luke 1:25, 38; 2:22; 4:19; 10:21; Acts 4:24; Rom. 14:6–8, etc.), but equally many passages identify Jesus as the Lord, suggestive of kingship (e.g., Luke 1:43; 6:46; 19:31; 24:34; Acts 10:36 [Lord of all], 1 Cor. 2:8 [Lord of glory], Rev. 11:15, etc.). However, Jesus himself came with the message of God's reign, for which people were to prepare by repentance and belief in the good news of the coming kingdom (Mark 1:15). It was not his Lordship or Kingship Jesus announced. The glorification of God's reign in terms of sheer might, justice, and the more severe characteristics of his sovereignty as found in the Hebrew Scriptures are somewhat moderated in Jesus' words. Power remains, as do sovereignty and judgment, but gener-ally a note of benignity influences these attributes. It is the poor or the poor in spirit who will enter the realm of God's kingship (Luke 6:20; Matt. 5:3). It is those of childlike simplicity and humility who will pass into the kingly domain (Matt. 18:3, 4; 19:14). The unrepentant, the proud, and the self-righteous will be under judgment, and even tax collectors and harlots will come into the kingdom before such as these (Matt. 21:31). It is a kingdom to be sought above all in the assurance of God's care, which drives away anxiety for worldly goods (Matt. 6:33; Luke 12:31). Paul continued the theme of the kingdom, pointing out that it does not mean food and drink, but righteousness, peace, and joy in the Holy Spirit (Rom. 14:17). It is a kingdom of power (1 Cor. 4:20), not to be inherited by the unrighteous (1 Cor. 6:9), or by flesh and blood (1 Cor. 15:50). Immoralities, the work of the flesh, have no place in it (Gal. 5:21), but the kingdom comes increasingly to be identified with both God and Christ (Eph. 5:5; 2 Tim. 4:1), or even as Christ's kingdom (Col. 1:13; 2 Pet. 1:11; Rev. 11:15). Thus the "kingdom" was a persistent and vivid figure of the New Testament, underlining the sovereignty of the deity.

Once the kingdom references are left behind, however, the New Testament reveals relatively few explicit examples of God as king. Although Jesus apparently preferred to speak of God as "Father," he did forbid the swearing of oaths in the light of God's kingship. "Do not swear at all, either by heaven, for it is the throne of God, or by earth, for it is his footstool, or by Jerusalem, for it is the city of the great King" (Matt. 5:34, 35). In the trial scene Jesus uses a circumlocution for God as king when he prophesies that the high priest will see "the Son of man sitting at the right hand of Power" (Mark 14:62). Paul implies God's kingly status when he establishes the authority of earthly rulers upon God's authority, "for there is no authority except from God" (Rom. 13:1). The most resounding and unequivocal expressions of God as king are found in 1 Timothy. Here in words of rolling sonority, God as king is heralded in all his glory. "To the King of ages, immortal, invisible, the only God, be honor and glory for ever and ever. Amen" (1:17). And again, looking forward to the appearing of the Lord Jesus Christ, the epistle continues, "this will be made manifest at the proper time by the blessed and only Sovereign, the King of kings and Lord of lords, who alone has immortality and dwells in unapproachable light, whom no man has ever seen or can see. To him be honor and eternal dominion. Amen" (6:15, 16). The book of Revelation contains references to God as king, in borrowings from the Old Testament (4:8, 11; 15:3), but also applies the phrase "King of kings and Lord of lords" to the exalted figure of Christ (17:14; 19:16).

To understand the meaning of God as sovereign, it is necessary to introduce certain other images over which that image ruled. Among these one of the most important is that of covenant-maker. Whether in point of time this image preceded that of king is difficult to determine, but the two were closely related. Wright saw God's covenant-making as dependent upon the King image: "The covenant based as it was on a terminology derived from a monarchical form of government . . . involved an interpretation of the meaning and significance of Israel's life."[24] From the history of kingship in the ancient Near East, it appears that covenant-making was characteristic of royalty. Of that practice we have an example when King David makes a covenant with the elders of Israel at Hebron (2 Sam. 5:3; cf. Jer. 34:8). This close association of earthly kingly status with that of covenant-maker carried over to the image of God in his role of king as being the prototypical covenant-maker. And the importance of this image has come to be the accepted basis of much Old and New Testament interpretation. "It is in the relation of the covenant God with a covenant history that the Old Testament is to be understood." But it has to be admitted that "the absence of references to the covenant is often perplexing."[25]

It seems probable that the image of God as covenant-maker was used to reshape the earlier narratives of the Patriarchal period, as later editors read back upon these stories the standpoint of the Mosaic dispensation. Consequently, when we read of God's making covenant with Noah at the time of the flood (Gen. 6:18), we are hearing the thought of a later period. But even in this episode, the appearance of the rainbow as a sign of the covenant is not limited to Israel, but is given a universal interpretation by the inclusion of "all flesh" and "every living creature" (Gen. 9:13–17). The narrower view is seen in the Lord's making a covenant with Abram, in which he promises to give the land of various tribes to his descendants (Gen. 15:18), as well as making him the father of nations (Gen. 17:4–7). The rite of circumcision, as a sign of the covenant, is associated with the same passage (Gen. 17:9–14). Isaac, the son yet to be born, will also be in covenant relation to God (Gen. 17:19–21). The Mosaic account of covenant-making by referring to "the book of Moses" implies that Moses had compiled the laws referred to in the previous chapters, and it tells of the sacrificial blood spattered upon the people to unite them with the covenant of God (Exod. 24:6–8). The practice of sacrifice as a symbolic act established the covenant so that no literary document describing the content of the covenant was necessary or survives, only the laws built about it. The Priestly hand reworks the material, making the Sabbath "a perpetual covenant" as a "sign for ever between me and the people of Israel" (Exod. 31:16, 17). The Deuteronomists moved the covenant arrangement into a time contemporary with their own by claiming "the Lord our God made a covenant with us in Horeb . . . not with our fathers did the Lord make this covenant, but with us, who are all of us here alive this day" (Deut. 5:2–3). And the theme of God as covenant-maker is echoed in the book of Judges (2:1) and in the work of the Chronicler (2 Chron. 15:12).

The eighth-century prophets may have assumed both the covenant and God as covenant-maker, but they do not develop their messages in these terms.[26] The later Isaiah, however, pictures God as the covenant-maker (42:6), and relates the covenant to God's love and peace (54:10), but he also refers to a future when God will make an "everlasting covenant" as though none had been made before (55:3; 61:8). Even foreigners who join with the Lord and keep his sabbath are to be included in it (56:6; cf. 59:21). Jeremiah harks back to the covenant made with the forefathers in some instances (11:2, 10; 22:9; 34:13), and in others looks forward to a new covenant, yet to be made, which will replace the old one, "not like the covenant which I made with their fathers . . ." (31:31ff.; 32:40; 50:5).[27] Ezekiel calls his people to remember the covenant of the past (16:8), but several of his references to God's making a covenant lie in the future (16:60, 62; 34:25; 32:26). A king who breaks the covenant will be punished (17:15, 19). In the Psalms the covenant God has made stands as a synonym for his "steadfast love" and his continuing care (89:3, 34; 105:45; 111:5, 9), although Ephraim is castigated for its failure to keep it (78:10). On the other hand, in a puzzling vision of Zechariah, the prophet reads the history of his people as one in which God annulled the covenant (11:10, 11). Malachi exalts the priestly group by claiming that God made a covenant with Levi, apparently a further limitation of the covenant, and he criticizes the refractory people for corrupting and profaning it (2:4, 5, 8, 10). Nevertheless, he holds out the hope that a messenger of the covenant·will come as one who will purify the sons of Levi (3:1ff.).

If God the covenant-maker by this means created and sustained a people in the Old Testament, the scene changes in the New Testament, where Christ comes to the foreground. At the Last Supper the old symbolism of blood associated with the covenant is retained, but a new age has opened for Christians (Matt. 26:28; Mark 14:24; 1 Cor. 11:25; Heb. 8:18, 20; 10:28). References to the old covenant are made in quoting Zechariah (Luke 1:72) and when Peter reminds his hearers that they are sons of the prophets and "of the covenant which God gave to your fathers" (Acts 3:25; also 7:8). But the emphasis falls repeatedly on the inadequacy of the old covenant in comparison with the new one now being established by God through Christ. Paul affirms that God "has qualified us to be ministers of a new covenant," since Christ has taken away the veil that "to this day" prevents the Jews from understanding the old covenant (2 Cor. 3:6, 14). The old covenant was in his view not a matter of law, but a promise made to Abraham, which points to Christ (Gal. 3:15–18), who in spite of the hardening of some, will save all Israel (Rom. 11:25–27). But it is the author of Hebrews who most fully spells out the superiority of the new covenant to the old. Jesus is the surety of a "better covenant" (7:22); the covenant he mediates is more excellent than the old, which had faults in it (8:6, 7), and is now obsolete (8:13). Christ is the mediator of the new covenant (9:15; 12:24), which God in Christ has made "the blood of the eternal covenant" (13:20).

Although God is described as king, nowhere is he hailed by the title of "covenant-maker", yet the evidence is clear that this image hovered over all the covenant passages. The Old Testament makes more of God's covenant-making than does the New, but in all those references found in the

Christian Scriptures, there is a strong and studied attempt to attach the new covenant to the old, if in no more than a way of setting forth the advantage of the new in respect to the old. Christ is the mediator and the agent by which a new Israel in covenant relation has been established. But it is God's act in Christ by which this new epoch and people have been created, and so he remains the ultimate covenant-maker. Thus the image of God as covenant-maker lies fully within the orbit of political thought.

As savior, at first glance, God seems to move into a totally spiritual realm, devoid of political associations. Yet it was by kings that people were often saved. Saul, the warrior chieftain (1 Sam. 9:16), and most decisively David (2 Sam. 3:18) were the agencies by which Israel was delivered from her enemies, particularly the Philistines. It was the royal line of David that brought unity to the tribes, short lived though it was. In the eyes of the biblical authors, insofar as David and his line performed this role, kings saved the Hebrew people. When to the role of king as savior is attached that of the covenant-maker, an even stronger case may be made for the transferral of these images to God. If the salvation looked for in parts of the Bible was that of "personal well-being and national and social freedom, justice and prosperity," it also looked beyond these worldly values to a communion with God, both in this world and the next.[28] In this manner the political image of king is stretched into a dimension that called for a new reading of the meaning of the image of savior.

In the image of savior God goes beyond warnings, punishments, or destructive wrath, although these are part of the total process, to acts of graciousness by which rescue from social and individual disaster, pain, suffering, frustration, despair, and immorality is effected. And the first of these was God's act in bringing the Hebrew people out of slavery in Egypt and binding them in covenant to himself. Thus he made them a nation. "Thus the Lord saved Israel from the hand of the Egyptians," ran the refrain. And Moses and the people of Israel sang "Thou hast led in thy steadfast love the people whom thou hast redeemed" (Exod. 14:20; 15:13). Moses recalls this crucial episode in Israel's history when he says, "You know no God but me, and besides me there is no savior" (13:4; cf. Isa. 43:11; 45:21; Ps. 106:21). The major prophets repeatedly use the image of savior. Isaiah names God as our king, who "will save us" (33:22), and Hezekiah in the same book announces "the Lord will save me" (38:20). In the later Isaiah God speaks of himself as "the Holy One of Israel, your savior" (43:3; 45:15; 49:26; 60:16; 63:8). Jeremiah comforts his people when he promises on the Lord's behalf "I will save you from afar" out of captivity (30:10, 11; 46:27). To Jeremiah himself God promises "I will surely save you" (39:18). To the captives in Babylon, he says, "I will save my flock" (Ezek. 34:22), as he will also save them from their sins (Ezek. 37:23). The Psalms chant the praises of God as savior or beseech salvation from him (e.g., 7:1; 17:7; 22:21; 28:9; 31:16; 54:1; 55:16; 69:1; 106:47;

116:4; 118:25). Salvation in these Psalms is sometimes sought for individuals and sometimes for the nation. One of the gentlest uses of the savior image occurs in the writings of Zephaniah, when God proclaims "I will save the lame and gather the outcast" (3:19). The gathering in a future time of the Lord's people from all over the world will take place, "for I will save my people from the east country and from the west country" and they at last "shall be my people and I will be their God, in faithfulness and in righteousness" (Zech. 8:7, 8, 13). If Creator is the image of beginnings, Savior is the apex of images for those actual and hoped-for victories of mankind, never completely to be won by human effort over tribulation.

Salvation in the New Testament tends to be a personal relation between the individual believer and Christ, although emphasis is also placed upon Christians as a new people and a chosen race (Rom. 12:4, 5; Tit. 3:14; 1 Pet. 2:9, 10). Christ is intimately associated with God in his redemptive work (Tit. 1:4, 2:13; 3:6; 1 Pet. 1:1), and sometimes he is singled out by himself as Savior (John 4:42; Phil. 3:20; 2 Pet. 2:20; 3:2, 18).[29] But explicit references to God as savior are found only in the Pastoral and Catholic epistles, with the exception of the Magnificat of Mary (Luke 1:47). First Timothy calls God savior three times (1:1, 2:3; 4:10), Titus salutes him as savior in three passages (1:3; 2:10; 3:4), and Jude ascribes the title to him once (v. 25). The saving action of God is also seen in his having sent Christ into the world (Acts 13:23; 1 John 4:14), and having exalted him as "Leader and Savior" (Acts 5:31).

The association of Lordship with Savior reflects the impression of kingship that the figure of Christ takes on in the Christian consciousness. It even impinges upon the role of God as Savior, giving an importance to Jesus Christ that at times threatens to diminish God's role in salvation. Although the danger may have existed, it is remarkable how few references there are in which the title of savior is bestowed on Jesus. Jesus himself did not use the title, and only a few passages in the Gospels, and these probably of a late date, call him savior.[30] Rather the figure of God stands behind or in close connection with Christ as savior. In the minds of those who wrote the New Testament, the ultimate source of salvation was God, who through Christ exercised his beneficent will. The author of 1 Peter represents this view when he tells his reader that if one suffers as a Christian, "let him not be ashamed, but under that name let him glorify God" (4:16). But time and tradition, rather than the emphatic testimony of the biblical texts, were to insure that Christ alone would eventually bear the title of Savior. Thus to many Christians the agent of salvation tended to assume the role of the original source of salvation as he was elevated in the religious imagination ever closer to the status of deity.

Kings save their people, sometimes by war. An earthly king who in times of danger does not lead or inspire his people to fight would be remiss in his royal duties. We have observed among the anthropopathic images of

God his tendency to belligerence (chap. 8), so it is sufficient at this point only to emphasize that God as king is the warrior king, without once more reciting all the warlike attributes that amplify the image. God is a man of war (Exod. 15:13; Isa. 42:13; Jer. 20:11; Job 16:14; Zeph. 3:17) who fights for his people (Exod. 14:14, 25; Deut. 1:30; 3:22; Josh. 10:14; 23:10, Zech. 10:5, 14:3; Neh. 4:20), and on occasion against them (Jer. 21:5). He not only is imaged as a warrior; he teaches the arts of war to his people (Judg. 3:1–2; 2 Sam. 22:35; Pss. 18:34; 144:1). Presumably a king who did not have the courage and strength to prosecute war had no place on a throne, and by the same token a god who did not fight was scarcely a god to be taken seriously.

The New Testament presents the clearest association of kingship with warmaking when Christ is envisioned as the conqueror who will sit down with his father on his throne (Rev. 3:21). A more belligerent role is given to Christ when, with the name "Faithful and True," he rides into battle on a white horse. "His eyes are like a flame of fire, and on his head are many diadems"—a sign of kingly status. He is clad in a robe dipped in blood and the name by which he is called is "the Word of God . . . on his robe and on his thigh he has a name inscribed, King of Kings and Lord of Lords" (Rev. 19:11–16). The scene described seems far removed from that of a savior, but it is as a savior-warrior that John envisions Christ's destroying the forces opposed to the faithful Christians.

Kings make war to protect their peoples and lands. They pursue aggressive warfare to enlarge their lands and lay alien folk under tribute. But they also aim at peace. In short, kings are, or should be, peacemakers. By insuring the tranquillity and prosperity of those under their reign, they promote security. Admittedly, the textual evidence for the connection between kingship and peacemaker is oblique, but once the political image of God's kingship is firmly established, his promotion of peace stands out as one of the functions of sovereignty. The covenant that was to insure the stability and prosperity of Israel was God's "covenant of peace" (Num. 25:12; Isa. 54:10; Ezek. 37:26), and no value for the individual or society was more highly esteemed than that of the peace God gave after struggle and conflict (e.g., 1 Kings 2:33; Ps. 147:14; Isa. 26:3; Rom. 15:33, etc.). If one were to count the forms or signs of salvation, peace within and without would surely be among the most positive evidences of God's action as savior.

The image of God as king extends into the realm of law and judicial proceedings. Wisdom and justice, the ideal virtues of the kings of Israel, found their apotheosis in God the lawgiver and judge. The Psalmist makes clear the association between God's kingship and the role of judge. "Thou hast maintained my just cause; thou hast sat on the throne giving righteous judgment . . . the Lord sits enthroned for ever, he has established his throne for judgment; and he judges the world with righteousness, he judges the peoples with equity" (9:4, 7, 8). So also Isaiah proclaims "the Lord is our judge, the Lord is our ruler, the Lord is our king: he will save us" (33:22). The title of judge is seldom used of God, but it occurs often enough to establish securely his right to it. He is judge of the earth in Abraham's discussion with the deity over Sodom's fate (Gen. 18:25; Ps. 82:8); he stands as judge between Israel and Ammon (Judg. 11:27); he is the "righteous judge" (Pss. 7:11; 50:6); he is asked to "rise up, O judge of the earth; render to the proud their deserts" (Ps. 84:2). The claim of judge-ship is even more emphatically established by the many instances of his exercising that role (e.g., Gen. 30:6; Exod. 5:21; 1 Sam. 2:10; 24:15; Hos. 6:5; Isa. 41:22; 66:16; Jer. 51:52) and many references in the Psalms. The New Testament carries on the theme, as in Paul's writings (Rom. 2:2, 3, 5; 14:10; 1 Cor. 11:32), in Hebrews (13:4), in the epistle of James: "the judge is standing at the doors" (5:9), and also in Revelation (6:10; 18:8).

As in the case of the title "Savior," Christ in some instances is seen as taking over the prerogatives of judgeship from God. Paul mingles kingship with judgeship in warning the Corinthians that "we must all appear before the judgment seat of Christ" (2 Cor. 5:10), and the same note is struck where Christ is referred to as the one "who is to judge the living and the dead" at the time of his appearing and the coming of the kingdom (2 Tim. 4:1). The most confusing presentation of Christ as judge is found in the Gospel of John. On one hand Christ claims that he judges no one (8:15), for "I did not come to judge the world but to save the world" (3:17; 12:47). On the other hand, he denies that God judges anyone, but "has given all judgment to the Son" (5:22) "for judgment I came into this world" (8:26; 9:39). Nor is that the end. After denying that he is to judge, the writer has Jesus continue by saying "Yet even if I do judge, my judgment is true, for it is not I alone that judge, but I and he who sent me" (5:30; 8:15, 16). It is by God's authority that he judges (12:49). And in one passage he claims that God himself will be the judge (8:50). It is most charitable to the Gospel writer's intent to take the passages of Christ's judgeship as being a dele-gated authority from God, and to diminish the force of the passages where he claims judgeship for himself alone.

Only one passage in the Bible uses the title of Lawgiver as applied to God, and that is associated with judgeship (James 4:12). But the manifesta-tions of God as lawgiver are so plentiful that the title may well be substan-tiated. The central passage, of course, to which the Old Testament repeatedly refers is that which portrays God as giving the law at Sinai (Exod. 20ff.), and the books of Deuteronomy and Leviticus bear out and expand upon the sanctity of the law given by the deity. Among the many references in the Psalms, the One Hundred Nineteenth in particular glories in the testimonies, precepts, statutes, commandments, and ordinances of the Lord. Nor were these laws burdensome to the devout Jew, for his "delight is in the law of the Lord" upon which he "meditates day and night" (Ps. 1:2). For Jeremiah the law is to be no external authority, but as part of the new covenant will be "written in their hearts" (31:33).

Jesus' respect for the law of God is unmistakable, although he urges an obedience that exceeds that of the defenders of the law (Matt. 5:17–20).[31] The Golden Rule he cites as coming from the "law and the prophets" (Matt. 7:12; 11:13), that is, the Scriptures. When asked as to the "great commandment in the law" he offers the two commandments, to love God and the neighbor, as the basis of the whole law and the prophets (Matt. 22:36–40). The Lukan passages concerning his youth make clear that he has undergone the rites prescribed by the law (2:39), thus establishing him fully within the heritage of Judaism. But with Paul the struggle over the law of God assumes the crucial role it was to play in the history of Christianity.[32] The law unquestionably had been given by God, but for Paul it did not bring the salvation the law promised. Only faith in Christ justified and saved (Gal. 2:15, 16). "Christ" for him was "the end of the law, that everyone who has faith may be justified" (Rom. 5:10). Thus Paul at times denigrates the law, since no human being will be justified by it before God. True, the law brings knowledge of sin (Rom. 3:20, 28), but it also brings wrath (Rom. 4:15), and only increases human trespasses (Rom. 5:20). In Paul it had served to incite his sense of his own sinfulness (Rom. 7:7), but at the same time he was willing to uphold it as holy, just, and good (Rom. 7:12). He agonized over the plight of his brother Jews who as yet had not recognized the new door that God had opened to salvation in Jesus Christ. They have had the benefits of God in the form of "the sonship, the glory, the covenant, the giving of the law, the worship and the promises," and Christ himself, according to the flesh, is of this race (Rom. 9:4–5). It was intolerable for Paul to believe that they will miss out on so great a salvation as God offered in Christ. To remedy the dire prospect of their rejection, he argues in an involved manner that at some future time they also will be brought to the acceptance of Christ in faith (Rom. 11:1ff.). What Paul could not surrender, even in his most extreme pronouncements on the importance of faith, was his conviction that the law had been given by God, but the new access to salvation, also from God, had superseded the law except in its negative functions. It remained to the author of Hebrews to reduce even that ritualistic function of the law to a mere "shadow of the good things to come," which gave a false rather than a "true form of these realities" (10:1). Thereby he jeopardized the biblical conviction of God as the lawgiver.

One does not entirely leave the area of political and judicial images in turning to the image of father. The earthly king of the people is seen as a son of God invested with certain rights and obligations, as in the case of the descendant of David when God says "I will be his father and he shall be my son" (2 Sam. 7:14; 1 Chron. 28:6, 9; Pss. 2:7; 89:26–28). Nor is God's lordship diluted in any sense by the use of the title "Father" in the Bible. A father, in the family circle, wields lordship over the family. He is the progenitor of the family, its protector, and the source of authority. He is a figure of strength to be treated with respect, yet also one who has affection for his own. There is a closeness of relation with his children, and this is borne out in the case of God in the Old Testament by his intimacy with Israel and in the New Testament by the frequent use of the image in relation to Jesus and human beings.

Moses is commanded to tell Pharaoh, "Thus says the Lord, Israel is my first-born son" and unless you let my son go "I will slay your first-born son" (Exod. 4:22). And the Deuteronomist rings the changes on Israel as God's son when Moses looks back on the wilderness wanderings as a time in which "The Lord your God bore you as a man bears his son" (1:31), but does not refrain from disciplining his people "as a man disciplines his son" (8:5). "Is he not your father who created you, who made you and established you?" (32:6) The Chronicler pictures David's praising God with the words, "Blessed art thou, O Lord, the God of Israel, our father, for ever and ever" (2 Chron. 29:10). But one goes to the prophet Hosea for the tenderest, yet most poignant, image of God as father. "When Israel was a child, I loved him, and out of Egypt I called my son . . it was I who taught Ephraim to walk. I took them up in my arms, but they did not know that I healed them" (11:1, 2; cf. Isa. 63:8, 9). Some scholars have, like Pier De Boer, flatly stated that carrying small children was a motherly, not a fatherly task.[33] The late Isaiah in contrasting the everlasting and redeeming God to the mortality of the patriarchs, claims the Lord as "our Father" (63:16). In the role of creator God is also hailed as "our Father" (64:8). Jeremiah, castigating Israel for its flagrant idolatries, puts in Israel's mouth a hypocritical appeal to the Lord, in which the people say "My father, thou art the friend of my youth" (3:4). In another passage the prophet pictures God as sadly meditating on what he had purposed for Israel. "I thought how I would set you among my sons . . . and I thought you would call me My Father, and would not turn from following me" (3:19). In spite of Israel's iniquities, the Lord will save him "for I am father to Israel, and Ephraim is my first-born" (31:9). God's fatherly love of Ephraim bursts out as he cries "is Ephraim my dear son? Is he my darling child? For as often as I speak against him I do remember him still. Therefore my heart yearns for him: I will surely have mercy on him" (31:20). A sterner note is struck by Malachi as he has the Lord asking "If then I am a father, where is my honor?" (1:6). The faithlessness among the Israelites moves the prophet to remind them that they all have one father, their creator (2:10). The connection between the king and God is illuminated by words suggestive of legal adoption, uttered by the Lord, "You are my son; today I have begotten you" (Ps. 2:7). They are words seized upon by the author of Hebrews as referring to Christ (Heb. 1:5; 5:5). The tender words of Hosea echo in the image of God as the "father of the fatherless and protector of widows" (Ps. 68:5), and again as the father who pities his children (Ps. 103:13).

A word perhaps should be interjected at this point in respect to the feminine or motherly images of God. Such references are exceedingly scarce. Much ink has been spilled over Genesis 1:27, where God created man in his own image, "in the image of God he created him; male and female he created them." The passage suggests an androgynous deity. In the Song of Moses, God chides his people for being unmindful "of the Rock that begat you." However, the Hebrew word for "begat," it is argued, is unquestionably to be translated "bore."[34] Another reference to mother-hood is discovered in the last chapter of Isaiah, where God says, "as one whom his mother comforts, so I will comfort you" (66:13). In the face of this lack of references to female attributes of God, DeBoer nevertheless insists that sufficient evidence exists to show "that ancient Israel and Judah have worshiped motherly aspects of their God."[35]

The image of father in the Old Testament paved the way for its use in the New Testament. The Synoptic Gospels, in various forms, unite in begin-ning Jesus' unique status at his baptism. There the heavenly voice an-nounces, "Thou art my beloved son" (Mark 1:11; Matt. 3:17; Luke 3:22). This unique relation of God and Christ as father and son becomes a favorite phrase in later writings (e.g., 1 Pet. 1:3; 2 Pet. 1:17; 1 John 1:3; 2:22, 24; 4:14; 2 John vv. 3, 9; Rev. 3:5, 21). The establishment of Jesus as the unique son of God, with approval and empowerment at the baptismal scene, is preceded in Luke's gospel by legends of Jesus' youth. The Gospel pictures Jesus as growing in wisdom and stature and "in favor with God and man" (2:52), suggesting that this realization of his status as a son of God came as a gradual development rather than at the episode of baptism. Luke also tells of the boy Jesus wandering off to the temple and later answering Mary's anxious inquiry as to his whereabouts with the words, "Did you not know that I must be in my Father's house?" (2:49)—words that undoubtedly were intended to carry a deeper meaning than the words convey on casual reading.

The mature Jesus lavishly used the term *father* to describe God, and it often runs in close parellelism with his teachings on the Kingdom. Cer-tainly, as Bornkamn noted, "Jesus' use of the name 'Father' for God cannot . . . be taken as the introduction of a new idea of God." However, he points out that Jesus did not apply the father-son relation to the nation, as did much of the Old Testament, nor did he make sonship the prerogative only of the pious.[36] The latter comment seems to be true of the Synoptic Gos-pels, but John's Gospel tells a different story. Only those who receive Christ and believe in his name "become children of God" (1:12), and the anti-Semitic cast of the Gospel ostracizes the Jews from the realm of God's fatherhood (e.g., 8:42). There are signs in the Synoptics of Jesus' moving away from Jewish traditions, as in the case of his attitude toward the Law and the Sabbath, and perhaps above all in his use of the title *Father*. He appears to have given a more intimate and less formal character to the title when he used the word *Abba,* a familiar form of address to an earthly father, but one uncommon in ceremonial religious language.[37]

The Matthean account of Jesus' teaching finds him using more references to God as father than are found in Mark's and Luke's accounts. In the Beatitudes the peacemakers shall be called "sons of God," suggesting a status yet to be achieved (5:9; cf. 5:45). The disciples are enjoined to do good works that will redound to the glory of "your Father who is in heaven" (5:16). The repeated use by this Gospel of the expression "Father in heaven" stresses the royal distance of God from mankind, even in the most sensitively intimate passages. The universal impartiality and beneficence of God who "makes his sun rise on the evil and the good, and sends rain on the just and unjust" is stressed (5:45; Luke 6:35). And the goal of the new life is pitched high when Jesus calls his followers to be perfect "as your heavenly Father is perfect" (5:48; cf. Luke 6:36). True piety is to be carried out in secret before God the Father (6:1, 4, 6, 18). The Lord's Prayer employs both the fatherly and kingly images, although the Lukan account uses a more personal form of address (6:9, 10; Luke 11:2). Forgiveness of others is to be matched with the heavenly Father's, as failure to forgive others is punished by God's lack of forgiveness (6:14; cf. Mark 11:25). Overweening anxiety about worldly goods and life itself is met by the assurance that "your heavenly Father knows that you need them all." In seeking first his kingdom and his righteousness "all these things shall be yours as well" (6:32, 33; cf. Luke 12:30). In contrast with parents "who are evil" yet give good gifts to their children, "your Father who is in heaven" gives good gifts to those who ask him (7:11; cf. Luke 11:13). Those who enter the kingdom are only those who do "the will of my Father who is in heaven" (7:21). As Jesus sends out his disciples, he encourages them to speak freely, since it will not be they who speak "but the Spirit of your Father speaking through you" (10:20). Nor are they to fear those who may kill them. The heavenly Father cares for them, even as he does for the humble sparrows. And those who acknowledge Jesus before the Father, Jesus will acknowledge in heaven, even as he will disavow those who deny him (10:28–33).[38] In a passage that brings to mind the Gospel of John, Jesus is described as thanking God the Father, "Lord of heaven and earth" for having withheld knowledge of the meaning of his sayings from the cognoscenti, yet revealing it to "babes." All things, he claims, have been given to him by "my Father," and in terms of a high Christology, he adds "no one knows the Son except the Father, and no one knows the Father except the Son, and anyone to whom the Son chooses to reveal him" (11:25–27; Cf. Luke 10:21–22).[39] We may be closer to the historical Jesus' teaching when he avows that his true brother, sister, and mother are "whoever does the will of my Father in heaven" (12:50). Jesus agrees that the confession of Peter near Caesarea Philippi is true, since flesh and blood had not revealed it to Peter, "but my Father who is in heaven" (16:17). The care of God the Father for little children is strongly emphasized, since "it is not the will of my Father who is in heaven that one of these little ones should perish" (18:10, 14). In a passage that puts in question Jesus' words about the establishment of his church (16:18, 19), he announces that "if two of you agree on earth about anything they ask, it will be done for them by my Father in heaven. For when two or three are gathered in my name, there am I in the midst of them" (18:19, 20). When the mother of the sons of Zebedee asks for her sons to be given seats of authority in the Kingdom, Jesus says that "my Father" alone can grant that wish (20:20–23). The bitter castigation of the Scribes and Pharisees, which may reflect the controversy between synagogue and the early Christian movement, puts the central emphasis upon one master rather than the religious authorities. "Call no man your father on earth, for you have one Father, who is in heaven" (23:9). The apocalyptic vision of the last days, which Matthew shares with Mark (chap. 13) and Luke (chap. 21), also puts the stress on God's preeminence rather than that of the son. No one knows the time of history's ending; not angels or the son, "but the Father only" (24:36). The judgment scene, unique to Matthew, pictures the Son of Man as King dividing the "sheep from the goats" with the summons to the saints, "Come, O blessed of my Father, inherit the kingdom," and the sinners are commanded to depart into eternal fire. Whether Jesus is here assimilated to the figure of the Son of Man may be left to biblical critics to ascertain, but if he is, he has become a glorified, transworldly, regal personage, rather than Jesus the teacher. At the Last Supper Jesus foretells that he will not drink wine again until he drinks it anew "in my Father's kingdom" (26:29; cf. Mark 14:25; Luke 22:18). The scene in Gethsemane finds Jesus entreating his Father in passionate prayer to be released from the fate he sees before him, yet yielding his will to that of the Father (26:39; Luke 22:42). The Markan account makes the scene more poignant by reporting Jesus' use of the intimate form of address, "Abba, Father" (14:36). The final act of Jesus' earthly life, according to Luke, was his loud outcry of "Father, into thy hands I commit my spirit" (23:46)—a saying that makes clear the distinction between Father and Son. John's Gospel clouds the distinction and confuses the issue, but this matter is best left to a separate treatment (chap. 11).

Other New Testament writings make less use of the father image than do the Gospels, with the exception of 1 John. It appears most often in salutation, often in the form of "Grace to you and peace from God the Father and the Lord Jesus Christ" (Rom. 1:7).[40] The risen Christ tells the disciples to await the promise of the Father, the coming of which is known only by the Father (Acts 1:4, 7), and Peter's sermon tells of Christ's having been exalted and having received the promise of the Holy Spirit from the Father (Acts 2:33). Paul used the image to highlight the relation of sonship into which his readers had entered when by the Spirit they utter the words "Abba, Father" (Rom. 8:15). Near the close of the same letter he urges that they live in harmony so that they may "with one voice glorify the God and Father of our Lord Jesus Christ" (15:6). His advice on eating food offered to idols is buttressed with the affirmation that there is only one God "the Father, from whom are all things and for whom we exist . . ." (1 Cor. 8:6). The Ephesian letter exalts God as the "Father of glory" (1:17), with whom reconciliation has been made by the blood of Jesus Christ, "for through him we . . . have access in one spirit to the Father" (2:18). God is the "Father, from whom every family in heaven and on earth is named" (3:14). And the principle of unity of the Christian community lies in this "one God and Father of us all" (4:6). All people will at last confess "that Jesus Christ is Lord, to the glory of God the Father" Phil. 2:11). Gratitude to the Father is sounded in Colossians (1:12; 3:17). In the midst of the troubles besetting the Thessalonians, the author prays that the Father will guide them and that the Lord Jesus will establish them in holiness before "our God and Father" (1 Thess. 3:11, 13). Comfort is to come from Christ and "God our Father" (2 Thess. 2:16, 17). The epistle of James hails God as "the Father of lights" and defines pure religion before God, the Father, as visiting orphans and widows (1:27). His practical advice on talking says of the tongue that it is used to "bless the Lord and Father" and also to curse men (3:9). In 1 John love and fatherhood are put to the foreground. The Christ that his readers know is "our advocate with the Father" (2:1, 13). Love of the world stands in contradiction to the "love of the Father," and cuts people off from relation to the Father (2:15, 16). A creedal element is introduced by the author when he offers a test by which the Antichrist may be recognized: "No one who denies the Son has the Father. He who confesses the Son has the Father also" (2:22, 23). In the divine love that the Father has given, the believers have become children of God (3:1). They are enfolded in God's care as they affirm "We have seen and testify that the Father has sent his son as the Savior of the world" (4:14). The elevated Christ of the book of Revelation continues the theme of fatherhood (1:6, 27). Before the Father he will confess the names of the saved (3:5), and will sit down on the throne with the Father (3:21).[41]

In a world that so often seems heartless in its waste of human hope and life itself, the image of God as Father reaches out, not always with a soft embrace, but with warm assurance of care that supports and sustains. It is never a cheap or sentimental figure, but one that touches the heartache and frustration of people with a love that resembles human paternal affection at its best. There is a safety and strength in the image of Father that speaks of One whose will has the last word and in whom one's total trust may be invested.

The area of family life produced another image, that of husband. It is less often used, probably because in the Old Testament it is associated with the sexual connotations of Baal worship. The temptations to the Israelites are manifest in the frequent uses of harlotry, not only as a physical act, but as an image of idolatry and immorality generally. It is natural that figures of speech that had the remotest connection with sex would be used most cautiously of God. Yet the figure of husband and wife did carry an aura of intimacy as well as of fidelity and companionship that was not entirely foreign to the Israelite sense of God.

One of the most striking usages of the figure of husband is found in the writings of the prophet Hosea. The interplay between the erring wife, Israel, and her husband, God, is vividly expressed. The language is un-compromisingly descriptive. "Plead with your mother," the Lord says to the prophet, "for she is not my wife and I am not her husband" (2:2). But then having been disciplined and cut off from her lovers, "then she will say, 'I will go and return to my first husband, for it was better with me then than now'" (2:7b). In a touching way the prophet pictures the Lord's drawing her back to himself in the wilderness for a honeymoon period. There he will "speak tenderly to her" and "she will answer as in the days of her youth." In that day she will call him "my husband" (2:14–16). The imagery used by Hosea is traceable in Second Isaiah when the Lord inquires "where is your mother's bill of divorce, with which I put her away?" (50:1), and again when the prophet boldly links the husband image with lofty titles: "Your maker is your husband, the Lord of Hosts is his name; and the Holy One of Israel is your Redeemer, the God of the whole earth is called" (54:5). The echo of Hosea again sounds when Jeremiah likens the faithlessness of Israel to a faithless wife's leaving her husband (3:20), and refers to the breaking of the old covenant at a time when "I was their husband" (31:32; cf. Ezek. 16:8ff.).

The husband image did not come over into the New Testament as a designation of God, but it is suggested in respect to Christ. The relation of Christ to the church can bear that meaning (Eph. 5:23, 25, 29, 32), and so also do apocalyptic scenes of the New Jerusalem coming down from heaven adorned as a bride for her husband, Christ (Rev. 21:2; 19:7–9). Paul's identification of the Jerusalem above as the mother may weakly associate Christ as the husband, who has brought into being the Christian community (Gal. 4:26). It remains a puzzle as to why with all the images of God as father in the New Testament the correlative husband image does not occur. Perhaps the father image, bearing a loftier significance than husband, ruled out the use of the latter with its questionable sexual connotations. And its scant use in the Old Testament, compared to that of father, may also have made it inconsequential for New Testament usage.

Miscellaneous images drawn from various forms of social experience depend upon the notion of salvation. The image of friend may be so construed when God acknowledges Abraham as his friend (Isa. 4:8; cf. James 2:23). The Lord asks "Have you not just now called to me 'My father, thou art the friend of my youth?' " (Jer. 3:4). The Psalmist sings, "The friendship of the Lord is for those who fear him" (25:14). God is also the guide and leader. "He will be our guide for ever" (Ps. 48:14; cf. Exod. 15:13; Isa. 42:16; 49:10; 58:11). And the image of shepherd in the Twenty-third Psalm (v. 1) puts in poetic form what the prophet Ezekiel stated in prose. The Lord will seek out his sheep and rescue them. He will feed them with good pasture and "they shall lie down in good grazing land. I myself will be the shepherd of my sheep and I will make them lie down, says the Lord" (Ezek. 34:11–15). The image is transferred to Jesus in the New Testament (cf. John 10:11, 14; Heb. 13:20; 1 Pet. 2:25; 5:4), where it supplements and enriches the image of Christ as Savior. The idea of redemption is fittingly expressed in the occasional use of the image of God as the healer. God promises the Israelites not to visit upon them the diseases with which he had plagued the Egyptians "for I am the Lord, your healer" (Exod. 15:26). Hosea sarcastically describes the superficiality of Israel's repentance when he has Israel blithely saying "Come, let us return to the Lord, for he has torn, that he might heal us; he has stricken, and he will bind us up," all of which will take merely a couple of days (6:1, 2; cf. 11:3). Jeremiah speaks the words of the Lord as he beseeches Israel's sons to return to God, who will heal their faithlessness (3:22). In personal distress the prophet cries "Heal me, O Lord, and I shall be healed; save me, and I shall be saved" (17:14). In spite of the disaster that has overtaken Judah, God promises to bring health and healing: "I will heal them" (33:6). God as healer shows in the cry of the Psalmist, who has asked the Lord for help and has been healed (30:2), as are many who suffer from their sins and are then in distress (107:20). The greatness of God is seen not only in the natural world, but in his gathering of the outcasts of Israel, whom he heals of brokenheartedness and whose wounds he binds up (Ps. 147:2–4). One needs only to mention the way in which the New Testament adapts the divine image of healer to Jesus, whose cures are seen as signs of the coming of the kingdom, or of Christ's own life-giving power.

As all these images pass before us, we are struck by the role social and historical experience has played in molding both anthropomorphic and anthropopathic images of deity. The harmony between earthly, mundane experience and the sense of God in his various functions is aptly demonstrated by them. We may also be struck by the manner in which the King image almost entirely preempts the field of images in the Old Testament, whereas the Father image tends to occupy the foreground in the New Testament. The Covenant-maker image shrinks in importance, but that of Savior runs through both Testaments, showing where the primordial center of all religion is, namely, in the soteriological question. A god who does not save, no matter how great he is in other respects, soon loses his devotees. The images of Lawgiver and Judge find more support in the Old Testament than in the New, although the judgmental aspects of God and Christ are given their place in the latter.

Because of the intimate association of these images with the social, political, judicial, and familial experience of a far distant time and culture, the tantalizing question arises as to whether these images can endure and carry the weight of human faith in a world in which kings no longer rule as once they did. The devout pray to or sing about the Great King of all, and his kingdom, but democracies or dictatorships actually frame our political lives. The prayer taught by Jesus says nothing about the coming of "thy democracy" or "thy dictatorship." Has not our experience made old images uncouth? And what of the image of Father in a unisex world? The roles of mothers and fathers seem ever more confused, so that the biblical traditions of the family, which gave rise to the father image, increasingly appear to undermine the meaning and validity of the title *Father* as applied to God. However, many of the preeminent biblical images of God and Jesus have so far sustained themselves through changing historical circumstances.[42] The sole exception to this observation is the present-day feminist revolt against the masculine element that suffuses the Bible. The images passed in review in this chapter are all certainly rooted in masculinity and male roles. The feminists of our day may attempt to rewrite the Bible, but for good or ill, kings, fathers, lawgivers, judges, and the like remain male figures, and they dominate the horizon of biblical experience. Esther and Deborah should not be forgotten, nor the women whose names appear in connection with the nascent Christian movement, but the actions seen as moving and determining the history in the biblical accounts are carried out by males: Moses, David, Solomon, the major prophets, and Jesus of Nazareth. Little wonder then that God should himself be hailed as masculine. The contemporary attack launched against male images in the Bible raises the interesting question as to how far the seeker of God is bound by the Bible's sexual images. It might be recalled that the word *gender* is a grammatical term, not one definitive of sexuality. *Ruach* in Hebrew is feminine, but it does not follow that "breath" or "wind" is to be characterized as female. In Greek *pneuma* is neuter, but sexual identity is not thereby ascertained. This occurs in other languages: in words such as *victime* in French (feminine) and *Mädchen* in German (neuter), sexual connotations are not designated. Perhaps proponents of women's rights would be well advised in translating biblical texts to refrain from placing too heavy emphasis on the vagaries of grammatical usage. The legitimacy of their claim does not hinge upon the confusion of gender and sex, nor upon the citation of biblical texts.

NOTES

1. André Lacocque, "A Return to a God of Nature," *The Chicago Theological Seminary Register* 68, no. 3 (Fall 1978): 29.

2. Henri Frankfort, *Kingship and the Gods* (Chicago: The University of Chicago Press, 1948), 343.

3. Wohlfahrt Pannenberg, *Faith and Reality*, trans. John Maxwell (London: Search Press; Philadelphia: The Westminster Press, 1977), 10. Cf. G. Ernst Wright's comment that "Israel's doctrine of God . . . was not derived from speculative thought; it was derived from the sole interpretation of historical events possible to them." *The Interpreter's Bible* (New York and Nashville: Abingdon Press, 1952), 1:352. For a contrary opinion see James Barr, "Story and History in Biblical Theology," *The Journal of Religion* 56, no. 1 (1976). The real distinctiveness of Israel is not the notion of divine action in history, but the idea of one God against many gods. He maintains: "Far from divine action in history providing a foundation for the perception of God, it may be that the peculiar perception of God was the foundation for the idea of divine action as the biblical story depicts it." 14.

4. Cf. The Faith and Order paper of the World Council of Churches, in *God, History, and Historians*, ed. C. T. McIntire (New York: Oxford University Press, 1977), 297.

5. Cf. ibid., 302–03.

6. "God's work in history deals directly with man and indirectly with nature . . . ," ibid., 313.

7. A. N. Whitehead, *Symbolism, Its Meaning and Effect* (Cambridge: Cambridge University Press, 1928), 76.

8. Some biblical critics view the use of *creation* here as referring only to human society, but see v. 23 and *The Interpreter's Bible*, 10:518ff.

9. John McIntyre, *The Christian Doctrine of History* (Edinburgh: Oliver and Boyde, 1957), 41.

10. Cf. *God, History, and Historians*, 304.

11. Georg W. F. Hegel, *Lectures on the Philosophy of World History, Introduction: Reason in History*, ed. Johannes Hoffmeister, trans. N. B. Wishart. Introd. Duncan Forbes (Cambridge: Cambridge University Press, 1975), 37–38.

12. "The concept of Yahweh as a king would hardly be adopted by the Israelites until they themselves had got a king, and with him, an obvious occasion to bestow on Yahweh this highest title of honor." S. Mowinckel, *The Psalms in Israel's Worship* (New York, Nashville: Abingdon Press; Oxford: Basil Blackwell, 1962), 1:125.

13. Frankfort, *Kingship*, 340.

14. John C. Meagher has pointed out that history, uninfluenced by theological interests, shows the prophecies of the longevity of the Davidic dynasty to be false: "There is no way to reconcile a promise that there will be an uninterrupted line of Davidic kings with the historical reality that there was not." "Pictures at an Exhibition: Reflections on Exegesis and Theology," *Journal of the American Academy of Religion* 47, no. 1 (March 1979): 8.

15. However, Solomon does act as a religious functionary when he prays at the dedication of the temple. 1 Kings 8:22ff.

16. So John Bowker, *The Religious Imagination and the Sense of God* (Oxford: Clarendon Press, 1978), 92.

17. Ibid.

18. Frankfort, *Kingship*, 342, 343.

19. A. R. Johnson, quoted in Bowker, *Religious Imagination*, 93; cf. also Norman Perrin, *Jesus and the Language of the Kingdom* (Philadelphia: Fortress Press, 1976), 16, 17.

20. This text is admittedly doubtful. The King James Version and The Bible: An American Translation read it to mean that Moses became king. If these translations are accepted, they make earthly kingship extant in the Mosaic period, a very doubtful reading. The New English Bible simply states, "Then a king arose in Jeshurun." So much for the vagaries of text and translation!

21. Vincent Taylor points out that the title of King for Jesus was avoided by Paul and the author of 1 Peter because of its dangerous political connotations. In Christian usage the preferred term was "Lord," since "all that was of value in it [King] could be embraced in the

title of 'the Lord,' with the added advantage of the liturgical associations of the Kyrios-title." *The Names of Jesus* (New York: St. Martin's Press, Inc., 1953), 77.

22. "Lord of hosts" was a favorite expression. Cf. Zechariah, chap. 8, and Haggai 1:2, 7, 14; 2:4, 6, 7–9, 11, 23.

23. In the gentle persuasiveness of God, Lewis S. Ford finds the connection between his process theism and divine kingship coming together. "Thus while process theism can only do partial justice to many of the images of divine kingship in the Bible, and none to some, it may be the model most appropriate to the final image emerging from this tradition." *The Lure of God* (Philadelphia: Fortress Press, 1978), 31.

24. *The Interpreter's Bible*, 1:355.

25. Ibid., 293, 299.

26. Bowker, *Religious Imagination*, 69. Hosea mentions the covenant of God only three times (2:18; 6:7; 8:1), Amos and Micah not at all, and Isaiah once (24:5).

27. A commentator on the use made of this passage in Hebrews maintains that in Jeremiah's day the old covenant was considered to be obsolete. "In speaking of a new covenant he treats the first as obsolete. And what is becoming obsolete and growing old is ready to vanish away." Heb. 8:13 and footnote.

28. G. W. H. Lampe, *God as Spirit* (Oxford: Clarendon Press, 1977), 16.

29. "In no passage in which St. Paul mentions Christ's redemptive work does he use the name 'the Saviour.' " Taylor, *Names of Jesus*, 107.

30. Taylor, *Names of Jesus*, 107.

31. Doubt has been raised about the authenticity of Jesus' comments on the law, especially cf. 5:18–19, which seem at odds with other statements of Jesus.

32. Paul uses the word *law* not only to refer to the Mosaic law, but sometimes more generally as the natural law of God, the law of conscience in his inmost self (Rom. 7:22), and the law of the "Spirit of life in Christ Jesus" (Rom. 8:2; 1 Cor. 9:21).

33. P. A. H. DeBoer, *Fatherhood and Motherhood in Israelite and Judean Piety* (Leiden: E. J. Brill, 1974), 41. But see Deut. 1:31 "as a man bears his son."

34. Ibid., 42.

35. Ibid., 37.

36. Gunther Bornkamn, *Jesus of Nazareth*, trans. Irene and Fraser McLuskey, with James M. Robinson (New York: Harper and Brothers, 1960), 126.

37. Ibid., 128.

38. The chapter is shot through with anachronisms. See especially vv. 17, 18.

39. The formative hand of the early church seems to have molded the passage.

40. Cf. 1 Cor. 1:3; 2 Cor. 1:2, 3; Gal. 1:1, 34; Eph. 1:2, 3; Phil. 1:2; Col. 1:1, 2, 3; 1 Thess. 1:1, 3; 2 Thess. 1:1, 2; 1 Tim. 1:2; 2 Tim. 1:2; Tit. 1:4; Philem. 1:3; 1 Pet. 1:2, 3; 2 Pet. 1:12; 1 John 1:1–3; 4:14; Jude 25, and the benediction of Phil. 4:20.

41. The images of King and Savior are sometimes applied to Jesus Christ, but never the image of Father. That is reserved to God.

42. In the case of Jesus, Vincent Taylor, showing his traditionalism, insists that the titles given to Jesus were the "signs and seals of the earliest Christology, and by their subsequent use throughout the centuries the Church has endorsed their permanent validity." He pointed out that Christianity has not been able to add other names in any significant degree. The list of designations of later, nonbiblical origin he called "depressing as a group of raw, self-conscious recruits." Taylor, *Names of Jesus*, 173–74.

12

Christ, the Image of God

The Old Testament offers the peculiar notion that God elected one group of people from all the nations of the world; the New Testament tells the even more perplexing story of God's revealing himself in only one man. Both are instances of the "scandal of particularity," as one nation or one person is entrusted with the fulfillment of divine purposes. Christianity further intensified the scandal by claiming that God not only revealed himself through Jesus Christ, but that Jesus Christ was actually identical with God. This astonishing assertion flew in the face of the Old Testament testimony that clearly distinguished between human beings and God. Nevertheless it found its way into both Christian piety and theology, becoming, with the doctrine of the Trinity, a determinant of orthodoxy. It became known as the Incarnation, a doctrine that curiously intermingled the ahistorical transcendence of God with a historical being who participated in physical nature. The latter fact has seemingly played little part in attempts to understand the doctrine, since ample confusion is presented in dealing with the first two parts of the trilogy. At what point in Jesus' career did he begin to incarnate God, or did he do so from birth? "Whatever theory of Incarnation we hold, we should find it hard to say that God learned the alphabet for the first time at Nazareth."[1] Did Jesus ever claim to be a substitute for God? Was he the only person in the Bible believed to be permanently possessed by the Spirit?[2] Or is Pannenberg correct in maintaining that the whole "Christ event," by which more is meant than Jesus' life and teachings, makes it possible to say who God is? That event explains "the statement that Jesus is himself God, the Son of God and one with the Father."[3] How Jesus is both God and God's son is somewhat baffling, but the doctrine of Incarnation is too firmly entrenched in Christianity to be dislodged by the squabbles that have accompanied it.

In one sense the biblical evidence for the Incarnation reaches a climax in the passages where Christ is pronounced to be the very image of God, but other images of Christ's intimate relation to God first call for attention. Two of these are associated with the titles "Son of God" and "Lord."[4] The evidence for the first of these titles runs throughout the Gospels, beginning with the baptismal scene and culminating in the Fourth Gospel with the words of justification for that Gospel, "these are written that you may believe that Jesus is the Christ, the Son of God, and believing, you may have life in his name" (20:31). In the remainder of the New Testament writings, the use of the expression is scantier, although it is widely used in Pauline material. It is the Son that Paul preached to the Corinthians (1 Cor. 1:19), but the phrase or its correlates does not occur in the Pastoral Epistles, and only once in the book of Revelation (2:18). It is lavishly used in the Johannine epistles, with the exception of 3 John. But with all the references to Jesus as the Son of God, it is not clear that the title means what the doctrine of Incarnation signifies. At times it reflects what may be called a "functional" usage, for Christ is the means of salvation decided upon by God. In many passages Jesus is clearly subordinate to God. Paul speaks of him as having been "designated Son of God in power" (Rom. 1:3, 4, 9), and at last to be "subjected to him who put all things under him, that God may be everything to every one" (1 Cor. 15:28).[5] Unquestionably, the intimate relation between God and Jesus as Son is sustained throughout the New Testament, but it does not amount to a full participation of the very nature of God in the Son.

The title of "Lord," which signifies ownership, power, and legitimate authority of a superior over a subordinate, is often used of Jesus, as it is of God.[6] Whether the title was employed during Jesus' lifetime seems moot. However, Vincent Taylor concluded that "it is highly improbable that this title was in use in the lifetime of Jesus. It is as the Risen and Ascended Lord that he is "ὁ κύριος, i.e. the Lord.'"[7] He insists, nevertheless, that the use of the title, implying confession and worship, was "the acknowledgement of His essential divinity."[8] But this conclusion runs beyond scriptural evidence because it is God who raises Christ from the dead (Gal. 1:1), and elevates him to the status of Lord, although that status appears to have been temporary (1 Cor. 15:28).[9] The many references that distinguish God from "the" or "our" Lord Jesus Christ stand as strong reminders that the doctrine of Incarnation had not fully emerged.

However, the Philippian letter presents an interesting problem because it contains words that some scholars have taken to be Incarnational.[10] The significance of parts of the passage hinges on the meaning to be given to the Greek word translated as "form." Jesus is described as being in the "form of God," yet not counting equality with God a thing to be grasped (2:6). Diverted for the moment into the realm of the meaning of Greek words, we find that the Greek word for form signifies not merely a similarity of appearance, but also a description of the true state of affairs. Armed with the latter understanding, some have concluded that Paul intended to say that Christ enjoyed identity with God's nature.[11] Unfortunately, the game of word meanings cannot stop there, since the same Greek word is used to describe Jesus as "taking the form of a servant." In this case, the natural meaning is that of the appearance, like that of a servant, not that Christ actually was a human servant. Allowance having been made for the elevated state of mind in which Paul may have penned the entire passage, it is strange that he employed the expression that Christ "did not count equality with God" something to be seized. If "being in the form of God" meant identity with God, then the statement on equality is pointless. There would be no question of equality. Only identity exists. The statement is also pointless unless equality was a state not at that time enjoyed, but a genuine possibility that Christ did not grasp. For a being identical with God, seeking equality makes no sense, but if equality could be sought by Christ, then he was not identical with God. Furthermore, on an even more abstract level, the notion of equality presupposes at least two different entities that may be said to be equal. They cannot be identical. But if we cast aside the confusing technicalities of the passage, we come to the climax to which Paul was leading his readers. Christ having humbled himself, "God has highly exalted him," and ultimately all peoples will bow before this exalted Christ and confess him as Lord "to the glory of God the Father" (2:9–11). Thus Lordship for Christ remains subject to the "glory" and kingly majesty of the Father.

The designations "Son of God" and "Lord" do not capture the full sense of Incarnation. They may point toward an identity between God and Jesus, but much scriptural weight points in a different direction. Not all of it need be rehearsed, but perspective is gained by noting enough passages to make the case for the distinction between Jesus Christ and God. We see Jesus claiming that "no one is good but God alone" (Mark 10:18). He prays to conform his will to that of the Father (Mark 14:36), and on the cross the cry of dereliction is wrenched from his lips (Mark 15:34; Matt. 27:46). In the "little apocalypse" some writer was not averse to saying that the Son did not know the time of the coming of the final day. Only the Father knew (Mark 13:32). On the whole, the Synoptic Gospels see Jesus set over against and distinguished from God the Father.[12] The Epistles and Acts also tend to regard Christ as subordinate to God, as already noted. The intimate association of Christ with God is ever present, but the final step to identity is usually carefully avoided. Peter can preach about "Jesus of Nazareth, a man attested to you by God with mighty works and wonders and signs which God did through him" (Acts 2:22). Jesus is "thy holy servant," or literally "child" (Acts 4:30). He is anointed and ordained (Acts 10:38, 42). He is raised from the dead; he did not rise by his own power (Acts 2:24, 32; Gal. 1:1; 1 Thess. 1:10; 1 Cor. 15:15). God is one, not divided into two or three persons (Gal. 3:20). As Christ is the head of man, so God is the head of Christ (1 Cor. 11:3). The evidence against an Incarnational interpretation begins to be impressive.

The Gospel of John brings Christ into the closest possible relation to God. This strange and often incoherent piece of writing laid the trail of charges that repeatedly exploded in bitter controversy over the doctrine of Incarnation.[13] The human and glorified aspects of Jesus are so intertwined that no one consistent picture emerges, either of Jesus himself or of his connection with God. Christ is at one and the same time humanly distinct from the deity and yet in union with him.[14] The best that can be done, therefore, in seeking out the image of God as Christ is to let the contradictory evidence speak for itself, a condition that no amount of harmonizing has ever satisfactorily ameliorated, even by the theory of diverse authors or editors.

The high Christology in this Gospel is unmistakable, even in passages that maintain distance between Jesus and God, although some interpreters hold that the whole Gospel should be understood throughout as referring to the Risen and Glorified Christ. No passage more startlingly expresses this view of Christ than the words that conclude the allegory of the Good Shepherd: "I and the Father are one," words followed by the claim that "the Father is in me and I am in the Father" (10:30, 38).[15] To see Christ is to see "him who sent me" (12:45), and he tells his disciples "henceforth you know him [Father] and have seen him" (14:7). In answer to Philip's request that he see the Father, Jesus replies "He who has seen me has seen the Father" (14:9). The attributes traditionally associated with God are ascribed to Jesus. He is the giver of eternal life (4:14; 5:21, 25; 6:27), and will resurrect those who believe in him (6:40, 44). He possesses all knowledge about mankind and what is to happen to him (2:25; 18:4). He is worshiped (9:38). Throughout such passages Jesus affirms that the Father is in him, as he is in the Father (17:21, 23). And if the words of the Prologue are to be taken as an essential part of the Gospel, the Incarnational theme is forcefully presented—"And the Word became flesh and dwelt among us" (1:14).

The Prologue also sets the problem of distinguishing Jesus from God. The identity between God and Jesus that the foregoing passages express is itself not a simple matter. Identity presupposes two beings, as in the Philippian passage, but it does not clarify in what respects the two beings are identical. As one philosopher has pointed out in his attempt to show the logic of the Trinity, "nothing is identical with something absolutely, but only in a certain respect." Identity is never absolute but relative.[16] In the case of the Jesus of the Fourth Gospel, it seems clear that identity is not absolute, else there is no point to the Gospel. Christ may be said to be God, but God is not totally exhausted in the figure of Jesus. To speak the words *God* or *the Father* is not to say "Christ." It is this lack of equality between the two terms with which the authors of the Gospel struggle. The result is that Christ must in certain ways be different from God, and yet identical with God. The Prologue immediately shows this quandary into which the writers of the Gospel must plunge.

One reluctantly becomes involved in matters of translation at this point, but the stately opening of the Gospel does invite such a consideration. "In the beginning was the Word, and the Word was with God and the Word was God" (1:1). Goodspeed translated the verse, "The Word was with God and the Word was divine." The grounds for this substantial change, which weakens perceptibly the identity of the Word with God, lies in the fact that the Greek word for God is not preceded by the definite article, which ordinarily would establish the status of the high and only God. This technicality is further spelled out. "The absence of the Greek article before the word God makes it perfectly clear," one scholar claims, "that θεός (God) is predicate, not subject, of the verb. The two terms are not interchangeable; else the writer could not say the Word was with God."[17] The New English Bible skirts the issue by a freer translation: "The Word dwelt with God, and what God was, the Word was." If the scholars are correct in these translations, it appears that Jesus, taken as the Word, is not elevated to identity with God, nor did God in his very nature become flesh. A unique, divinely endowed being did assume physical form—but in that direction lies the Arian heresy! And after all, as Dodd pointed out, nowhere else in the Gospel is Jesus expressly asserted to be this divine Word.[18] Jesus may be the image of God, but at best he is a likeness, not an Incarnation. In what respects he is the likeness of God may be inferred from the attributes of God we have seen ascribed to him.

The evidence in John's Gospel for the distinction between Jesus and God, the subordination of the Son to the Father, and the dependence of Christ upon God is not difficult to discern. All three of these ideas have been met previously, but in the context of the Fourth Gospel, they take on decisive significance. They stand in an anomalous relation to the claims of identity. God's love of the world is seen in his giving and sending his only Son to save those who believe in him (3:16, 17). Jesus himself certifies that the Father has sent him (5:36), and that he did not come of his own accord (8:42). In fact, he can do nothing on his own authority, but only speaks as God instructs him (5:30; 8:28; 14:31). That there is a will in Jesus that is not identical with God's seems clear when Christ claims to have come down from heaven "not to do my own will, but the will of him who sent me" (6:38). He alone has seen the Father, apparently a different being from himself (6:46; 8:38). Those who believe in him really believe in God (12:44). And in numerous places Jesus speaks of going to his Father (13:3; 14:12, 28; 16:2, 10; 20:17). Jesus himself says that there is only one true God (17:3). The human Jesus shows through in his being "wearied" (4:6), and in the inescapable fact that he died (19:30).

In these passages, hints of Jesus' identity with God, or his being the image of God, are elusive. Christ is the Son by means of whom God carries out his purposes, and although the intimacy between the two remains, Jesus cannot be interpreted as being totally at one with the deity. Yet as we seek other grounds for establishing the unity of God and Christ, we find

Paul at times approaching that goal. Christ for Paul is "the power and the wisdom of God" (1 Cor. 1:24), or in an oft-remembered passage he says "God was in Christ reconciling the world to himself" (2 Cor. 5:19).[19] In the Colossian letter the union is made even more explicit, "For in him [Christ] all the fullness of God was pleased to dwell (1:19; 2:9).[20] Clearly, here the notion of God imaged in Christ, as in certain of the Johannine passages, is in the ascendancy.

The word *image* itself is used in man's being in the image of God in the familiar passages of the Genesis story of creation (1:26, 27; 9:6).[21] A similar usage is found in Paul's writings. When the apostle gives instructions on head coverings at worship, he advises that since man "is in the image and glory of God" he ought not to cover his head. He plays on the Adamic, physical nature of man, "the image of the man of dust," against "the image of the man of heaven," which Christians will become (1 Cor. 15:49)—a passage consonant with being conformed to the "image of his Son" (Rom. 8:29; 2 Cor. 3:18). The Colossian letter tells the Christians that the new nature is being revealed "in knowledge after the image of its creator"— although whether God or Christ is the "creator" is not clear. Man as the image of God is also employed in the epistle of James, where the word *likeness* is substituted for the word *image* (3:9). Thus man (male only?) is the image of God. But what then of Christ? There are only two passages where Christ is specifically called the image of God. The first of these occurs in 2 Corinthians 4:4, where the Greek word for image is translated as "likeness." Why this translation was preferred by the Revised Standard Version is not clear, since other translations follow the Greek more closely at this point.[22] The other passage is found in Colossians (1:15). "He is the image of the invisible God. . . . " This figure is expanded in meaning by the words "For in him the whole fullness of deity dwells bodily" (Col. 2:9). If Christ is the image of God, then the issue of identity arises once more. Does the Greek word for image actually bear the meaning of identity, and if so, in what degree? Vincent Taylor warns against assuming that the word *image* means a "faint copy of an original" or taking it as an artificial imitation or representation. In ancient thought εἰκων [image] meant more than "likeness," he claims. "It described the essential nature of a thing."[23] Therefore when Paul uses the expression 'the image of God,' he is not stating that Christ merely reflects God, but that in him, so to speak, God comes to light and is fully expressed."[24] If Taylor is correct, some measure of identity is implied by the word *image*. Following his definition of the word *image* leads to several interesting questions. If *image* signifies "the essential nature of a thing," then by consistency of usage are not all images of God also descriptions of the essential nature of God? The use of the word in connection with Christ can then be taken as a paradigm for its use for all other imageful language about God. Or is Taylor's interpretation of the word governed by an antecedent belief in the Incarnation, which makes its use exceptional rather than a paradigm for biblical images generally? If the answer to the first question is in the affirmative, then all images of God participate in and describe "the essential nature" of God—a conclusion usually hotly contested by those who hold that images are metaphorical or are likenesses, imitations, or representations. On the other hand, if the second question is answered in the affirmative, then no conclusions should be drawn about image language generally, since *image*, when used of Christ, is used in a unique sense. Identity occurs only at one place in Scripture, that between Christ and God. Thereby the doctrine of Incarnation is firmly established. However, the troublesome problem remains as to why image language should mean "the essential nature of" a thing here, but nowhere else.

One other passage may be introduced that sheds a slightly different light on the meaning of *image*. The writer of Hebrews asserts that Christ reflects the glory of God and "bears the very stamp of his nature" to such a high degree that he upholds "the universe by his word of power" (1:3). Apart from the sense of Christ's being a reflection of God, the crucial word is *stamp*, which stands for the Greek word for "character." This word carries the meaning of "exact reproduction," "very facsimile of the original," or "representation" of God. The implication here seems to be that Christ is not God, but that he bears in himself the stamp, as in a seal of wax, of what God is.

The difficulties associated with Christ as the image of God have produced another interpretation in which Christ is moved away from his human nature to the realm of pure symbol. Christ functions, it is said, as an image or symbol, pure and simple, and the vexing problem of his relation to God and history is left aside as of little importance for contemporary thought. "Jesus, as we know him, is no less a symbolic form than the other socially constructed fictions which have emerged from the genius of individuals within the Christian community."[25] Whether this view coincides with what the biblical authors had in mind is doubtful. Nor is Christ as a fictionalized symbol apt to arouse enthusiasm or nurture piety among the orthodox. In any case he would not be the fully Incarnate One.

The mysteries of the doctrine of Incarnation cannot be unraveled here, beyond indicating the biblical evidence.[26] It may be concluded, however, that the notion of Christ as the image of God cannot be taken at face value. The whole meaning of an image is lost if there is absolute identity between the image and that which is imaged. The image (Christ) cannot be substituted *in toto* for the being imaged (God) without making the word *image* nugatory. Furthermore, the Scriptures themselves cast serious doubt upon any attempts to make Christ absolutely identical with God. As Hepburn pointed out, "our texts do not give us license . . . to translate *without change* statements about Jesus into statements about God."[27] However, as I have maintained in respect to other images of God, unless there is some degree of identity between the image and God, the image fails of its purpose, validity is left hanging, and the image then becomes merely fanciful or poetic. But the religious meaning for the writers of both Testaments was too serious a matter to be relegated to the realm of merely aesthetic adornment. Imagery depends upon the distinction between the image and what is imaged, but by the same token there cannot be total separation. The more complete the identity between the image and the imaged, the less the image can do its work, but if there is no participation of the image in the imaged, there is no foundation for assuming the validity of the image. Consequently, in the orthodox tradition we are left with what Pannenberg called a paradox. "When the divinity of Jesus is expressed as Jesus' unity with the Father, it is still distinguished as the Son from the Father and nevertheless as one with the Father."[28]

We are left to understand that Christ was the image of God for the faith of some early Christians, and so to consider him, regardless of the metaphysical difficulties involved, was to make a valid assertion about God's nature. Similarly some also entertained the idea of Incarnation, with its equally difficult implications, although the word itself is never used in the texts. But neither of these views can be said to have controlled the thought world of the entire corpus of New Testament writings. Those outside the early Christian community apparently did not see Jesus either as the "image" of God or as God Incarnate. Only the impact of Christ on some of the human lives he touched aroused that sense of worship held to be appropriate before God himself. Out of these experiences, and above all the Resurrection, were forged the titles that ultimately were attached to Jesus, and high among them, doing justice to his uniqueness and the sense of God's presence mediated through him, were "Christ the image of God" and only later the doctrine of Incarnation.[29]

NOTES

1. Frank Herbert Brabant, *Time and Eternity in Christian Thought* (London, New York, Toronto: Longmans, Green and Co., 1937), 273.

2. G. W. H. Lampe, *God as Spirit* (Oxford: Clarendon Press, 1977), 52, 53.

3. Wohlfahrt Pannenberg, *Faith and Reality*, trans. John Maxwell (London: Search Press; Philadelphia: The Westminister Press, 1977), 60.

4. "In terms of the history of traditions, the path to the perception of Jesus' divinity ran by way of the titles 'Son of God' and 'Kyrios.'" Wohlfahrt Pannenberg, *Jesus—God and Man*, trans. Lewis L. Wilkins and Duane H. Priebe, 2d ed. (Philadelphia: The Westminster Press, 1977), 69, n. 49.

5. Pannenberg admits "At first the 'Son of God' concept did not express a participation in the divine essence. Only in Gentile Christianity was the divine Sonship understood physically as participation in the divine essence." *Jesus—God and Man*, 117.

6. Cf. Kittel, *Bible Key Words*, trans. and ed. J. R. Coates and H. P. Kingdon (New York: Harper and Brothers, 1958), 92–97.

7. Vincent Taylor, *The Names of Jesus* (New York: St. Martin's Press, Inc., 1953), 43.

8. Ibid., 51.

9. "The description of Jesus as Lord in the Palestinian tradition has nothing to do with a

predicate of divinity but has grown out of a secular mode of address." Ferdinand Hahn, *The Titles of Jesus in Christology* (New York and Cleveland: The World Publishing Company, 1969), 88. The Hellenistic Judaic Christian Church tried to avoid the interpretation of Jesus in a divine sense. Cf. 107, 113.

10. Cf. Werner Foerster in Kittel's *Bible Key Words*, 98.

11. Cf. *The Interpreter's Bible* (Nashville, Tenn.: Abingdon Press, 1955), 11:48.

12. Cf. Pannenberg, *Jesus—God and Man*, 158. Unfortunately, Pannenberg evades the force of his own statement here by referring to "the deity of Jesus Christ." 160.

13. Norman Perrin in *Jesus and the Language of the Kingdom* (Philadelphia: Fortress Press, 1976), confessed that the Gospel had proved intractable to the historical criticism of biblical texts, but held out hope for future scholarship. Cf. Walter Bauer, *Orthodoxy and Heresy in Earliest Christianity*, ed. Robert A. Kraft and Gerhard Krodel (Philadelphia: Fortress Press, 1971), 211.

14. So careful a scholar as Raymond E. Brown reminds the reader of John's Gospel to be cautious in evaluating the Johannine acceptance of Jesus as divine or equal to God. See The Anchor Bible (Garden City, N.Y.: Doubleday and Co., Inc., 1966), 29:408.

15. C. H. Dodd comments that these passages are intended "to describe a unity between Father and Son so close that to see the Son is tantamount to the *visio Dei.*" *The Interpretation of the Fourth Gospel* (Cambridge: The University Press, 1953), 194; cf. 257, 389.

16. A. P. Martinech, "Identity and Trinity," *The Journal of Religion* 58, no. 2 (April 1978): 175.

17. *The Interpreter's Bible*, 8:464.

18. Dodd, *Interpretation of the Fourth Gospel*, 267.

19. Jerry H. Gill, in pointing out the multiple uses of language, insists on the metaphorical meaning of the preposition *in* as used here. He claims that we need to take the word neither literally nor poetically, but as an example of transcendence mediated through a metaphor. "Myth and Incarnation," *The Christian Century* 94 (December 21, 1977): 1193–94. Whether Paul understood it so is another matter.

20. The New English Bible translates the passage "For in him the complete being of God, by God's own choice, came to dwell."

21. Robert Javelet comments upon image and likeness in Genesis 5:1–3. Seth is the image and likeness of his father, Adam, and by that heritage is himself in the image of God. "C'est tout l'homme qui est à l'image et ressemblance de Dieu; il est le majordome de Dieu sur terre." *Image et Ressemblance au Douzième Siècle* (Paris: Editions Letouzey et Ané, 1967), 17.

22. Cf. King James Version; The New English Bible; and Peake's Commentary on the Bible, 969. Goodspeed used "likeness."

23. Taylor, *Names of Jesus*, 125. Dorothy L. Sayers emphasizes the notion of Christ as the image of God, but tells us little of what it means. "Christian theology says very emphatically the Son, who is the express image, is not the copy, or imitation, or representation of the Father, nor yet inferior or subsequent to the Father in any way. In the last resort, in the depths of their mysterious being, the unimaginable and the image are one and the same." *The Whimsical Christian* (New York: Macmillan Publishing Co., 1978), 84.

24. Ibid., 127.

25. Donald E. Miller, "The Truth of the Christian Fiction: Belief in the Modern Age," *The Christian Century* 96 (January 31, 1979): 98.

26. James M. Gustafson is correct when he writes, "Every effort to formulate a coherent Christology is selective of the biblical materials, and is determined in part by the issues that the theologians and the churches face in particular times and places. Debates about Christianity are never exclusively debates about what the New Testament really says about Jesus." *Ethics from a Theocentric Perspective*, vol. 1, *Theology and Ethics* (Chicago, Oxford: The University of Chicago Press, 1981), 275.

27. Ronald W. Hepburn, *Christianity and Paradox* (London: Watts, 1958), 66–67: "To reduce *all of God* to human incarnation is virtually inconceivable, a fact to which trinitarian doctrine is the traditional response." Cf. Frances Young, "A Cloud of Witnesses," in *The Myth of God Incarnate*, ed. John Hick (Philadelphia: The Westminster Press, 1977), 35.

28. Pannenberg, *Jesus—God and Man*, 183. For a Whiteheadian interpretation of the Incarnation, see Lewis S. Ford, *The Lure of God* (Philadelphia: The Fortress Press, 1978), 49–51, 67.

29. On the relation of historical knowledge of Jesus to the Christ of faith, and also the Trinity, see chap. 14.

13

God as Creator

The image of God as Creator once more raises the issue of the relation between nature and salvation history. The Bible opens with the picture of God as Creator of the world and mankind, yet the principal line of thought soon centers upon the covenantal theme and the images of God as Savior and Judge and King. The Gospel of John also opens with a creation announcement in which the Word was held to be the agency by which "all things were made" (1:3). Two distinct perspectives appear. One is cosmogonic and the other is covenantal, or as some have called it, salvation history.[1] In interpreting the Hebrew Scriptures, Von Rad showed his theological predilections by pointing out that the position of the creation story at the beginning of our Bible has often led to misunderstanding, "as though the 'doctrine' of creation were a central subject of Old Testament faith. That is not the case. . . . Rather the position of both the Yahwist and the Priestly document is basically faith in salvation and election."[2] This view is supported by others, who claim that God was first apprehended as the deliverer, King, and Lord, before he was understood to be the Creator.[3] This position is sometimes buttressed by noting that the Priestly story of creation (Gen. 1:1–2:3) is of a later date than the many examples where the salvation is emphasized. However, in taking into account the biblical scholars' dating of documents, it should be noted that what comes first in the order of writing may not be primary in respect to existential or metaphysical reality. What was taken for granted may be more important than what was expressed. Moreover, to divide the creator God from the redeeming God may tend to drive a "Marcionite wedge" between the two.[4] Nor do all who insist upon the priority of the role of God as King or Savior fail to see the manner in which the two themes are interwoven. After all, because God is the God of history, and history is wrought out in the sphere of nature, Yahweh must at least control nature, even if he did not create it.

There are good reasons why the image of God as Creator was used. Apart from possible dependence upon Babylonian creation myths, there seems to have been a need for a more inclusive term than King. What was needed was an image that took into consideration the sovereignty of God over the whole world. And as previously argued, there could be no salvation history without nature. But if nature could be used by God only to judge, redeem, and direct Israel, it conceivably could in its brutish, mindless way rebel against the divine purposes. He must be the Creator of nature, not simply the Lord over it. But nature proved to be more than a stage upon which the drama of salvation was played out. It entered into the plot itself. The generations born and to be born were part of the story (Isa. 48:19), and without nature the cultic acts of worshiping God could not be carried out (e.g., Lev. chaps. 1–7). And in the Christian literature, the Resurrection, with all its attendant problems, shows in one form or another that God's sovereignty over nature in the form of death is not the end of the salvation drama. If physical resurrection is accepted, God is master over physical death, and the empty-tomb stories attest to this version of the Resurrection. The disciples, startled and frightened by Jesus' appearance, mistakenly suppose that they see a spirit, according to Luke's Gospel. Jesus invites them to see his hands and feet and handle him, and he says "a spirit has not flesh and bones as you see I have" (24:37–43). God triumphs over the very nature he has created, including death. Without the raising of Christ the salvation story for Christians would be incomplete.[6]

That God is the creator of nature is well attested, not only in the Priestly story of creation, but in numerous passages throughout the Old Testament. But the Genesis passage does give rise to the question as to what sense is to be given to his creatorship. The familiar theological expression that entered into orthodox Christian thought is that of "creation *ex nihilo.*" By this term it is asserted that all that can be said to be, with the exception of the deity, began by an act of God. There is literally nothing prior to God upon which he exercised his initial act.[7] Furthermore, the concept itself establishes the uniqueness of God's creativity, since there is no creation *ex nihilo* within the world. Human creation may devise novelties, but always by using and rearranging what is already created. Therefore "we should admit at once that the creation of the world ought not to be construed by analogy with creations within the world."[8] But if this is so, then whence the idea of creation? It would seem to be a purely logical rendition of what ought to have been the case, but one that cannot be definitely decided. And there still remains the possibility that the idea of creation did arise from the realm of ordinary experience, and then, as Ian Ramsey explained the logic of the term, it was given an extended meaning to make clear the absolute dependence of all creatures on God.[9] Some biblical scholars maintain that the Genesis passage does strongly imply creation *ex nihilo,* while others deny it.[10] In the latter case, if we follow the text more carefully, God is a creator by virtue of his bringing order out of an already existing chaos.[11] Fortunately or unfortunately, the Bible was not concerned with the logical and religious niceties of the doctrine. It proceeded in other contexts to treat

God as creator of the world without technical explanations of the Genesis passage.

God imaged as the creator of the natural world, including mankind, repeatedly reflects the Genesis passages. The Psalms in particular glorify God in this role. "By the word of the Lord the heavens were made, and all their host by the breath of his mouth" (33:6). "The heavens are thine, the earth also is thine; the world and all that is in it, thou hast founded them" (89:11). "In his hand are the depths of the earth; the heights of the mountains are his also. The sea is his, for he made it; for his hands formed the dry land" (95:4, 5). Even the formation of the human embryo is due to his handiwork (139:13–16). Of all the Psalms the 104th best expresses the sustained glorification of the Creator. He makes light and darkness, he stretched out the heavens like a tent, he set the earth on its foundations, he creates springs and causes the grass and trees to grow, he cares for the beasts of the forest, and when he sends out his Spirit [breath], all creatures are created. "O Lord, how manifold are thy works! In wisdom hast thou made them all" (v. 24). If ever an image sprang from objective worship, this Psalm expresses it, for it is worship for the sole purpose of glorifying God for his own sake as Creator. Creation praises him (Ps. 148:3–10), and all nature participates in this worship of its Creator. "Praise him, sun and moon, praise him, all you shining stars! Praise him, you highest heavens, and you waters above the heavens . . . for he commanded and they were created. And he established them for ever and ever; he fixed their bounds which cannot be passed" (148:3, 4, 5b, 6). Sea monsters, fire, hail, snow, creeping things and flying birds—all join in this hymn of praise (148:7–10).

In the wisdom literature, Job describes God as hanging the "earth upon nothing" (26:7), and when God answers Job's complaint, he crushingly reminds the suffering human of his creative power and wisdom. No word of compassion or justification for Job's plight is given. Before that onslaught Job is moved to confess, "I have uttered what I did not understand, things too wonderful for me, which I did not know." Heretofore, his had been hearsay knowledge, now replaced by a firsthand sight of God himself. "Therefore I despise myself, and repent in dust and ashes" (42:3–6). Creatorship produces awe and alone brings Job to repentance. In Proverbs the prudent advice to "my son" to seek wisdom is in turn founded upon the wisdom of God in his creation of the world (3:19, 20).

The earliest of the writing prophets spells out the sanction of his judgment as the creator of the world. It is he "who builds his upper chambers in the heavens and founds his vault upon the earth: who calls for the waters of the sea and pours them out upon the surface of the earth" (Amos 9:6; 4:13). But among the prophets it is Deutero-Isaiah who most fully plays upon the theme of God as creator. God, in the prophet's words, commands his people to "lift up your eyes on high and see who created thee" (40:26). "I made the earth and created man upon it; it was my hands that stretched out the heavens, and I commanded all their host" (45:12, 18). Nothing lies beyond the scope of his creation, since "I form light and create darkness. I make weal and woe" (45:7). In the new day Third Isaiah prophesies that God will create "new heavens and a new earth" (65:17). Jeremiah centers upon God as creator when the Lord says, "It is I by my great power and my outstretched arm have made the earth, with the men and animals that are on the earth, and I give it to whomever it seems right to me" (27:5; cf. 10:12, 51:15). And Malachi bases his criticism of his listeners' faithlessness and profanation of the covenant upon God's creatorship (2:10).

God as creator of the world is assumed in the New Testament, but less often mentioned. The "little apocalypse" of Mark refers to it (13:19), and the book of Acts makes several references to it. When Peter and John are released, their friends praise God, in words fashioned upon Old Testament passages: the "Sovereign Lord, who didst make the heaven and the sea and everything in them" (4:24). The same words are used when Paul and Barnabas rebuke those who have heralded them as gods (14:15). On the Areopagus, Paul proclaims "the God who made the world and everything in it, being Lord of heaven and earth" (17:24). The Roman letter censors human wickedness and idolatry in the name of God the Creator (1:20, 25). When the author of 1 Timothy gives advice on abstinence from marriage and certain foods, he argues that "everything created by God is good" (4:4), and refers to the deity as one "who gives life to all things" (6:13). Hebrews repeats part of Psalm 102, which attributes the creation of the world to God (1:10b), and prefaces the account of the heroes of faith with a reference to the fact "that the world was created by the word of God" (11:3). The scoffers at the notion of Christ's return have ignored the fact that God created the world, thus reckoning without God's power (2 Pet. 3:5, 6).

God's creatorship of all the world, even to its most intimate detail, is unquestionable. As such he is imaged in his exalted wisdom and power. But the meaning of this image is not exhausted by referring only to its cosmic proportions. He is the Creator in another, even more important, sense as well. As Savior he creates salvation by producing a new level of life for people beyond their purely physical or sentient existence. By his free choice he creates a people bound to the covenant and law and set apart from other nations by virtue of the higher ethical and religious living expected of them. A new life principle enters into the individuals who make up this chosen race, even as they are to be bound together in a unique social body. The pattern, in general outline, is repeated in the New Testament. God creates a new people, although one not entirely cut off from the people of the Old Testament. Through Christ a new life principle is believed to enter into each member of the New Israel, by which they are bound together in one body over whom Christ is Lord. By faith and in a new spirit Christians form a society, as did the descendants of Abraham. Thus the cosmogonic meaning of God's creatorship is linked with the salvation story. Of course, a strong case could be made that the two stories had never been totally separated. Yet those who make this case are equally quick to maintain that the cosmogonic myth, as it has been called, was a late, if not an independent element, attached to the story of salvation. If true, it would seem that the two were not always intertwined, but the texts would not seem to support that conclusion. However, the limited use of the cosmogonic factor in the New Testament and the marked preference for the epic of spiritual salvation would also strengthen the view of the subordination of God as creator. Here God remains as creator of heaven and earth, but it is primarily as the creator of a new life and a new people through Christ that he is known. Yet, as suggested, the God who creates the natural world is also the God who creates salvation in both Testaments. Therefore the created world of nature is bound to be an ingredient of the salvation story, although its importance seems to vary in respect to the two Testaments, the Old Testament offering a more this-worldly view than the New.

It is not difficult to see the manner in which God created the Hebrew people into what was to be a definite society. The book of Exodus might be considered one extended version of God's creating this society. By rescuing the Hebrews from slavery, by binding them to himself by covenant and law, he has provided a way to save them from anarchy and the destruction that awaited them at the hands of foreign tribes and nations. In what may be a late intrusion into the text, the Lord is heard to say, "you shall be to me a kingdom of priests and a holy nation" (Exod. 19:6). The Deuteronomist sees the choice of these people as due not to their number or power, but to God's love. Therefore "you are a people holy to the Lord, your God; the Lord your God has chosen you to be a people for his own possession, out of all the peoples that are on the face of the earth" (Deut. 7:6–8). The Song of Moses tells of the father-God "who created you, and made you and established you" (Deut. 32:6), and of the Rock "that begat you" (Deut. 32:18). Throughout the book of Leviticus, the priestly authors bolster the uniqueness of the new people by the prescriptions and laws they develop. By their obedience to these legalisms God will own them to be his people (Lev. 26:12, 13). In his words of judgment the prophet Amos reminds them that they have been brought out of Egypt by the Lord, and that "you only have I known of all the families of the earth." Therefore "I will punish you for all your iniquities" (3:1, 2). The creation of the world is fused with the salvation to come to this people by Deutero-Isaiah (40:28–31; 43:23, 24; 45.:4, 8–17). Jacob has been created by God: "But now thus says the Lord, he who created you, O Jacob, he who formed you, O Israel: Fear not, for I have redeemed you; I have called you by name, you are mine" (43:1, 15). In an elevated moment Jeremiah cries, "If the heavens above can be measured, and the foundations of the earth below can be explored, then I will cast off all the descendants of Israel for all that they have done" (31:37). And the creation of the world once more appears in connection with God's saving actions as the prophet says, "O Lord God, it is thou who hast made the heavens and the earth by thy great power and by thy outstretched arm! . . . who showest steadfast love to thousands, but dost requite the guilt of the fathers to their children after them . . ." (32:17, 18). In the vision of the valley of dry bones, the prophet Ezekiel uses the image of God as the creator who gives to the bones a new life by breathing his breath into them (37:1-5). The Psalmist repeatedly joins God's creation of the world with salvation. He makes the world and his counsel stands forever: "Blessed is the nation whose God is the Lord, the people whom he has chosen as his heritage!" (33:6-12). The elements are afraid, the thunder and lightning play about, and the earth trembles, yet "Thou didst lead thy people like a flock by the hand of Moses and Aaron" (77:16-20). The theme of creation and the salvation of the people is rehearsed in Psalm 89, and again when having affirmed that the depths of the earth and the heights of the moun-tains, the sea and the dry land are of his making, the people are called upon to worship the Lord, our Maker, "For he is our God, and we are the people of his pasture, and the sheep of his hand" (95:3-7; 100:3). In a more individualistic vein, the Psalmist asserts the steadfastness of God, whose word is "firmly fixed" as the earth itself and whose law and precepts he claims he never forgets, "for by them thou hast given me life. I am thine, save me, for I have sought thy precepts" (119:89-94). The history of Israel is compressed into a few lines that tell of God's use of nature to save his people and whose strength conquered enemy tribes. And at last he "gave their land as a heritage . . . to his people Israel" (135:5-12). In a more expanded form the story is retold in which God's creation of nature as well as of his people is linked with salvation, as each line of the poem is com-pleted with the words "for his steadfast love endures for ever" (136). The uniqueness of this people is set against the background of the Lord's use of nature and his giving of statutes and ordinances to Israel, since "he has not dealt thus with any other nation; they do not know his ordinances. Praise the Lord" (147:16-20).

In such passages as these God is seen as Creator and user of nature, but also as the one who creates a people imbued with a principle of life that centers upon fidelity to him expressed in awe, repentance, and a high level of ethical and religious conduct. Only by holding to this Creator God who saves, will Israel be kept from the destruction that the same God may launch upon them. Yet it is his arbitrary love that sustains them and for-gives them, lest their destruction be complete. Traces of the idea of a new people created by God through Jesus Christ are found in Matthew's gos-pel. Peter's confession of Jesus as the Christ brings forth the words of Jesus about the church he will found under Peter's authority (16:18-19), although later in the Gospel the disciples are given a similar authority where two or three are gathered together (18:18–20). The twenty-third chapter, wherein Jesus is described as bitterly criticizing the Jewish religious leaders, probably also indicates the growing self-conscious identity of the Christian community in contrast with the synagogue. But in Acts we find the Christians still within the fold of Judaism as they attend the temple (2:46; 3:1), although they make up a closely knit fellowship of their own (2:44; 4:32). The sense of a new and unique people created by belief in Christ becomes apparent in the writings of Paul. He imparts a secret and hidden wisdom of God, "which God decreed before the ages for our glorification" (1 Cor. 2:7), and claims that "we have the mind of Christ" (1 Cor. 2:16). The very spirit of God dwells in them (1 Cor. 3:16), and they have become kings (1 Cor. 4:8). In the same letter the apostle lays down advice as to how they are to live as the new community (chaps. 5–8, 10–11). So closely knit are these Christians with each other and Christ that they are the body of Christ (1 Cor. 12:12–27). They are "a new creation," since everything old in their lives has passed away, and they have become "ambassadors for Christ" (2 Cor. 5:17, 20). They, by their faith, have become "sons of God" and at the same time Abraham's offspring—an idea developed more fully in the Roman letter. There, by heralding Abraham as the father of faith, Paul connects the new Christian community with the patriarch, the "father of us all" (Rom. 4:16; 9:6; 11:1, 2). Christ was raised from the dead so that they "might walk in newness of life" (6:4), and having died with Christ they shall "live with him," a life lived to God (Rom. 6:8, 10, 11), which is eternal life (Rom. 6:22, 23). A new spirit-filled life of righteousness marks the Christian (Rom. 8:9–17). But this new life comes not from human desire or choice, for God has predestined and chosen those who at last will be justified and glorified (Rom. 8:29, 30; cf. 1 Thess. 1:4; Col. 3:12; 1 Pet. 1:2). The theme of new life into which the Christians have been introduced by Christ is echoed in the Ephesian letter (2:1, 4, 5), and also in the Colossian letter (3:4). Again the unity of the new community is to be found in love and peace, "to which you were called in the one body" (Col. 3:14, 15). The separation of the new people in Christ from the inferior Jewish dispensation is clearly reflected in the book of Hebrews. The ancient covenant is obsolete, and Christ the true high priest is more excellent than the old priesthood (8:6, 7, 12). The law is now counted as but a shadow of good things to come (10:1). The astonishing sense of the superiority of the new people is to be seen in the fact that although the heroes of the Old Testament were all participants in faith, "God had foreseen something better for us, that apart from us they should not be made perfect" (11:40). And what could be stronger evidence of the people God in Christ has created than the words "You are a chosen race, a royal priesthood, a holy nation, God's own people. . . . Once you were no people, but now you are God's people" (1 Pet. 2:9, 10; Rev. 1:6).

If faith is the principle that pulsates through this self-conscious community, so also are other equally important characteristics. The new life is one of love, whose source is God shown in Jesus Christ. The Gospel of John sounds the theme (3:16; 13:34, 35; 15:9–14; 16:27), but even more strongly it represents Christ as the one in whom to believe to secure eternal life. A spiritual quality above anything physical denotes the possession of this new dimension of Christian experience. It is one that not only applies to a life after death, but is an actual dynamic lived out in the world. John symbolizes it in variant forms: as a spring of water spontaneously welling up (4:14), as a resurrection (5:21), as words spoken by Jesus and believed (4:24); as belief in Christ (6:47); as the eating of Christ (6:57, 58); as God's commandment (12:50). Jesus himself defines eternal life by saying "this is eternal life, that they know thee, the only true God, and Jesus Christ whom thou hast sent (17:3). The crucial sign of Christ's giving of life is the raising of Lazarus, an event introduced by Jesus' words to Martha: "I am the resurrection and the life; he who believes in me, though he die, yet shall he live, and whoever lives and believes in me shall never die" (11:15, 16, 38–44). Personal immortality is here promised, but taken with other references to eternal life, it is a life not to be postponed until after physical death, but a quality of life lived in the world, worthy to be crowned in another world. As such, it marks the newly created community and expresses itself in the love of which the gospelers wrote. And of course this love, in other sections of Scripture, is also seen as what ideally holds the Christian community together. One of the fruits of the Spirit is love (Gal. 5:22), and it is elevated to a higher position than faith and hope in the thirteenth chapter of 1 Corinthians.

The first epistle of John, like the Gospel of John (15:18, 19), sets off the Christian community from the world by virtue of the love God has for his people and their love for each other. "Do not love the world or the things of the world," the writer commands, for then the love of God will not rest in them (2:15, 16). The Antichrist is of the world, but "we are of God" (4:6), so "let us love one another; for love is of God, and he who loves is born of God and knows God." God loved us and sent his Son to expiate our sins, and because of that love "we ought to love one another" (4:7–11). "We love, because he first loved us" (4:19). God has created a new people through Christ by the love he has shed upon them. With faith and love comes release from the law and entrance into a hitherto unknown freedom. As God freed ancient Israel from slavery, so now, as Paul would have it, through God's Christ, Christian folk are emancipated from the bondage to the Jewish law and the weight of sin it imposed upon human beings. Speaking for himself, the apostle claims that he has been set free from "the law of sin and death" by "the law of the Spirit of life in Christ Jesus" (Rom. 8:2; cf. 1 Cor. 9:1, 19). Moreover, the new people are no longer slaves to "the elemental spirits of the universe" and to those beings which are "no gods," since now God has come to know them (Gal. 4:3, 7, 9). In words that were to stir the Protestant Reformation, Paul proclaimed, "For freedom Christ has set us free; stand fast therefore, and do not submit again to a yoke of slavery" (Gal. 5:1). But it is a freedom not to be abused, but one in which in love these spirit-filled people are to be "servants of one another" (Gal. 5:13).

In spite of the connections between the two "peoples" God has created, dissimilarities are evident. The people of the Old Testament are to be given more worldly and material benefits than those of the New Testament. If they are obedient, they will be fruitful as a people, and will be a great nation (Gen. 12:1–2; Deut. 30:16). They will possess a land that God gives them (Exod. 33:1; Deut. 31:20, 21, 23). No similar promises are made to the new people in Christ. More "spiritual," less worldly blessings descend upon the new Israel. Salvation is for the inner person within the Christian community. It is the new spirit that fills this group, since "flesh and blood cannot inherit the Kingdom of God, nor does the perishable inherit the imperishable" (1 Cor. 15:50). The line between the fleshly and the spiritual is sharply drawn (Rom. 7:18, 24; 8:6, 8), although life will be given to mortal bodies (Rom. 8:11).

The image of God as Creator, the maker of heaven and earth and the new people, proved to be one that enlarged the scope of both the cosmogonic myth and the salvation story. More than the images of King, Father, or Savior, it opened the way in the direction of the more metaphysical images or symbols that have come to be the stock in trade of theology. It wove together in one concept the notion of a God who presided over the nature he had brought into being, and who at the same time made possible, each in its own way, a new life for Israelite and Christian alike.[12] In this way the image of Creator not only established the absolute priority of God, but also served as a transitional figure to the realm of image-symbols that have entered into the language of both theology and worship.

NOTES

1. Cf. Leonard L. Thompson, *Introducing Biblical Literature* (Englewood Cliffs, N.J.: Prentice-Hall Inc., 1978), 40.

2. Gerhard von Rad, *Genesis* (Philadelphia: The Westminster Press, 1961), 43–44.

3. Cf. G. Ernest Wright in *The Interpreter's Bible* (New York, Nashville: Abingdon-Cokesbury Press, 1952), 1:355; "The conception of creation springs out of the experience of God as Redeemer," E. C. Rust, *Nature and Man in Biblical Thought* (London: Lutterworth Press, 1953), 18; cf. *God, History and Historians*, ed. C. T. McIntire (New York: Oxford University Press, 1977), 297.

4. Cf. G. W. H. Lampe, *God as Spirit* (Oxford: Clarendon Press, 1977), 22.

5. Rust, *Nature and Man*, 38.

6. The recital of these passages from Luke does not settle the Resurrection problem. The earlier account of Paul (1 Cor. 15:3–8) takes precedence over the incoherent Gospel accounts.

7. Creation *ex nihilo* is ordinarily accepted as an implication of omnipotence. Cf. E. J. Khamara, "In Defence of Omnipotence," *The Philosophical Quarterly* 28, no. 112 (July 1978): 221.

8. Robert C. Neville, *God the Creator* (Chicago and London: The University of Chicago Press, 1968), 109; cf. 115.

9. Cf. Ian T. Ramsey, *Religious Language* (London: S.C.M. Press Ltd., 1957), 71ff.; like Ramsey, T. R. Martland sees the doctrine of *ex nihilo* as a confession of intellectual and psychical incompleteness and dependence, which religion generates as it promotes ever open-ended awareness and sensitivity. Cf. "Five Observations in Search of a Method to Justify Religious Activity," *Philosophy and Phenomenological Research* 39, no. 2 (December 1978): 254–55.

10. Cf. Von Rad, *Genesis*, 47, 49; Eichrodt, mentioned in Rust, *Nature and Man*, 31. Cf. Wright, *The Interpreter's Bible*, 1:466, 467.

11. "As with the J myth, we have no indication of a creation *ex nihilo*. When the work of creation began, already a primeval chaos existed, and God created the world out of this formless world-stuff." Rust, *Nature and Man*, 29; cf. Wright, *Interpreter's Bible*, 1:365.

12. "Salvation is that part, or aspect, of the divine creative activity by which man comes to be informed by God's presence, made in his image and likeness, and led to respond with trust and willing obedience to the love and graciousness of his Creator." Lampe, *God as Spirit*, 17.

14

The Transformation of Images

The image of God as Creator remains as vivid as any image, but unlike many images, it carries with it a metaphysical and theological connotation. The expansiveness of this image tends to open the way to what Whitehead called the unfortunate habit of paying "metaphysical compliments" to the deity.[1] Whether or not this practice, especially in Christianity, is unfortunate, the fact remains that with the development of metaphysical attributes something of the dramatic, forceful imagery of the Bible was blanched out in these linguistic forms. In the conversion of relatively simple confessions of faith into creedal forms, one can detect a movement of doctrine from living experience into the more static forms, as philosophical terminology was put to use. The needs of the early Christian community for teaching, worship, and exorcism; the facing of persecution; and the detection of heresy—all played their part in this development.[2] This is not to say that confessions bordering upon creedal formulations are entirely foreign to the Scriptures. The Old Testament passage, "A wandering Aramean was my father . . ." (Deut. 26:5ff.) might be considered to be incipiently creedal, and even more certainly the Shema (Deut. 6:4). The references in 1 John by which the Antichrist is to be disclosed sound like creedal formulae (4:2–3, 15; 5:1–5). The writings of the early Church Fathers and the major creeds show the biblical ascriptions to God, such as "Almighty," "Eternal," "Holy," and "Glory," have survived the transposition into Creeds. But to these have been added terms that bear a metaphysical connotation. Among these "Omnipresent," "Omniscient," "Omnipotent," "Infinite," "Impassible," "Incomprehensible," and "Transcendent" stand out, although none of these occurs in Scripture. The dynamic flavor of religious experience is certainly not totally eliminated from these terms, yet theological and philosophical influence has removed them by several degrees from their anthropopathic sources. Attempts have been made to distinguish biblical thought from philosophical speculation, lest the "static qualities" of Greek thought intrude upon the uniqueness of biblical expression.[3] But Christianity went its way, accepting as orthodox these "metaphysical compliments."[4] However, it should be noted that none of the images depicting

192

God as immoral or carrying out despicable acts survived transcription into the Creeds or Confessions. These were eliminated as unworthy or false, and only those which elevated him were incorporated into "metaphysical compliments."

Where these quasi-metaphysical descriptions are used, we are no longer in the area of biblical images, but are forced to use the cumbersome term "image-symbol" or "image-concept," as one modern theologian suggests.[5] On the one hand they retain the religious feeling of the image, and on the other, they become intellective formulae. They are halfway steps between images and symbols. As images move toward symbols, they lose perceptual detail and vivacity, but gain in breadth of expression. By inference as well as by enlargement of religious scope, they widen the focus of the images. They express the sense of "beyondness" and "illimitability," sheer wonder and unspeakable awe that mark much of religious experience. At the same time they serve to prevent any form of idolatry that might spring from anthropomorphism or anthropopathism. However, some damage is done to the images themselves. What was presumably reasonably clear and precise in the images now becomes indefinite and clouded in language that is fertile soil for theological and philosophical wranglings in search of intelligible meanings. The image-symbols, more weakly tethered to any concrete human experiences, expand the feelings of worshipers as God is seen as elevated far beyond what goes on within the world. Ejaculations of praise and breathless adoration of supreme power and wisdom replace the personal intimacy expressed in some forms of anthropopathic imagery. The element of transcendence introduced by the image symbols finds God elevated to an ontological and spiritual level, where love to God seems pointless and prayer fruitless except as an expression of adoration of the indefinite. In some transformations from image in the direction of symbol, paradoxically God may become sheer Being, as with Tillich and Ricoeur. On the one hand, as we have seen, he is a completely featureless blank, and on the other the repository of undiscriminated and indefinite meanings. No focus for faith, love, or prayer seems possible under these conditions. As one critic of Ricoeur's notion of God as Being crisply commented, obedience to such an entity is "as nonsensical as love of minus two."[6]

Yet the movement from image to image-symbol may be understood in a different manner. The use of image-symbols does enter into the worshipful and confessional modes of religion. An example of how this development may occur and how it is to be understood was offered by Ian Ramsey. If the term *infinite wisdom* is taken for an illustration of how the logic of these metaphysical affirmations works, the word *infinite* functions as a "qualifier" of the word *wisdom*, the meaning of which is reasonably clear. The qualifier is a directive pointing the way in which one's mind should move, starting from human wisdom, through quite wise, very wise, and so on endlessly until a disclosure or insight occurs that evokes a religious or, as Ramsey put it, a theological situation. "Logical qualifiers are not further descriptions," he held, "but words which qualify models so as to do justice to what is 'disclosed' in worship."[7] The procedure, which may be applied to other images of God, in fact assumes at the outset acts of worship. It merely offers an explanation to show that the act of worship is intelligibly grounded in concrete experience, but it is not a substitute for worship itself. However, the farther the "qualifier" extends the original image or experience toward the limitless, the less chance there is of ever finding the truth of the final symbol or understanding its meaning. "Infinite wisdom" in this case vanishes into ambiguity, where one still has some idea of wisdom, but finds no point at which to grapple with its infinity. The qualifier has become a negator, to show that nothing limits God's knowledge or wisdom, and it may lead at last to the conviction that nothing at all should be uttered. The formless, contentless, imageless character of God that results may well express the deep oceanic feelings of worship and guard against a literalistic reading of images, but a price must be paid for surrendering the sharp focus the image gives. It appears that in the main the biblical authors more often were content to express their highest and deepest religious attitudes in images, rather than in such metaphysical symbols. But then it is curious that theological discourse still claims "hermeneutical fidelity for its concepts in relation to the originating religious language of the scriptural texts."[8]

The preeminent biblical images of God are those of power raised to the highest degree of intensity by the many references to him as Almighty. And it is from these images that the image-symbol or image-concept of Omnipotence arises. God identifies himself to Abram as "God Almighty" (Gen. 17:1), and again to Jacob (Gen. 35:11). Balaam sees the vision of "The Almighty" (Num. 24:4), Isaiah sees destruction coming upon Babylon from the Almighty (13:6), Ezekiel's visions are attended with a sound like that of the thunder of the Almighty (1:24). The author of Job particularly liked to refer to God as Almighty (5:7, 6:4; 13:3; 16:23; 22:7, 23; 24:1; 33:4), as did the Psalmist (Pss. 68:14; 91:1). Paul draws on Old Testament citations (2 Cor. 6:18), and the book of Revelation has God announcing himself by the same term (1:8; 11:17; 15:3; 16:7; 19:6).

The word *omnipotence* does not occur in these passages, but the transition from Almighty to Omnipotent is not difficult to recognize. However, with the entry of Omnipotence, a new dimension is added to *Almighty*, a metaphysical one that has moved away, in some degree, from the religious significance that the word *Almighty* originally possessed in the context of Scripture. Correspondingly *Omnipotent* has become not only a favorite word in the Creeds and Confessions, but it degenerates into a staple of philosophical argument.[9]

Omnipotence might be regarded as the all-inclusive concept or symbol, including all other image-symbols. This was not to be the case. While the

Bible sanctioned the use of such descriptions of God as Eternal, Everlasting, and Immortal, piety as well as theology was not satisfied with them. The terms *Infinite* and *Imperishable* were called into service in the Creeds, although it is difficult to see that they add anything to the biblical terms. The images from which the image-symbol *Eternal* appears to spring are those of sheer unending endurance in time. As von Rad pointed out in respect to the Old Testament use of the Hebrew word for everlasting, usually translated as "eternal" or "eternity," the sense is not that of timelessness or otherworldliness. Rather it signifies time extending forward and backward without end.[10] Bevan agreed when he stated, "So far as the language of the Bible goes, there is nothing to show that the eternity of God is understood in any other sense than that of unending time." He continued by arguing that Christian theologians under Neoplatonic influence erred in separating God's being from time by referring to eternity. But *eternity* says nothing, although it sounds like a positive attribute. It is a "mere X denoting something of which all we know is that it cannot be Time like the time we experience."[11] However, a philosophical theologian, anxious to preserve the extended meaning of *eternal*, argues on the basis of the doctrine of creation *ex nihilo*, that whatever being creates in this manner must be eternal, that is, nontemporal, and astonishingly concludes that "time itself is not temporal—it is eternal."[12] In any case, the notion of "everlasting" seems to have given rise to a whole set of image-symbols, including "infinite" and "imperishable," that express the inexhaustible power of the deity. In later theological discussion the doctrine of analogy was used to give content to these words, although this use, as with Aquinas, was a doubtful contribution to the understanding of a nonfinite being.[13]

There is little difficulty in discerning in both Testaments the root imagery for these image-symbols, which have grown into metaphysical descriptions of God. He is hailed as the "everlasting God" (Gen. 21:33), the Lord who will reign for ever and ever (Exod. 15:18). He is the eternal God who is the dwelling place of believers (Deut. 33:27). David blesses God, "our father, for ever and ever" (1 Chron. 29:10). Deutero-Isaiah exalts the power of God as "the everlasting God" (40:28), and Third Isaiah sees him as inhabiting "eternity" (57:15). The Psalmist sees the Lord sitting enthroned forever (9:7; 29:10; 45:6): "from everlasting to everlasting thou art God" (90:2). Although his works will perish, "he doth endure" (102:26). The New Testament carries over, with fewer references, the sense of everlasting and eternal, but perhaps in the more transcendent sense. Paul speaks of God's "eternal power and deity" and his "immortal nature" (Rom. 1:20, 23; 16:26). The author off 1 Timothy ascribes immortality to God, who is the only being who possesses it (1:17; 6:16); John in Revelation calls him the one "who lives for ever and ever" (4:9, 10; 10:6; 15:7); and Jude caps his resounding ascription of God's glory, majesty, dominion, and authority with words that leave no doubt of his transcendent character: "before all time and now and for ever" (v. 25). The "eternality" of God has become more than unending time. From figures such as these the metaphysical symbols of a God who was impervious to time's passage were forged. At the same time a theological and philosophical problem was set in motion as to how an eternal, infinite, imperishable God could have anything to do with a finite, ever-changing world. And even the presence of Jesus Christ as a historical personage in the world as the image of God has only exacerbated the issue.

The problem became even more intransigent when the image-symbols "impassible" and "immutable" were introduced.[14] Eternality in some respects retained a remnant of dynamism in the biblical images, but now God became the unchangeable one. He is considered to be devoid of emotions and incapable of a change of mind or will, because these were taken to be signs of weakness or imperfection. In spite of scriptural evidence to the contrary, the framers of Creeds and Confessions proceeded to adopt two metaphysical terms that virtually obliterated the anthropopathic character of the deity. The impersonal images, which stressed the immovable nature of God, such as rock, fortress, or tower, or in personal terms, his steadfast love, were converted into impassibility. The absolutely dependable God who was to be trusted through thick and thin became an inert being without feeling or purpose. Even a personal pronoun would seem to be out of place in addressing this entity. Yet if impassibility signifies rigidity, it also expresses the objectivity of a God that was not to be manipulated or used. The source of this image-symbol can be seen in the images themselves. God shows his "steadfast love" to Joseph (Gen. 38:21). He has led his people by his "steadfast love" (Exod. 15:33), and will continue to show it to those who love him and keep his commandments (Exod. 20:6). And as we have seen, the phrase is repeatedly used in the Old Testament (e.g., Num. 14:18); 2 Sam. 2:6; Ps. 136; Jer. 33:11), as are the references to the rocklike character of God (Deut. 32:15, 18, 42; 2 Sam. 22:3; Ps. 18:2, etc.) But in the book of Job, God is announced to be "unchangeable" (24:13). Here, it would seem, a firm basis for immutability or impassibility is offered. However, translations are not agreed as to the meaning of the word. The King James Version renders it as "he is of one mind"; the New English Bible reads "he decides," while the University of Chicago version says "he has chosen." The unchangeability of God appears to vanish in the light of these translations, unless they are to be taken to signify in a very loose manner that he is complete in himself, as the King James Version suggests. Even this possibility is ruled out by a commentator who states "the idea of divine immutability is neither expressed nor implied in the text."[15] And even Malachi's forthright statement, "for I the Lord do not change" (3:6) is regarded as difficult to understand. The nearest approach to immutability in the New Testament lies in a reference in Hebrews to the "unchangeable character of his purpose" (6:17, 18) and in James's reference to "the Father of lights with whom there is no variation or shadow due to change" (1:17).

Undoubtedly the notion of immutability or impassibility as developed in Christian theology derived from Greek sources that held to the view that whatever could change was not all it could be and was therefore in a metaphysical sense imperfect. In raising God to the level of perfection, divine mutability and passion were thus cast aside as a blemish upon divine nature.

That God was a perfect being came to be a capstone attribute or image-symbol, but like the other image-symbols, it raised once more critical questions as to how a perfect being could without defect have dealings with an imperfect world of mankind. The image-symbol strives to express in the strongest terms the supremacy and excellence of God, but in so doing it sets him at a great distance from all that makes up the world. He is complete in himself, in contrast to the being presented by biblical imagery that suggests his unlimited nature. God has vanished as an object of religious devotion if perfection is the supreme accolade given to him. As one philosopher notes "A perfect God, a God who in a perfect way fulfills his end, is an irreligious concept. God is here transformed into a thing, into a lifeless but expedient and therefore perfect object."[16] This may be the reason that God himself is seldom called perfect in Scripture. His work is perfect (Deut. 32:4; Eccles. 3:14), his way is perfect (2 Sam. 22:31; Ps. 18:30), and his law is perfect (Ps. 19:7), but there is no "perfect" God in the Old Testament. In the New Testament no passage designates God as perfect except the one in Matthew, where Jesus says, "You therefore must be perfect, as your heavenly Father is perfect" (5:48). This statement becomes suspect, however, in Luke's rendering, "Be merciful, even as your Father is merciful" (6:36). It is barely possible that Paul employs the image-symbol "perfect" when he calls the Roman Christians to be transformed so that "they may prove what is the will of God, what is good and acceptable and perfect" (12:2). Or, as an equally valid translation runs, "the good and acceptable and perfect will of God." The assumption must be made, as in the case of the Old Testament references to the perfect works, way, and law of God, that only a God who is perfect could exercise a perfect will. The same assumption applies to James's speaking of "every perfect gift from above" (1:17). It is remotely possible that the divine perfection is implied in the references to the fullness of God indwelling in Christ (Col. 1:19; 2:19), but supposition would be stretched beyond the limits of reasonable conjecture by that step.

In both Scriptures the specific evidence for God's perfection remains without an underlying image upon which to build the image-symbol. Yet there is plenty of circumstantial evidence to allow the notion of God's perfection to take shape. The burden of that evidence consists in the religious conviction that there is no insufficiency in the deity. Amid the ever-shifting experiences and wayward passions of the world, there hardened into the image-symbol of perfection a God of imperturbable serenity far removed from these distractions, a God whose very nature needed nothing beyond himself to be himself. Metaphysically, his perfection in its impassibility and immutability stands in sharp contrast to the emotional heavings and passionate struggles found in the world. Yet Christian worshipers have continued to sing "change and decay in all around I see: O thou who changest not, abide with me." So as the world changes and passes, the perfection of immutability is sought, even when the hymn as a prayer is directed to a God who is not impassible! The paradox of perfection remains, or is best understood as a purely negative attribute.

The perfection of the deity makes God an isolated figure, far distant from the common world of humans. His very perfection would be endangered if he came in contact with that imperfect world. And as the distance, religiously and ontologically, between human beings and God enlarged, it would seem that no commerce with this exalted being could be initiated by mankind, a conclusion that the early Barth adopted. Only some act from "beyond," from God, could span the gulf, in the giving of the law in Judaism and the coming of Christ for Christianity. Revelation alone could make God known, and this through intermediaries.[17] But perfection could not cordon off God from his creation. Two other image-symbols were necessary, those of omnipresence and omniscience, by which this God maintained relation to the world. Neither of these image-symbols occurs in Scripture, but the images out of which they grew are present.

To know all (omniscient), God must be everywhere (omnipresent), and an example of the linkage between the two may be found in the words "the eyes of the Lord are in every place, keeping watch on the evil and good" (Prov. 15:3). However, the two image-symbols can be treated separately even though they appear to be mutually intertwined. Omnipresence can be understood religiously as the presence of God in the world for the worshiper, even when at times he is hidden (Pss. 10:1; 13:1; 27:9; 30:7; Isa. 1:15; 30:20; 57:17; Mark 15:34). So it is claimed, "God is never absent from his world; he does not leave it and come back again."[18] On the other hand, Rudolf Otto emphatically denied that omnipresence as a metaphysical symbol had religious value. The doctrine, he claimed, was "a frigid invention of metaphysical speculation, entirely without religious import." God, so considered, was deity bound to every time and place like a natural force pervading space. "Scripture knows no 'Omnipresence,' neither the expression nor the meaning it expresses," he wrote.[19] Probably it cannot be denied that metaphysical thought entered into the image-symbol of omnipresence, but it is also true that its source lay in those images of Scripture that are most closely aligned with religious feelings and insight. It ministered to and expressed the sense that God was no absentee being, without care or sustaining power directed to his creation. "Underneath are the everlasting arms" (Deut. 33:27). To Abraham God promises that he will be with him and will keep him wherever he goes (Gen. 28:15). The same promise is made to Joshua (1:9), and David is reminded that God has been with him wherever he went (2 Sam. 7:9). The Chronicler speaks of God as having been "in all places, where I have moved with all Israel" (1 Chron. 17:8). No expression of the inescapability of God's presence is more graphic than that of the Psalmist. "Whither shall I go from thy Spirit? Or whither shall I flee from thy presence: If I ascend to heaven, thou art there! If I make my bed in Sheol, thou art there" (Ps. 138:7, 8). Amos sounds the same theme in threatening God's punishment. "Though they dig into Sheol, from there shall my hand take them; though they climb up to heaven, from there I will bring them down" (9:2ff.).

The general position of the Christian Scriptures hovers between assuming the ever-present and accessible deity and the maintenance of his distance from the world, only overcome in Jesus Christ. But there are no passages that definitively imply omnipresence with the clarity of the Old Testament imagery. Even there the presence of God "everywhere" is often limited in scope to the fate of Israel. In spite of the relatively meager grounds provided for omnipresence found in Scripture, Christian theologians proceeded to incorporate the doctrine in some of the creeds. It served to lessen the gulf between a perfect God and the world, and allowed for human accessibility in prayer to the deity. It expressed the haunting proximity of God.

In the case of the yoke-fellow to omnipresence, the image-symbol of omniscience fared better as to scriptural basis. The biblical authors were enamored of the image of God's knowledge and wisdom, an exception being that of God's ignorance as to the whereabouts of Adam in the Garden of Eden (Gen. 3:9, 11). By knowledge, wisdom, and power, God created the world, nations rise and fall under his watchful eye, and people are judged and saved according to his purposes. To encompass both nature and history in a universal oversight, even down to the most intimate detail, called for a knowledge that so far exceeded human wit and imagination that the acceptance of the image-symbol of omniscience was irresistible to worshiper and theologian alike. Moreover, it was one that continued to express something of the anthropopathism of the images themselves, although the word *omniscient* found no place in Scripture. Thus the prayer of Hannah contains the words, "The Lord God is a god of knowledge" (1 Sam. 2:36), without reference to his infinite knowledge or omniscience. The expression "the wisdom of the angel of God" who knows "all things that are on earth" may be a circumlocution for God's encompassing knowledge (2 Sam. 14:20). The Psalmist pictures God as looking down from heaven and seeing "all the sons of man" and observing "all their deeds" (33:13–15). He knows the "secrets of the heart" of human beings (44:21;

93:11; 103:14). He knows when the Psalmist sits and rises, what he thinks and what he says before "a word is on my tongue." He is "acquainted with all my ways" (139:2–4). The book of Job has God peering into the depths: "Sheol is naked before God, and Abaddon has no covering" (26:6). He is a god who looks to the ends of the earth, and "sees everything under the heavens" (28:24). Nothing escapes the Lord's sight, even when some persons foolishly try to hide (Isa. 29:15). Jeremiah believes that before he was conceived, God knew him (1:5), and on God's behalf he asks, "Can a man hide himself in secret places so that I cannot see him" (23:24). Before people ask of God, he knows their need (Matt. 6:8, 32). Paul's doctrine of predestination is based on God's foreknowledge (Rom. 8:29), and he praises God as "the only wise God" (Rom. 16:27). It is by the church that "the manifold wisdom of God" may be made known to the principalities and powers in the heavenly places (Eph. 3:10). And in Hebrews the theme of the impossibility of hiding from God is sounded again (4:13). But the words in 1 John come close to the image-symbol "omniscient" when the author claims that God "knows everything" (3:20).

In the Fourth Gospel Christ himself is seen as possessed of a knowledge far beyond that of ordinary humans. Insofar as this picture of Christ shows him in intimate relation to the deity, he enjoys virtual omniscience. He spies Nathaniel under the fig tree, and immediately knows that he is an Israelite without guile (1:48). He knows all men and what went on in their minds (2:25). The Samaritan woman is amazed that he knew she had had five husbands (4:16–18). The same uncanny perceptiveness allows Jesus to know in advance that the crowd wished to make him king by force (6:15). From the beginning he knew those who would not believe in him and who would betray him (6:64, 71), even as he knew the decisive time for his destiny (7:6). He knows God, but the Jews do not (8:55). The disciples, satisfied that he was now speaking plainly, say, "now we know that you know all things" (16:30). The scene of the arrest finds Jesus "knowing all that was to befall him" and virtually taking charge of the whole procedure (18:4).

So in the images of both God and Christ we have the foundations of the image-symbol of omniscience, which has come to play a large part in both Judaism and Christianity. Human knowledge, stretched to the uttermost in this image-symbol, as with others, is meant to show that in God or Christ there is no limitation—an implicit negative assertion clothed in an affirmation. But to make the knowledge of God even more mysterious, the image-symbol "incomprehensible" was added. Incomprehensibility is a paradoxical term. On the one hand it suggests that God is totally unintelligible to humans, yet on the other it assumes that mankind understands that it is God, not some other being, to which incomprehensibility properly belongs. It denies that com-prehension of God is possible, if com-prehension is taken as the human ability to understand in a totally encompassing manner. God's knowledge, wisdom, and being are boundless or infinite, and therefore impenetrable to humans. God lives in mystery, and again the paradox appears, because his very incomprehensibility lures one to further acquaintance with him, to seek after him that he may be found (Acts 17:27; Deut. 4:29; Isa. 55:6; 65:1; Jer. 29:13), and at the same time it makes impossible an exhaustive knowledge of the plenitude of his hidden being.

Passages that emphasize the hiddenness of God or that set him apart from mankind form the basis of the doctrine or image-symbol of the incomprehensible God. He is a God who dwells in thick darkness, who addresses Moses (Exod. 20:21; 1 Kings 8:12; Ps. 18:11). To him belong "the secret things" (Deut. 29:29). He does great and unsearchable things (Job 5:9). Job, in his agony, cannot find him (23:3, 8, 9), and only "the outskirts of his ways" are known to him, and "the thunder of his power cannot be understood" (26:14). The Lord hides himself in times of trouble (Pss. 10:1; 13:1; 22:1, Mark 15:34), and his knowledge "is too wonderful for me; it is high, I cannot attain it" (139:6). His greatness is unsearchable (145:3), and "his understanding is beyond measure" (147:5; Isa. 40:28). His thoughts and ways are not mankind's (Isa. 55:8), and although he has put eternity into man's mind, yet "he cannot find out what God has done from the beginning to the end" (Eccles. 3:11). It is the Lord's glory "to conceal things" (Prov. 25:1). Paul ecstatically proclaims "how unsearchable are his judgments and how inscrutable his ways" (Rom. 11:33). The Gospel of John has Jesus proclaiming to the Jews, "His voice you have never heard, his form you have never seen" (5:37). It remained for the author of 1 Timothy to come as close as any to the explicit notion of incomprehensibility when he praises God, dwelling in unapproachable light, "whom no man has ever seen or can see" (6:16).

The Hebraic and Christian views of God hover between two notions of God. On the one hand, God is known and identifiable by specific characteristics that distinguish him from all other beings. On the other, he is a God either shrouded in darkness or dwelling in "inapproachable light." In the second alternative he so far exceeds human understanding that his ways, whatever they may be, are completely separate from those of mankind. Indeed if incomprehensibility were the last word on the nature of God, literally nothing could be said about him, including the attribution of incomprehensibility itself. Such a totally incomprehensible God is no god at all. But religious experience could not settle for an atheism based on incomprehensibility. Instead it settled for the conviction that the image-symbol of incomprehensibility expressed a mysterious meaning beyond anything permitted by the more definite images or literal expositions of his attributes or nature. The term *incomprehensible* enhanced the sense of mystery believed to be indispensable to the depths of religious faith, and defended as such by the pious as a safeguard of the uniqueness of the deity.

Before his fathomless nature the knee was to be bowed, and the voice silenced in awe. Any attempt to define this being, even tentatively, could only be understood as an act of lèse majesté, an unfailing indication of sinful pride. "Le Dieu défini est le Dieu fini." It is as though God himself would vanish if human comprehension actually knew or understood him—perhaps a fulsome tribute to the formidable powers of mankind, but scarcely an accolade to God's independent reality! The notion of God's incomprehensibility is not simply testimony to God's difference from human and finite reality. It grows out of the common experiences of helplessness and frustration and ignorance before the enigmas of human existence. It expresses the realization that one is faced with an ineluctable power that does not yield to human manipulation, no matter how artfully undertaken. Prayer, ritual, or conduct cannot bend the will of God to human purposes. God blesses and judges as he freely wills. His mystery suffuses even the clearest intimations of his presence. So religious faith is nurtured as much by the celebration of God's obscurity as it is by the fleeting knowledge and awareness of his presence. "No form of devotion which does not offer or achieve this mystery for the worshipper," Rudolph Otto claimed, "can be perfect or can give lasting contentment to a religious mind."[20] "Incomprehensibility" is the image-symbol that feeds this sense of God's mystery.

Closely connected with incomprehensibility is the uniquely religious term *holy* or *holiness*. Unlike some other attributes of God that have been turned into image-symbols, this one retains the vivacity and focusing power of an image, while approaching a literal description of the very essence of the deity. The idea of holiness suggests separation from all that is common, defective, or polluted. It may incorporate ethical conduct, but its connotation extends beyond the moral domain.[21] It can be used in connection with a human sense of guilt and wrongdoing, as when a divine sanction is broken or overlooked, but it signifies more than an ethical shortcoming. In its impersonal sense it was applied to objects and persons, implying that they were set apart as clean or pure for divine purposes.[22] Holiness is an invisible, mysterious power that at one and the same time both attracts and repels the worshiper. And nowhere is this clearer than in respect to God, who calls human beings to himself and yet forbids an impertinent intimacy. Before this God of holiness, humans are sinful, not only because of their misdeeds, but because his holiness judges them for the suffocating circumscription by which false centers of loyalty bind their existence. When Isaiah is confronted with God's holy presence in the temple, he cries, "Woe is me! For I am lost: for I am a man of unclean lips, and I dwell in the midst of a people of unclean lips; for my eyes have seen the King, the Lord of hosts" (6:5). Thereby a paradigm is set for the experience of God's holiness. Isaiah's uncleanness does not consist simply in ritualistic or moral deficiency; rather he sees his life as totally incommensurate with that of God, and as such unworthy to be in the Lord's presence. Humility, abasement, and repentance, not the exertion of moral effort, are to be the steps by which a new center of existence is to come about. Before holiness the old defenses are worthless; only a pure and clean heart open to God is acceptable.

Not all expressions of God's holiness are so described in Scripture. Moses is forbidden to enter Canaan because he did not revere God as holy (Deut. 32:51). The holiness of God is associated with his jealousy and unforgiving nature in the words of Joshua (Josh. 24:19). The absolute uniqueness of the deity sounds in Hannah's words of devotion: "There is none holy like the Lord" (1 Sam. 2:2). For looking into the ark of the Lord, seventy men are killed, moving others to be amazed at the mysterious power of the Lord: "Who is able to stand before the Lord, this holy God?" (1 Sam. 6:19, 20). Isaiah calls Assyria to book for her mockery and pride "against the Holy One of Israel" (2 Kings 19:22). The Priestly authors of Leviticus use the supreme sanction of God's holiness for their charge to Israel to be holy. "You shall therefore be holy, for I am holy" (Lev. 11:45; 19:2; 20:26; 21:8). Here the sense is not only that God is set apart by his holiness from all common or secular things, or that the people should also be set apart from all other peoples, but, more important, that they should be set apart or consecrated to God. To that end the ritualistic and moral laws were developed. The judgment called down upon the "cows of Bashan" by Amos is rooted in the Lord's swearing by his holiness that horrendous punishment will befall them (4:2). But there is a tenderness also in God's holiness, as Hosea sees it, for God will not destroy Ephraim precisely because "I am God and not man, the Holy One in your midst" (11:9). But scenes of judgment are rehearsed in the writings of Isaiah (1:4; 5:19, 24, 25; 30:11, 12ff.). Although God's holiness is not exercised solely in punishment, he is the Holy God whose holiness is recognized in his righteousness (5:16). The survivors of the house of Jacob will "lean upon the Lord, the Holy One of Israel" (10:20), and shouts of joy will go up, for this Holy One is in the midst of Israel (12:6). The time will come when the products of human hands will be forgotten and men's eyes will look only to the Holy One of Israel (17:7, 8), and they shall find rest and salvation as the Holy Lord has promised (30:15). Second Isaiah sees the Lord, the Holy One of Israel, as the Savior of his people (43:3), and although dwelling in the high and holy place, he is also with those of a contrite and humble spirit (57:15). The note of judgment and punishment continues to ring in the prophecy of Jeremiah (50:29; 51:5). Ezekiel foresees the time when the scattered Hebrew people will be gathered and so manifest the holiness of God before nations (20:41), while he piles destruction on their enemies (28:22). And it is characteristic of this prophet that, having castigated his people for having profaned God's holy name, he envisages God as saving them from Babylon for the sake of that holy name (30:21–23; 39:7). Repeatedly the Psalmist praises God for his holiness, even when the deity is far away (22:2, 3). He sings joyfully to God for his holiness (71:22), but it is a holiness both righteous and terrible in its majesty that is worshiped (99:3–5, 9). And the wisdom proclaimed in Proverbs has its basis in the insight that the knowledge of the Holy One brings (9:10).

The ascription of holiness in the New Testament is given to Jesus (John 6:69), and particularly in innumerable passages to the Spirit, but very few passages dwell upon God's holiness. The writer of Ephesians calls the church to a likeness of God "in true righteousness and holiness" (4:24). Hebrews holds forth the promise that after divine discipline the faithful will share in God's holiness (12:10). First Peter makes use of passages in Leviticus in calling readers to be holy, as is he who called them—although it may be Jesus Christ, not God directly, who has called them to this new life (1:15, 16). It is only in the book of Revelation that God himself is hailed as holy. In the last days an unceasing chant goes up: "Holy, holy, holy is the Lord God Almighty" (4:8). He alone is holy as the King of the ages (15:3, 4), "thou who art and wast, O Holy One" (16:5).

The holiness of God is associated with him as king, and by that association the image of glory swings into full view. Holiness and glory are equal partners in the exaltation that objective worship feels and expresses. Both set God apart in his majesty as the fit subject to command the sole devotion of humans. Glory, like holiness, is an end in itself; it is the intrinsic value in which all in the world come to rest. Yet it is the most difficult ascription of all to delineate or analyze. Its connection with the image of king, however, provides a tentative grasp of its meaning. Like holiness, it suggests a sense of height above all that surrounds it, and in terms of social and political imagery, it stresses the distinction between subordinate and superior beings. Glory is what pertains to a ruler, an emperor or king, setting him apart from his subjects.[23] It is what a political theorist has called the domain of "miranda," that is, what is to be wondered at in distinction from "credenda," those things that are to be believed. Before the "miranda" of power and authority, criticism or rebellion is quelled as inappropriate. Glory enjoys the trappings of "pomp and circumstance." It exhibits itself in the raiments and symbols of office, which make unquestionable a right to rule that is stronger than sheer power. By its regal ostentation and magnificence, it overawes and at the same time elicits adoration and devotion. In its glory royalty is a pageant resplendent with the bright colors of regalia, sashes, medals, jewels, swords, and crowns. Glory is brilliance and light that takes the observer away from the dullness and drabness of everyday life. As the gods of old were called the shining ones, so their human counterparts appear in radiant beauty to their subjects. To witness the glory of royalty brings forth tears of joy, gasps of admiration, while pride at vicariously participating in the tradition of authority and continuity swells the breast. Yet with pride comes humility, as one is reminded to bow and be abased before such splendor, for the splendor is itself only the impressive, outward appearance of a mystery that fends off all encroachment by lesser beings. One can but yield oneself to its overwhelming authority. It is the last and ultimate goal of life for which to live and die. It is as evanescent as a gossamer, yet its strength has held kingdoms and empires together by the loyalty it has elicited from subjects. And when transposed into the religious realm, where God's glory penetrates the religious consciousness, it transcends the panoply and splendor of earthly kings. It is a motive that animates the life of faith, even as it promises a final vision of God's glory, for which all being exists.

Yet glory, as seen in both earthly and heavenly terms, can be a dangerous goal. People have died for it and killed for it, whether for man's or God's glory. In its pursuit humans have turned brutal, losing all sense of ethical discernment. Seduced by its lure, people have ecstatically abandoned common sense and have been engulfed in a passion that takes over their higher faculties. The simplicities of life are set aside to revel in its insidious enchantment. So Jesus recalled his listeners from the contemplation of Solomon's earthly glory to the wonders of God's world about them. "Even Solomon in all his glory was not arrayed" in the simple beauty of the lilies of the field (Matt. 6:29). The vision of the mighty "King of Glory" (Ps. 24:7–10) may lift hearts and voices to new emotional heights, but it can also lead to the exaltation of power for its own sake, a danger that moved Whitehead to observe, "The glorification of power has broken more hearts than it has healed."[24] Nevertheless, seen through the perspective of the kingly image, "glory," often with "holiness" is the highest accolade paid by biblical authors to the deity, even as the vision of it for humans is the crowning event of existence. If it stands for unlimited power—which it does—nevertheless it is also cloaked with beauty. "Out of Zion, the perfection of beauty, God shines forth" (Ps. 50:2). And seldom is it far from God's righteousness. Before God's glory, one does not seek worldly glory or power, for the divine glory humbles pride.

As is fitting, God the king over the powers of nature calls upon them to reveal his glory. In the wilderness when food was scarce, the glory of God is seen "in the morning" when food is provided (Exod. 16:7ff.), and in a cloud that reveals his glory (Exod. 16:10). The association of God's glory with a cloud takes on an almost tangible presence as it covers the tent of meeting, and glory fills the tabernacle so that Moses is unable to enter (Exod. 40:34; cf. Ezek. 10:4; 43:5). The cloud not only leads the Israelites by day; it is the sign of the mystery of God's glory. When it covers the mountain, the glory of the Lord settles upon Sinai (Exod. 24:15, 16). And there is also brightness as fire (Exod. 24:17), a description fully displayed in the visions of Ezekiel, when a cloud, lightning, fire, gleamings, and brightness are all brought into play as "the likeness of the glory of the Lord" (Ezek. chap. 1; 43:2). For Ezekiel the glory of the Lord is personalized, as when it stands before him (4:23), or when it enters the temple (43:4). Nowhere is this glory more beautifully expressed than in the lines of the Third Isaiah: "Arise, shine, for your light has come and the glory of the Lord has risen upon you" (Isa. 60:1). The very heavens tell of his glory (Ps. 19:1), and prayers are offered that his glory be seen over all the earth (Pss. 57:5, 11; 72:19; 108:4). By its presence there shall be deliverance (Ps. 108:6), and although his glory is above the heavens, "He raises the poor from the dust and lifts the needy from the ash heap" (Ps. 113:4, 7). And his protection will be about his people, for "the glory of the Lord shall be your rear guard" (Isa. 58:8). Thus do morality and glory intertwine. But mere humans will not participate in the divine glory. "My glory I will not give to another" (Isa. 48:11).[25]

The writers of the New Testament quarried the innumerable references to divine glory in their inherited Scriptures. The kingly image was retained, accompanied by its ideas of light, power, mystery, and righteousness. However, the Christian authors had a problem on their hands, not found in the Old Testament. Not only was there a glory of God; there was a glory of Jesus Christ. As earlier observed, the relation between God and Christ was not clearly worked out in the New Testament. Hence the glory of Christ at times appears as a state into which he was elevated by God after the resurrection, a state that Paul for one saw as the goal of the believers when they also would be raised in immortality.[26] His glory is derivative from God's. At other times the Scriptures present Christ as already enjoying a glorified state, that is, a kingly one, during his lifetime. In yet other instances his glory had not been revealed, but awaited disclosure beyond history. There remains, at the same time, the glory that pertains only to God, for it appears that he is glorious quite apart from Christ. The consequence is that the New Testament offers no simple, unified picture of divine glory. In brief, it can be said that God's glory is shown in Christ, both during his lifetime and in some final state of affairs, but God remains as the ultimate source of glory.

The tone of God's glory is set in Luke's legend of Jesus' birth. The heavenly host chants "Glory to God in the highest and on earth peace among men with whom he is pleased" (2:14). It is to God's glory, not to Jesus', that men are to do good works (Matt. 5:16). He alone is to be glorified; for him, through him, and to him are all things (Rom. 11:36). In being in harmony with each other and in accord with Jesus Christ, the Christians can lift one voice to glorify "the God and Father of our Lord Jesus Christ" (Rom. 15:5, 6). His is the glory for evermore (Rom. 16:27; Gal. 1:5; Phil. 4:20; 1 Pet. 4:11). The righteousness that comes through Christ is all "to the glory and praise of God" (Phil. 1:11), and the exaltation of Christ as Lord is "to the glory of God the Father" (Phil. 2:11). The regal ascription is plainly stated in 1 Timothy: "To the King of ages, immortal, invisible, the only God, be honor and glory for ever and ever" (1:17).

Stephen's recital of Israel's history opens with the words "The God of glory appeared to our father Abraham" (Acts 7:2), and ends with Stephen's seeing the glory of God in heaven, Jesus standing at the right hand of God (Acts 7:55). Paul charges that all persons have sinned and thereby fallen short of the glory of God (Rom. 3:23). By the power of the divine glory Christ was raised from the dead so that "we too might walk in newness of life" (Rom. 6:4). And in that life all is to be done to the glory of God (1 Cor. 10:31). The image of light in connection with glory is used by Paul when he affirms it "is the God who said 'let light shine out of darkness' who has shone in our hearts to give the light of knowledge of the glory of God in the face of Christ" (2 Cor. 4:6). The God of Jesus Christ is the "Father of glory" (Eph. 1:17). And the stately ascription of Jude praises God "our savior through Jesus Christ" to whom "be glory, majesty, dominion and authority, before all time and now and for ever, Amen" (v. 25). Revelation echoes the theme of eternal glory (1:6, 4:9, 11; 7:12). The scenes of terror of the last days will move those who escape to give glory to God (11:13), and an angel proclaims "Fear God and give him glory, for the hour of his judgment has come" (14:7). Those who are punished "did not repent and give him the glory" (16:9), but those whom he saves will cry, "Salvation and glory and power belong to our God" (19:1, 7). Once more we see the smoke of God's glory filling the temple in heaven as it did in Moses' time, or that of Solomon and Ezekiel, so that no one could enter (15:8). When the heavenly Jerusalem descends, it has the glory of God, "its radiance like a most rare jewel, like a jasper, clear as crystal" (21:11), and in it "the glory of God is its light and its lamp is the Lamb" (21:23). So God the king shines in splendor, although beside him, equal in glory, stands Christ.

These passages in the main exalt the glory of God, although several of them include the glory of Christ. To the eyes of the early Christians, Christ is seen occasionally as glorious or to be glorified without reference to God, although more often the glory attributed to him is closely bound to that of God. In the Son of Man sayings, Jesus as the Christ announces that he will come in "clouds with great power and glory" (Matt. 24:30; Mark 13:26), although the accounts of Matthew, Mark, and Luke include his glory with that of the Father (Matt. 16:27; Mark 8:38; Luke 9:26). The Gospel of John has one passage that sets apart Christ's glory (2:11), but the general tenor of that Gospel clearly shows Christ's glory to be from God. The Second Thessalonian letter has the opponents of the church excluded "from the presence of the Lord and from the glory of his might" (1:9), and the brethren are urged to obtain "the glory of our Lord Jesus Christ" (2:14). Paul sees the rulers of this age as having "crucified the Lord of glory" (1 Cor. 2:8), and he pictures the believers as being changed into the glory of the Lord as they have beheld his face (2 Cor. 3:18). The churches themselves are "the glory of Christ" (2 Cor. 8:23). Glory is to be given to Christ (2 Tim. 4:18; Heb. 13:21; 2 Pet. 3:18). James summons the Christians to hold the faith "of our Lord Jesus Christ, the Lord of glory" (2:1). The glory of Christ to be revealed will be the occasion of rejoicing and joy (1 Pet. 4:13), and that promise is made good when angels cry "worthy is the Lamb who was slain, to receive power and wealth and wisdom and might and honor and glory and blessing" (Rev. 5:12).

The Gospel of John, of all the Gospels, makes clear that Christ's glory is entirely derived from the Father. Even the Prologue, which sets the tone of a high Christology, confesses that the glory beheld in the Word is a glory "as of the only Son from the father" (1:14). In the body of the Gospel Jesus is treated as an already glorified being, yet one still to be glorified. His glory comes from the only God (5:44); it is "my Father who glorifies me" (8:54). Jesus does not seek his own glory; God seeks it (8:50). The resurrection of Lazarus is prefaced by Jesus' statement that Lazarus's illness has taken place for the glory of God "so that the Son of God may be glorified by means of it" (11:4). In the raising of Lazarus, however, Martha is told that she would see the glory of God; his own is not mentioned (11:40.) After the triumphal entry into Jerusalem, Jesus announces that the time has come for him to be glorified, indicating that to this point in John's sequence of events, Christ has not yet been glorified (12:23). At the Last Supper, Judas having retired, Jesus proclaims, "Now is the Son of Man glorified, and in him God is glorified"; this glorification is to take place at once (13:31, 32). Yet on Jesus' lips are placed the words of a prayer in which he asks that he may be glorified so that he may glorify God (17:1), with the glory that he had before the world was created (17:5), he having already glorified God on earth (17:4). He asks that those who have believed in him, and to whom he has given the glory conferred by God on him, may behold the glory he possessed before the foundation of the world (17:22, 24). It is the glory of God that is to be found in Christ, "who is the likeness of God," Paul affirms. It is God who brings the light of glory, now seen in the face of Christ (2 Cor. 4:6). And to the Philippians Paul promises that their needs will be cared for by God "according to his riches in glory in Christ Jesus" (4:19). Christ reflects—and the connotation is that of light and brilliance—the glory of God, says the writer of Hebrews (1:3). It is God who raised Christ and gave him glory "so that your faith and hope are in God" (1 Pet. 1:21), a glory conferred by God at the beginning of Jesus' ministry (2 Pet. 1:17). Thus we see that it is God's glory that has been shared with Christ, not that Christ attained glory unaided (Rev. 5:13).

The glory made available in Christ, God has prepared for Christians (Rom. 9:23; Eph. 1:12, 14). The goal of life is the ultimate sharing in God's glory (Rom. 5:2; Col. 1:12; 3:4; 1 Pet. 5:4, 10; 2 Pet. 1:3). Such was the lofty aim set before those not powerful or of noble birth, the foolish in the world, the low and despised, whom God had chosen to show the wise and strong "so that no human being might boast in the presence of God" (1 Cor. 1:26–29). Their bodies, perishable though they are, will be raised at last imperishable; "sown in dishonor," they will be raised in glory; "sown in weakness," they will be raised in power, as was Christ (1 Cor. 15:42, 43). The glory of God will be manifested in them as they participate in the royal glory, as did Christ.

"Holiness" and "Glory" carry few metaphysical associations compared to other image-symbols. They arise most directly out of the raw material of worship, relatively untouched by philosophical and theological tampering. In the case of holiness, the sociological influence of taboo may be detected, molding the form but not the heart of the image-symbol. It is not entirely reducible to taboo, although the difference between the clean and pure as sacred, and the flawed and impure as profane lies at the center of religious experience. Similarly, glory may arise in connection with the political imagery of royalty, but its expression goes beyond that of praising earthly rulers. It is never reducible to the imagery that informs and frames it. In the strain that both holiness and glory put upon the language, the mystery of transcendence is discoverable. Both set God apart from the ordinary and prosaic events of daily life. Built upon the experience of self-transcendence found in all normal human beings, transcendence takes on the semblance, if not the reality, of another realm of being. But if such a realm of transcendent being exists, to state a hoary truism, it is experienced only within the limits of worldly time and space, no matter how elevated the sensations felt. In this sense immanence always has the last word in religious experiences that purport to give insight into realms beyond. But religious experience of transcendence is not identical with the theoretical constructs that some forms of philosophy or theology have created. Transcendence as a religious phenomenon is built upon the hunger for it, natural to human beings, whose clearest insights are always tinged with the sense of the "more" that prosaic words fail to capture. The religious images that best convey and express this intimation of a mystery lurk among even the commonest of earthly experiences. Transcendence, as the neutral product of theological and philosophical speculation, does not summon people to worship it; only the vivacity of imagery performs that task. Consequently, we find the word itself used in only one passage of Scripture, when Paul speaks of God's transcendent power, sharply distinguished from that of humans (2 Cor. 4:7).[27]

The biblical images that have led to the idea of transcendence in worship are those which are associated with height. Bevan observed that considering moral and spiritual worth to be greater or less in ratio to the distance outward from the earth's surface is an odd proposition. Yet height does suggest powers beyond those of mankind. From the sky above come thunder, lightning, rain, or snow, for example. Height allows for a longer and wider range of vision (omniscience). It is an ingredient in social ranking, as between superiors and inferiors, and this fits with kingship. The light of sun, moon, and stars in the sky above suggests the inaccessible mystery, stability, and endlessness of that which lies beyond, and consequently is put in the service of God's transcendence. Hence the images we find in Scripture bespeak a transcendence molded on the natural fact of height. As Bevan put it, "It is the difference of God from man, the essential infinite unannullable difference, which the term transcendence proclaims."[28] Yet it is a difference, not a total separation from the world, of which the images speak. If anything, including God, were entirely out of relationship to the world, then the force of Whitehead's dictum would have to be acknowledged, that only complete ignorance would result.[29] Whatever may have been the limits of the knowledge of God, the biblical authors felt confident that they were not bereft of God's presence even in the darkest periods. Accordingly, when holiness and glory are praised and sought, the transcendence these images or image-symbols evoke is not a compliment paid a nongod or an absent deity. No matter how high God was placed by religious imagination, his objectivity was never questioned, nor were his interest and concern for earthly events and human beings ever ruled out. His thoughts may not be our thoughts, his ways may be higher than our ways (Isa. 55:8, 9); he may dwell "in the high and holy place," but he is also "with him who is of a contrite and humble spirit."

The imagery that gave rise to the theological usage of the terms *transcendence* and *transcendent* lies plentifully upon the pages of Scripture, regularly adorning the language of kingship. The editors saw fit to include an episode in Abram's career where he meets Melchizedek, a king and also a priest of "God Most High." This person blesses Abram in the name of "God Most High." The affair breathes the air of idealization rather than of a factual account, but the presence of the phrase is symptomatic of a whole range of such expressions scattered throughout the Bible. When Moses blesses the Tribes, he pictures God as one "who rides through the heavens to your help and in his majesty through the skies" (Deut. 33:26). Solomon's question, "But will God indeed dwell on earth?" is appropriately answered with the words, "Behold, heaven and the highest heaven cannot contain thee: how much less this house which I have built" (1 Kings 8:27). The Psalmist's imagery makes clear the association of height and kingliness. "The Lord is in his holy temple; the Lord's throne is in heaven" (11:4). He "looks down from heaven" (14:2; 33:13), because he is "high above all nations and his glory above the heavens," where he "is seated on high" (113:4, 5). Prayer is addressed to "thou who art enthroned in the heavens" (123:1), the Lord "above all gods" (135:5). A classic instance depicting transcendence is that of Isaiah's temple vision in which "the Lord sits upon a throne, high and lifted up" (Isa. 6:1). And the figure is repeated, this time in connection with the ethical attributes of God: "The Lord is exalted, for he dwells on high; he will fill Zion with justice and righteousness" (Isa. 33:5). In an echo of Amos, Jeremiah proclaims "the Lord will roar from on high" (25:30). The book of Daniel is replete with references to the Most High God (3:26; 4:17, et al.). Micah bows before God on high (6:6). The opening passages of Luke's Gospel depict "the power of the Most High" overshadowing Mary and John to be called "the prophet of the Most High" (1:35, 76). Jesus follows the Jewish practice of exalting God when he teaches the nature of prayer, addressing God as "Our Father who art in heaven" (Matt. 6:9). In the sermon on the plain, Jesus says that those who forgive their enemies will be "sons of the Most High" (Luke 6:35). In the country of the Garasenes, a demented man identifies Jesus as the "son of the Most High God" (Luke 8:28). A slave girl following Paul and his companions cries "These men are servants of the Most High God" (Acts 16:17). The author of Hebrews, in exalting Jesus, pictures him as having sat down at the right hand "of the Majesty on high" (1:3).

Beside these figures of speech, how bland and wan does the term *transcendent* appear! The biblical writers come closer to the core of heartfelt religious worship than does all the speculation about the transcendence and immanence of God. Their language set a safeguard against the assimilation of the deity to finite realities, except in the case of Jesus as the image of God. They expressed in forceful imagery the polarity between earth and heaven without surrendering one to the other, and left to later scholars to make what they could of both. In the fervent religious consciousness, God was felt to be far above and distant from mankind, but at the same time ever heedful of his people in their wanderings, apostasies, and idolatries, persecutions and sufferings, righteousness and unrighteousness. Earthly kingdoms and empires might rise and fall, but there was One who in his "transcendence" did not rise or fall, and in Him both Jew and Christian trusted. Fortunately, the transformation of images into image-symbols has not allowed the freshness of their originals to disappear entirely into the murky disputes of theological speculation on one hand or the less focused generalities of pure symbols on the other.

NOTES

1. Alfred N. Whitehead, *Science and the Modern World* (New York: The Macmillan Co., 1945), 258.

2. Cf. Oscar Cullmann, *The Earliest Christian Confessions* (London: Lutterworth Press, 1949), 18; R. P. C. Hanson disputes Cullmann on several of these points. Cf. *Traditions in the Early Church*, (London: S.C.M. Press, 1962), chaps. 2, 3.

3. So G. Ernst Wright in *The Interpreter's Bible* (Nashville, New York: Abingdon-Cokesbury Press, 1952), 1:387. However, James Barr applied a corrective to this view when writing of the New Testament. "The apostles do not seem to have seen that they could materially assist their hearers or strengthen their case by pointing out that Greek thought is static and biblical thought dynamic; or that biblical thought is concrete while the traditional thought of their hearers has been abstract. . . ." *Biblical Words for Time, Studies in Biblical Theology* 33 (Naperville, Ill.: Alec R. Allenson Inc., 1962): 159.

4. Examples follow: *Almighty* was carried over into the confessions of Irenaeus, Tertullian, Novation, Lucian of Antioch, Arius, Eusebius of Caesarea, The Apostles' Creed; *Eternal* and *Infinite* appear in the Athanasian Creed, the Heidelberg Catechism, Augsburg Confession, Scotch Confession of Faith, the Thirty-nine Articles and Westminster Confession of Faith; *Incomprehensible* finds place in the Athanasian Creed, the Longer Catechism of the Eastern Church, The Belgic Confession, the Scotch Confession of Faith; *Immutable* or *Unchangeable* occurs in the Belgic Confession and the Westminster Confession of Faith; *Omniscient* and *Omnipresent* show up in the Longer Catechism of the Eastern Church, and *Omnipotent* in the Scotch Confession of Faith. Cf. Philip Schaff, *The Creeds of Christendom*, 4th ed., vols. 1, 2, and 3 (New York, Harper and Brothers, 1877, 1905, 1919). Cf. Robert M. Grant, *The Early Christian Doctrine of God* (Charlottesville: University Press of Virginia, 1966), chap. 1, appendixes I, II.

5. Julian N. Hartt draws a provisional distinction between images and concepts, which he calls an image-concept. Theology, as he sees it, "is a way of reflecting on the story and construing the images of faith." It is a conceptual enterprise at the secondary rather than primary level of religious language. *Theological Method and Imagination* (New York: The Seabury Press, 1977), 16, 17. Cf. G. Van Der Leeuw, *Religion in Essence and Manifestation* (London: George Allen and Unwin, Ltd., 1938), 153.

6. Anthony Kenny in *The Listener*, February 5, 1970, 187.

7. Ian Ramsey, *Religious Language* (London: S.C.M. Press Ltd., 1957), 65–66, 164.

8. David Tracy, *Critical Inquiry* 5 (Autumn 1978): 1, 95.

9. E.g., E. J. Khamara, "In Defence of Omnipotence," *The Philosophical Quarterly* 28, no. 112 (July 1978): 215ff. Cf. also Richard Swinburne, "Omnipotence," *American Philosophical Quarterly* 10 (1973): 236–37.

10. Gerhard von Rad, *Genesis*, trans. John H. Marks (Philadelphia: Westminster Press, 1949), 232. Cf. Frank Herbert Brabant, *Time and Eternity in Christian Thought* (London, New York, Toronto: Longmans, Green and Co., 1937), 235–38.

11. Edwyn Bevan, *Symbolism and Belief* (New York: The Macmillan Co., 1938), 97, 112. James Barr more cautiously claims "when writers say that God is 'eternal,' they may well be saying rather more, or meaning more, than his existence is coterminous with the totality of time." But he also writes "that the Bible appears to offer no explicit group of statements expressly devoted to the problem of the relation of time and eternity." *Biblical Words*, 146, 147.

12. Robert C. Neville, *God the Creator* (Chicago and London: University of Chicago Press, 1968), 115.

13. "After God had widened to an infinity and even an indivisible infinity, there was no possibility for an analogical knowledge of God." Martin Foss, *The Idea of Perfection in the Western World.* (Princeton, N.J.: Princeton University Press, 1946), 42; cf. 41–43.

14. G. W. H. Lampe, *God as Spirit* (Oxford: Clarendon Press, 1977) 21. "It is significant that Christian theologians customarily set down the doctrine of the impassibility of God as an axiom, without bothering to provide much biblical support or theological proof." Jaroslav Pelikan, *The Emergence of the Catholic Tradition (100–600)* (Chicago, University of Chicago Press, 1971), 52.

15. *The Interpreter's Bible*, 3:1083.

16. Foss, *Idea of Perfection*, 26.

17. F. Gerald Downing has mounted a penetrating attack upon the idea of revelation in the New Testament, concluding that there is no valid meaning to the term *revelation*. The Christian must offer commitment to God "but still in uncertainty, without the comfort yet of 'revelation' and 'knowledge of God.'" *Has Christianity Revelation?* (London: S.C.M. Press Ltd., 1964), 290.

18. Lampe, *God as Spirit*, 7.

19. Rudolf Otto, *The Idea of the Holy*, trans. John W. Harvey (London: Oxford University Press, 1925), 219, 220.

20. Ibid., 219; "One of the results of the philosophy of religion . . . is that any manifestation of God that does not also reveal that God is still essentially hidden cannot be sustained as central to religion." Neville, *God the Creator*, 197. Negative theology feeds upon the hiddenness and incomprehensibility of God. "Because we cannot know what God is, but rather what He is not, we have no means for considering how God is, but rather how He is not." "Summa Theologica," pt. 1. q. 3, *Basic Writings of Saint Thomas* Aquinas, ed. Anton C. Pegis (New York: Random House, 1945), 25; "This is what is ultimate in the human knowledge of God: to know

that we do not know God." (Quaestio Disputata de Potentia Dei) quoted in Josef Pieper, *The Silence of St. Thomas,* trans. Daniel O'Connor (London: Faber and Faber, 1957), 69.

21. Michael B. Foster may unwisely have claimed that "morality in the Bible is secondary to holiness," *Mystery and Philosophy* (London: S.C.M. Press, 1957), 71. Otto's study of the holy lists God's "fury," "jealousy," "wrath," as examples akin to holiness. Otto, *Idea of the Holy,* 78.

22. Examples of this usage are oil, garments, priests, the Temple, the altar, the Sabbath, mountains, nation, people, offerings, vessels, convocations, etc., and above all, God's name and Spirit.

23. On political majesty see C. Keith Boone, "Political Majesty: Promise or Peril to Contemporary Society," *Thought* 56, no. 221 (June 1981).

24. A. N. Whitehead, *Religion in the Making* (New York: The Macmillan Co., 1926), 55.

25. "There is hardly . . . in the Old Testament any notion of man's sharing in the glory of God," David Cairns, *The Image of God in Man* (New York, Philosophical Library, 1953), 25.

26. J. M. Cameron's comment upon Christ's glorification sheds light on the relation between Jesus' earthly life and his glory, "and just as the glorified state of Christ is not a transcending or an abolition of his human existence, but the taking of his human nature, that nature in which he was obedient and suffered, into the life of God himself, so the end for which the Church strives as a human institution is also the end willed by Christ and given by the Father, a glorified human life and not a gaseous miasma in which the flesh will be no more." *Images of Authority* (New Haven, Conn.: Yale University Press, 1966), 42–43.

27. "Since transcendence, though a characteristically Hebrew idea, is nowhere philosophically expounded in the Bible, a term had to be adopted to express its definition." The word used, according to G. L. Prestige, is "uncreated." *God in Patristic Thought* (London: S.P.C.K., 1952), xx.

28. Cf. Bevan, *Symbolism and Belief* 30, chap. 3, 68. Norman H. Snaith overstates his case when he claims that transcendence in the Old Testament does not mean remoteness, but too many images do express the Lord's distance from mankind. He is correct when he claims that transcendence signifies otherness. *The Distinctive Ideas of the Old Testament* (London: The Epworth Press, 1950), 47.

29. Cf. Whitehead, *Science and the Modern World* (New York: The Macmillan Company, 1945), 38.

15

Conclusion: The Search for Authoritative Images and Symbols

When approached in the mode of secondary naiveté, the Scriptures yield no criteria for determining the relative authority of images of God. Its evenhanded descriptions and expositions lead either to the granting of authority to all images or none at all, depending upon the interpreter's religious proclivities. If one were inclined to explore the question of gradations of authority, enumeration of the instances in which images appear might provide an answer. However, the history of Christian worship and theology makes clear that matters have not been settled in so simplistic and quantitative a manner. Some images, seldom mentioned in Scripture, have achieved authoritative status, while others, often occurring, have been eliminated or reduced in significance. Something more than simple arithmetical calculation appears to have been at work.

The evidence for such a selective process may be indicated by reference to the often-used phrase *the biblical point of view*. This phrase is taken to embrace only those images, symbols, or ideas chosen to be of superior authority upon which then, as the phrase implies, full biblical support is conferred. Surreptitiously however, the phrase also implies that what has been selected truthfully represents the unity and uniformity of biblical belief—a conclusion completely at odds with the testimony of the Scriptures themselves.[1] Discrimination among images has been made on the basis of some principle which, it is then affirmed, is itself biblically sanctioned. Thus "the biblical point of view," and the images selected, enjoy biblical authority.

An example of the outcome of this involuted process may be observed in the conclusions of the Ecumenical Study Conference on Biblical Studies, sponsored by the World Council of Churches in 1949. This body decided that the center and goal of the entire Bible was Jesus Christ. Accordingly, it was maintained, the Jewish Scriptures were to be interpreted in the light of this conviction. They were to be understood as speaking of the "total revelation in Christ, the Incarnate Word of God, from which arises the full trinitarian faith of the Church." Furthermore, "any teaching that clearly contradicts the Biblical position cannot be accepted as Christian."[2] It would seem clear that this reading depends less upon full confrontation with the texts than it does upon confessional interests used as a discriminating principle and then certified as "the Biblical position." The primary question is not first of all the legitimacy of interpreting the whole Bible as a testimony to Christ along with several theological doctrines, but the legitimacy of appropriating the authority of Scripture for this confessional position. "The Biblical position" has here been invested with supreme authority for the life of the Christian community.

A slightly different version of the use of "the biblical point of view" obtains in the editorial advice offered to readers of the Oxford Annotated Bible, Revised Standard Version, published in 1962. The phrase in question does not occur, but its sense is discernible in the use made of the more pliable principle of progressive revelation, by which the New Testament is regarded as providing the discriminatory elements by which to interpret the Jewish Scriptures. Readers are instructed that "much in the Old Testament is superseded in the New and there are ideas of God in the Old Testament which are not to be approved." To be sure, the editor added, "part of the Old Testament was outgrown before the Old Testament was itself complete," but more of it was "superseded in the New Testament."[3] Biblical authority, or "the biblical point of view," therefore, does not extend to cover all images or symbols of the Jewish Scriptures. It might be asked in turn whether it includes all those found in the New Testament, such as those in the book of Revelation. The images or ideas that are to be accorded superior authority are not specified, but the intent of the editorial commentary is clear. But again the first question to be met is not that of selectivity itself, but rather that of crowning results of this supersession with the aura of total biblical authority.

Biblical fundamentalism meets this problem of selectivity by the blanket assertion that the Bible "is absolutely infallible, without error in all matters pertaining to faith and practice, as well as in areas such as geography, science, history etc."[4] Equal authority then is granted to all images without discrimination, although no fundamentalist actually treats the Bible in this way. Evangelical perspective reduces the scope of biblical authority substantially by according it only in matters of faith and practice.[5] But whichever way one turns, the problem of granting biblical authority to the selection still arises. In plain fact, however, historical-critical biblical study, varieties of textual interpretation, ethical and theological developments, newly discovered manuscripts, and fresh translations have taken their toll of both primary biblical authority and the biblical authority accorded to the images, symbols, and ideas selected. So radical has been this dismantling or limitation of biblical authority that one biblical scholar has maintained that "it is safe to say that the unity and authority of the Bible can no longer be taken for granted as central theological data."[6]

In spite of this dire conclusion, the Bible continues to maintain a position of authority for the Christian community. The selective use of its images as authoritative has not destroyed or displaced claims for its authority. But granted the fact of images selected as of superior authority to others, wherein does this authority consist? Two directions, often closely inter-twined, may be suggested in answer. One of these lies in the authority granted to the Bible by the corporate judgment of the Church as developed over the centuries of its existence. The Church has pronounced on what images or symbols can be counted as of preeminent authority. This is an answer developed by David H. Kelsey's fine study of biblical authority. He has argued that the lack of unity and the inherent contradictions found in the Bible do not detract from its authority when that term is properly understood as integrally and functionally related to the Church.[7] The Bible is the canon, the rule of faith for the Church. Consequently, "if one gives up a concept of 'church' of which the concept 'scripture' and especially the concept 'canon' is a part, then one is also logically obliged to give up the concept of the 'authority' of scripture."[8] This argument looks to be a short-circuited one in which the Church, by an authority of its own, pronounces Scripture to be canon and then claims its authority derives from Scripture. However, a preliminary step is introduced by which the Church deter-mines what is to be accepted as biblically authentic. This step is what Kelsey calls a synoptic judgment antecedently made as to what Christian-ity is "basically all about," a judgment, it appears, not made on the basis of texts alone, but on a perspective suggested by the texts and the Christian life itself, and one that in effect would rule out *a priori* some images of God and Jesus.[9] In the light of this synoptic judgment it is maintained that the patterns of Scripture "can be relied upon to act as outside limits to the range of ways" in which the Church can construe God's presence among the faithful.[10] Then one other principle is invoked. The theologian must present his/her work intelligibly, as open to reasoned elaboration and ar-gued defense within the cultural conditions of what is seriously imaginable and traditional.[11] When all is said, Kelsey's textured differentiations of the meanings of authority leave that term with a greatly attenuated meaning of biblical authority harnessed to the theological needs and interests of the Church.

This conclusion does not stand by itself, since the images of God in the Bible apparently enjoyed authority in their own right prior to the Church's existence or the formation of the canon. Another direction should be ex-plored that takes into account the kind of authority with which individual worshipers have invested these images. This more individualistic source of authority may be introduced by the remarks of another theologian. He asserts that "the Bible no longer has unique authority for Western man" and acknowledges that biblical claims cannot be assessed by reference to the Bible itself. Instead, he writes, "we must devise our own criteria for interpreting and answering" these claims, criteria that "must truly be criteria *for us*. . . ."[12] The locus of authority has thus been shifted from both Church and Scripture to the informed and sensitive judgment of individuals. Biblical authority, if there be such, resides in the contemporary assessment of religious needs, for as another theologian observes, "it is futile for a system of faith to employ modes of thought that contradict the fundamental experience of the people of our age."[13]

What remains is then to show that many images or modes of thought found in Scriptures become authoritative as interpretations or expressions of lived experience. Images of God that describe him in unworthy terms, and jar contemporary religious and ethical presuppositions, may nevertheless have their place in expressing the harshly devastating experiences of life. The tendency to exalt only God's beneficent attributes has led to the belief that his goodness matches only what humans approve, and as a result generations of people have been prepared for atheism when life experiences have not concided with that belief, and texts have been virtually expurgated from worship to meet the demands of that conviction. God, conceived anthropopathically, never is "really" angry, vengeful, jealous, or a dealer in suffering and death, although for some Christians the suffering and death of Christ is an essential part of the epic of salvation, which they believe God planned and executed. But, as one theologian blandly explained, images or symbols of this kind "are not used to shed light on the character of God's love, although they all have meaning only as illuminating that same love."[14] Just how they illuminate, except by contrast and contradiction, is far from evident. He is still experienced as implacable and uncaring. "The volcanic forces of human nature and history require austere and shocking transcription."[15]

In the face of war, famine, drought, flood, and personal tragedy, people are sometimes willing to take the advice of Job's wife, "Curse God and die" (2:9), but others wrestle with their agonies, never giving up God, although deeply tempted to do so. C. S. Lewis reflected upon the nature of God after his wife's death. He did not cease to believe in God, but he sensed the danger that he would come to believe "dreadful things about Him." He feared to find himself saying "So this is what God's really like. . . . Deceive yourself no longer." The consolations of religion came to him only from those who did not understand and did not touch his despairing and even defiant mood. "If God's goodness is inconsistent with hurting us," he wrote, "then either God is not good or there is no God: for in the only life we know He hurts us beyond our worst fears and beyond all we can imagine." All moral judgments about God are turned topsy-turvy in which God's bad attributes—unreasonableness, vanity, vindictiveness, injustice, and cruelty—all would really be good! Lewis was forced to admit that his image of God had been ruthlessly torn apart, whereas he had assumed it to be sacrosanct, like God himself. "He shatters it himself. He is the great iconoclast." Plaintively he asked, "Could we not almost say that this shattering is one of the marks of his presence.?"[16] So Merleau-Ponty had the right of it when he wrote, "The world is not what I think but what I live through."[17]

While faith holds, in Job's experience and that of Lewis, abhorrent images of God establish their authority not by the testimony of the canon, but because they address and reflect the raw materials of human distress. The experiences of God give authority to Scripture, not vice versa. The Bible was not squeamish in portraying God in his full sovereignty, even to the point, as Paul discovered with his thorn in the flesh (2 Cor. 12:7–9), that God sometimes did not ease human suffering. In this respect it is more consistent and honest, if less indulgent, in depicting God than are those who have sentimentally poeticized him.

"The fundamental experience" of persons is by no means exhausted in scenes of pain, suffering, frustration, and death. The darker sides of God's nature did not and do not completely fill life's horizon. The images of God find their authority by marking the unsuspected high points of human experience. His fidelity and his "steadfast love" continue to sustain people in the anxieties and evils of daily life. The sense of the world's incorruptible moral order finds its rootage in his enduring justice. People still delight in the law of the Lord. The cry of the heart for mercy and forgiveness is matched by the images of God's tenderness and his redirection of life from waywardness and despair. In his presence people can still sing with joy (Ps. 5:11), and dance in his praise (Ps. 149:3). And Paul's triumphant words lift the human spirit above the depressing pressures of our common life: "neither death, nor life, nor angels, nor principalities, nor things present, nor things to come, nor powers, nor height, nor depth, nor anything else in all creation, will be able to separate us from the love of God in Christ Jesus our Lord" (Rom. 8:38–39).

The religious and cultural landscapes have indeed changed from those of biblical days, but a secularized age, in which references to God have become polite formalities or merely explosive outlets for human exasperation, has not totally eclipsed the deep matters of human destiny that the images of God address. Signs of favor, hope, and life, in the presence of death, are detectable in the vicissitudes of human existence, and are couched in the images of God's solicitude. Nor have all traces of his power and glory been extinguished from nature in spite of its ruthless despoiling by mankind. Thus the authority of the Bible remains by virtue of its continued capacity to express, inspire, and interpret in images and symbols our most profound experiences.

For individuals, the authority of Scripture may be rooted in the existential relevance its images have for private experience. But this factor alone does not explain the fact that certain of these images and the symbols based upon them have become the marks of authentic belief for the Church as a whole. Social confirmation has been needed to substantiate the authoritative preeminence of such images and symbols for Christian belief. Confronted by a plethora of biblical images, many of which stand in confrontational opposition to each other, the Church, through its theologians, biblical interpreters, and councils, has striven to unify into a coherent picture the nature of God and Jesus Christ. Over a long period of time, often with bitter controversy, a winnowing process has taken place by which some images and symbols have been accepted as the marks of true belief. The details of that process need not detain us here, and may better be left to the historians of doctrinal development. What can be suggested are the major areas that have affected the selective process. Political, social, and philosophical interests have undoubtedly played their parts in determining which images have been granted authoritative status, but other factors seem to have more decisively fashioned the outcome.

The coherence that has been sought arises from the need for images suitable to the worship of God, for worship is the milieu in which they arise and flourish and by which their aesthetic modality is created. *Theological reason* operates upon this basis to insure that the ruling conception of the God worshiped be itself a coherent idea as it seeks among many images of God those which mutually support each other as a cohesive whole. Inherent in the work of theological reason is the need for *ethical reason* to rule out demeaning or immoral aspects of the deity or to interpret them as compatible with loftier standards appropriate to the divine nature, lest the deity appear morally unworthy of human devotion. Intellectual contradictions among images have had to be resolved by logical reasoning to insure that Christian faith not be based upon intellectual confusion or sheer nonsense. The images and symbols that achieve normative status with their implied doctrines must exhibit logical structure both to strengthen the believer's faith by rational explication and to enter into intelligible discourse with the world of other faiths. Logic may so prize its own kind of coherence that it tempts worshipers to substitute correct belief for vital faith, but as long as it has kept company with the life of devotion it need not do so. On the other hand, without logical reasoning, images left to themselves do not create the coherence necessary to the Church's life. But reason's search for logical coherence has not been easy, for faith confronts it with intractable nuggets of experience and belief that do not yield smoothly to linear elucidation. This has been the case with two landmarks of Christianity, the Incarnation and the Trinity. Reason in these instances has the task of showing that the paradox each entails is an unavoidable accompaniment of Christian experience, and yet meets the criterion of intelligible discourse.

This search for the coherence of faith has never settled only for the Incarnation and the Trinity, but these two stand out as the principal standards of Christian orthodoxy. Other images, however, have also achieved authoritative positions and been regarded as supplementary to those essential paradoxes. The image of God as the Covenant-maker has served to bind together the God of the Jewish Scriptures and the God revealed in Jesus Christ with his people in unbreakable fidelity. The image of God as King with his Kingdom announced by Jesus Christ has concentrated God's sovereign rule in one figure of speech. As one theologian observes, "The Christian faith is a worldview. It is a massive appropriation of a political image: the Kingdom."[18] But significant as such images are in the economy of Christian belief, they have not been held to be the crucial authorities by which Christian faith has been defined. The Incarnation and the Trinity occupy that role. Images, as previously observed, are often converted into symbols (chaps. 4 and 14). And this has been the case, apparently, in respect to the Incarnation and the Trinity. Jesus is first understood as a human figure, as Paul suggests when he writes "we once regarded Christ from a human point of view." But then he adds, to show that this perception has taken on spiritual significance, "we regard him thus no longer" (2 Cor. 5:16). Then in Colossians Jesus the Christ is transformed into "the image of the invisible God" (1:15). From human figure, Jesus passes into image of God, and then finally, in the symbol of Incarnation, becomes the embodiment of God. So image is converted into symbol. In the symbol of the Trinity the three images of Father, Son, and Holy Spirit coalesce into the symbol of one God. In each instance a major step toward coherence as well as comprehensiveness has been taken, driven not by logic alone, but by the dynamics of faith as well. And both of the resultant symbols have become authoritative for orthodox Christianity in spite of their paradoxical character.

The biblical sources of the Incarnation are largely found in the Gospel of John (chap. 12). From this and other materials, at some time the paradox of the Incarnation was formulated. It is one in which two beings, each possessed of discrete and unique attributes, were merged into one entity, the God-Man. Reason has inquired how on logical grounds it can be asserted that an undeniably historical, finite human being can be the repository of an ahistorical, infinite, nonhuman being. Was there not here a discontinuity that no amount of subtle reasoning could bridge? The philosopher Lessing set a similar problem when he argued that a "ditch" existed between the accidental, time-limited truths of history and the necessary truths of reason, since the latter could never be based on the former.[19] His problem, translated into terms of the Incarnation, might read that the truth of God could never be based on the actions and teachings of the historical Jesus, for history and faith occupy completely diverse dimensions. However, it remained for Sören Kierkegaard to raise this separation of history and faith to new heights of importance by his insistence on the Absolute Paradox, the Incarnation, as the supreme object of Christian faith. He asked whether it was possible to base an eternal happiness upon historical knowledge, and answered his question in the negative. Faith, for him, could not depend on the vagaries of historical knowledge, but on a leap to what logic regarded as an absurdity, the Absolute Paradox that could not be mediated or understood by human reason. Yet the form this faith assumed was necessarily built upon historical knowledge found in Scripture and churchly tradition. Without this knowledge of a historical being, Jesus, there could be no paradox in which to believe. Nor did Kierkegaard's awareness that there was a paradox come to him by private inspiration, since he insisted that he was set on the reintroduction of New Testament Christianity into Christendom. Furthermore, without historical knowledge passed on from generation to generation, the "disciple at second hand" would have no opportunity to enjoy that "eternal happiness" that faith in the Incarnation brings.[20]

However, in the main Kierkegaard was correct. He saw that the Absolute Paradox was not simply an object of intellectual inquiry, but rather a subject of religious worship. In spite of his idiosyncratic arguments about history, he saw that faith did not arise solely from historical knowledge. Faith may arise on the occasion of such knowledge, but its significance for the believer is not limited to this information. The paradoxical character of the Incarnation is not first of all a logical puzzle, but it functions in religious awareness and worship. The paradox of the Absolute Paradox is essentially the product of religious experience wherein cognitive, conative, and affective elements constitute a unity. The logical problems about the Incarnation arise only when one stands outside the orbit of worship. What had been intuited as a unity of experience is the impact of God through the historical Jesus upon human life. For that experience paradox is the logical expression of personal involvement, not the noninvolvement of the philosophical analyst. The paradox of the Incarnation rendered into a comprehensible form the believer's experience of two juxtaposed realities, an experience that has no counterpart in the life of the unbeliever. In a logical sense faith without the fact of the historical Jesus would be without any concrete features by which to discriminate its object from a shadowy, disembodied idea, while without the reality of God's presence the power and love experienced in Jesus would be inexplicable, or would not be, as Kierkegaard would have it, the source of "eternal happiness." To be sure, the symbol of the Incarnation is not clearly formulated as the only norm of Christian faith in the New Testament, but it claims biblical authority when a judicious selection is made of the available texts. But its continued authority depends upon the depth of worship it inspires.

From the standpoint of coherence the symbol of the Trinity shares with the Incarnation similar logical problems, but it can lay claim to far less textual support. In spite of this lack, it has become the dominant authoritative symbol of Christianity, a fact all the more surprising since the Christianity of the New Testament seldom mentions it. A survey of the biblical material even casts doubt on its acceptability by Jesus, Paul, and the earliest representatives of the new faith. The most precise statement of the Trinity occurs in the conclusion of Matthew's Gospel, where Christ commands the disciples to spread the Gospel and baptize in the name of the Father, Son, and Holy Spirit (28:19). Paul seems to attest to the Trinity in his benediction in 2 Corinthians. There he asks that "the grace of the Lord Jesus Christ, the love of God and the fellowship of the Holy Spirit" rest upon his readers (13:14). More obliquely the salutation of 1 Peter refers to "God the Father," who has chosen, destined, and sanctified Christians by "the Spirit for obedience to Jesus Christ" (1:2). Yet the Jesus of the Synoptics did not teach the Trinity (cf. Matt. 19:16–22; 22:37–40), but rather advises his listeners to repent and have faith in God (Mark 11:22; Luke 8:21). Nor were his healings accomplished in the name of the Trinity. The signs attributed to him in John's Gospel carry no trinitarian authority, even in the raising of Lazarus (11:43). There Jesus teaches, not the Trinity, but belief in himself as the one from God. Peter's healings in the book of Acts (e.g., 3:6; 4:10) and his teachings (5:28) were in the name of Jesus alone, as were the recorded baptisms (2:38; 8:12, 13, 38). The purpose of Jesus' coming was to bless people and turn them from wickedness (3:26), and to give repentance and forgiveness of sins (5:31). Neither does Paul in Acts heal in the name of the Trinity (16:18, 33; 19:11–17). Naturally, if the ending of Matthew's Gospel was written after these events, Paul would have known nothing of it! Furthermore, Paul turned his back on the idea of a triune God when he asserted, as a Christian Jew, "God is one" (Gal. 3:20), a theme echoed elsewhere (Eph. 4:5; 1 Tim. 1:17; 6:15).

The pervasive silence about the Trinity in these instances is remarkable. Apparently the earliest strata of Christian belief did not include the Matthean commission, or, if it was known, it was flouted. Customarily, the name of Jesus was employed in baptisms and healings, or, as in the salutations and benedictions of the epistles, Jesus Christ and God were often linked without mention of the Holy Spirit. Paul's benediction in 1 Corinthians, however, seems to be an exception to this generalization. It probably antedated the passage in Matthew, and more certainly that in 1 Peter. Yet it was scarcely offered as a theological doctrine describing God as triune. Rather it was a sensitively molded expression that captured the grace, love, and fellowship of three distinct but related realities, the Lord Jesus Christ, God, and the Holy Spirit. It does not appear as a creedal formula bearing doctrinal authority, but rather as a literary unit that breathes the atmosphere of worship and devotion. It blesses rather than demands acceptance. Nowhere, not even in the conclusion of Matthew's Gospel, is God referred to as a triune God. The theological expression

"God the Father, God the Son, God the Holy Spirit" is never used, and salvation is never construed as dependent upon belief in a triune God.[21]

In spite of this paucity of explicit Trinitarian texts, the Church in its orthodox form has continued to invoke the Trinity as the principal authoritative symbol by which to speak of God. The Trinity, inclusive of the Incarnation, has concentrated the spiritual coherence of Christian belief and faith in one paradoxical form. It has been embraced less from a desire for logical neatness than for its capacity, when fully explicated, to unify and comprehend all other images of the deity. In it the three agencies by which salvation was wrought have been brought together as an affirmation of religious faith. The power, majesty, and love of God, the Father, the principal author of all good, was crucially exemplified in his Son, Jesus Christ, empowered by the Holy Spirit (chap. 10). Concrete religious experience in worship, rather than canonical or ecclesiastical authority, first molded and sanctioned this touchstone of Christian faith. It rose to its present position out of the devotional needs of the Christian community, and when clearly formulated, focused the religious imagination upon the mystery of the divine presence. Its seeming absurdity may elicit strenuous philosophical efforts, but as the unifier of Christian belief, it induces worship of God's beneficent power exercised in Jesus Christ and ever present through the Holy Spirit. Awe, wonder, adoration, and the elevation of the human spirit are its milieu, perhaps better confessed in song than trivialized by rote repetition as prose or made the subject of the proddings of an inquisitive reason. So pervasive and authoritative has been its presence that some, like Martin Luther, have thought to detect its presence even in the Jewish Scriptures. On the other hand, others have challenged its biblical authority and turned to other images or symbols believed to be more appropriate and less paradoxical.

A proposal of this kind has been tendered by a modern scholar who states, "The Trinitarian model is in the end less satisfactory for the articulation of our basic Christian experience than the unifying concept of God as Spirit."[22] When this clue is followed, many images of God, brought with great difficulty under the aegis of the Trinitarian symbol, may be accommodated and fewer eliminated. Long before the Trinity was formulated, God was imaged as Spirit. So the many images of God found in Scripture may be brought within the scope of the ruling image of Spirit. God, the Creator, Covenant Maker, King, Lawgiver, Judge, Warrior, Giver of Life and Death, Loving Father, and Christ, all may be regarded as empowered by the Spirit. The Trinity itself might be understood as the exemplification of Spirit, for God is the Spirit that infuses and moves the Son (e.g., Mark 1:12; Luke 4:1, 18; John 1:33), and continues as Holy Spirit to abide with the devout. The Spirit's multiple and ambiguous nature summons up impressions of power, benign and severe, personal and impersonal. Its invisibility stands for the reality of that which is unseen, while its derivation from words like *wind* or *breath* provides a palpability affecting the healing of the physical and spiritual nature of humans. Spirit resonates with the human consciousness of one's innermost intractable reality as a self. It emanates from a person, affecting the attitudes and perceptions of others, and in his or her absence continues to pervade the life of those left behind, as it did with Jesus' Spirit after his death and resurrection. Although it may localize itself, it also moves freely, unlimited by human devices, spontaneously moving human desires, longings, and volitions, thus becoming representative of divine sovereignty and transcendent objectivity. "Our God is in the heavens, he does whatever he pleases" (Ps. 115:3; cf. John 3:8). The image of Spirit warns against attempts to limit God's majesty by other images or symbols that would confine and rigidify his power and love. In worship, at its peak of ecstatic intensity, the human spirit is met with his Spirit, whereby the deepest satisfactions are realized, while on the other hand, in the duller routines of daily life, it companies with those who have not reached such heights. Its daily presence reminds the faithful that God is not only the Ancient of Days of the past, but the dynamic contemporary of the present and future.

Whether or not acknowledged as Spirit, there is that in the experience of God which sets the poet, philosopher, or lay person in search of other images conformable not only to those of the Bible, but to the uniqueness of individual experience. The dynamism of Spirit, to which the Bible attests, drives to new forms of confessional language. We find Francis Thompson coining the image of God as "the hound of Heaven" to reflect his own fugitive existence. Alfred North Whitehead attempted to mark the breadth and depth of the spiritual life in less poetic, prosaic images when he wrote of God the Void, God the Enemy, and God the Companion. It need not be supposed then that creation of images of God ceased with the closing of the canon, for Spirit continues to outspeed even our most cherished biblical images, making of them, as of newly created ones, tentative steps in the spiritual life. When ancient symbols or images, shorn of their past cultural accretions, reveal fresh apprehensions of the divine reality, when new images press to be created, God appears as the Iconoclastic One who breaks through them all. He destroys the idolatrous devotion with which we invest them, calling us by his Spirit to the deeper grounds of faith from which their authority ultimately arises. God imaged as the Iconoclastic Spirit may never become the single authoritative image of faith for the Christian church, but it is an image that rings true to the depth and height of mankind's experience of God as expressed both in Scripture and in contemporary worship and devotion.

NOTES

1. Many of the viewpoints of both Old and New Testaments "are not only diverse but also in some cases mutually exclusive." Joseph Blenkinsopp, *Prophecy and Canon* (Notre Dame, London: University of Notre Dame Press, 1977), 140; "Paul is far from being under the illusion that even in his own communities everyone believes and thinks exactly as he does." Walter Bauer, in *Orthodoxy and Heresy in Earliest Christianity,* ed. Robert A. Kraft and Gerhard Krodel (Philadelphia, Fortress Press, 1971), 235.

2. *Biblical Authority for Today,* ed. Alan Richardson and W. Schweitzer (Philadelphia: Westminster Press, 1951), 241.

3. *The Oxford Annotated Bible, R.S.V.* (New York: Oxford University Press, 1962), 1515, 1516.

4. Jerry Falwell, *Listen, America* (Garden City, N.Y.: Doubleday-Galilee, 1980), 54.

5. See Stephen T. Davis, *The Debate about the Bible* (Philadelphia, Westminster Press, 1977), 23.

6. Blenkinsopp, *Prophecy and Canon,* 142.

7. David H. Kelsey, *The Uses of Scripture in Recent Theology* (Philadelphia: Fortress Press, 1975), 175–176; cf. 207ff., 164, 182, 212.

8. Ibid., 176.

9. "In each case the decision about how to construe texts taken as authoritative scripture is determined by a logically prior decision about how best to characterize in a single judgment the singularity and complexity of the modes of God's presence." Ibid., 168; cf. 159, 205.

10. Ibid., 213.

11. Ibid., 175.

12. Gordon D. Kaufman, "What Shall We Do with the Bible?", *Interpretation* 25, no. 1 (January 1971): 96, 97.

13. Nathan A. Scott, "Arnold's Vision of Transcendence—the Via Poetica," *The Journal of Religion* 59, no. 3, (July 1979): 266.

14. Roger Hazelton, *Semeia,* no. 13, 2 (Missoula, Mont.: Scholar's Press, 1976), 40.

15. Amos Niven Wilder, *Theopoetic* (Philadelphia: Fortress Press, 1976): 40.

16. C. S. Lewis, *A Grief Observed* (New York, The Seabury Press, 1961), 9–10, 23, 28, 52.

17. Cited in Mary Warnock, *Imagination* (Berkeley and Los Angeles: University of California Press, 1976), 148.

18. Julian N. Hartt, *Theological Method and Imagination* (New York: The Seabury Press, 1977), 15.

19. Cf. G. E. Michaelson, Jr., "Lessing, Kierkegaard, and the 'Ugly Ditch': a Reexamination," *The Journal of Religion* 59, no. 3 (July 1979): 324ff. Unfortunately, Michaelson does not address the possibility of overcoming the divorcement between historical knowledge and religious faith in these two thinkers. Richard Campbell takes a different view from Michaelson. Cf. "Lessing's Problem and Kierkegaard's Answer," in *Essays on Kierkegaard,* ed. Jerry H. Gill (Minneapolis, Minn.: Burgess Publishing Co., 1969), 74ff.

20. For a philosophical analysis of Kierkegaard on paradox and The Absolute Paradox, see R. T. Herbert, *Paradox and Identity in Theology* (Ithaca and London: Cornell University Press, 1969), chaps. 3 and 4.

21. In spite of the lack of Trinitarian texts and evidence that the doctrine was not recognized as normative in the New Testament, the theological mind occasionally persists in affirming its biblical authenticity. Daniel L. Migliore, for example, sees one theological task to be the critical examination of the doctrine of God "to see if it is genuinely biblical and evangelical, that is, trinitarian." "The Trinity and Human Liberty," *Theology Today* 36, no. 4 (January 1980): 497.

22. G. W. H. Lampe, *God as Spirit* (Oxford: Clarendon Press, 1977), 228.

Bibliography

Anderson, B. W., ed. *The Old Testament and Christian Faith*. London: S.C.M. Press, 1964.

The Ante-Nicene Fathers. American Reprint of Edinburgh ed. Grand Rapids, Mich.: Wm. B. Eerdman's Publishing Co., 1951.

Bachelard, Gaston. *La Poétique de L'Espace*. 2d ed. Paris: Presses Universitaires de France, 1958.

Barfield, Owen. *Poetic Diction*. London: Faber and Gwyer, 1927.

Barr, James. *Biblical Words for Time*. Naperville, Ill.: Alec. R. Allenson, Inc., 1962.

Berger, Peter L. *A Rumor of Angels*. New York: Doubleday Anchor, 1969.

Bevan, Edwyn. *Symbolism and Belief*. New York: The Macmillan Co., 1938.

Blenkinsopp, Joseph. *Prophecy and Canon*. South Bend, Ind. and London: University of Notre Dame Press, 1977.

Bornkamm, Gunther. *Jesus of Nazareth*. Translated by Irene and Fraser McLuskey and James M. Robinson. New York: Harper and Brothers, 1960.

Bowker, John. *The Religious Imagination and the Sense of God*. Oxford: Clarendon Press, 1978.

Brabant, Frank Herbert. *Time and Eternity in Christian Thought*. London, New York, and Toronto: Longmans, Green and Co., 1937.

Buber, Martin. I and Thou. Translated by Ronald Gregor Smith. Edinburgh: T. and T. Clark, 1950.

Bultmann, Rudolf. *The Theology of the New Testament*. Translated by Kendrick Grobel. New York: Charles Scribner's Sons, 1951.

Caird, G. B. *The Language and Imagery of the Bible*. Philadelphia: The Westminster Press, 1980.

Cairns, David. *The Images of God in Man*. New York: Philosophical Library, 1953.

Cameron, J. M. *Images of Authority*. New Haven: Yale University Press, 1966.

Cassirer, Ernst. *Language and Myth*. Translated by Susanne K. Langer. New York: Dover Publications, 1946.

———. *The Philosophy of Symbolic Forms*. Translated by Ralph Manheim. New Haven: Yale University Press, 1955.

Coates, J. R., ed. *Kittel's Bible Key Words*. New York: Harper and Brothers, 1958.

Copleston, Frederick, S. J. *A History of Philosophy*. Vol. 6, pt. 2, *Kant*. Garden City, N.Y.: Doubleday Image Book, 1964.

———. *Religion and Philosophy*. Dublin: Gill and Macmillan, 1974.

Cullmann, Oscar. *The Earliest Christian Confessions*. London: The Lutterworth Press, 1949.

Daiches, David. *Essays by Divers Hands*. New Series 33. London: Oxford University Press, 1965.

Daly, Robert. *God's Altar*. Berkeley, Los Angeles, and London: University of California Press, 1978.

David, Charles. *Body as Spirit*. New York: The Seabury Press, 1976.

Davis, Stephen T. *The Debate about the Bible*. Philadelphia: The Westminster Press, 1977.

DeBoer, P. A. H. *Fatherhood and Motherhood in Israelite and Judean Piety*. Leiden: E. J. Brill, 1974.

Dickie, Edgar P. *God Is Light*. New York: Charles Scribner's Sons, 1954.

Dictionnaire de Spiritualité. Paris: Beauchesne, 1977.

Dodd, C. H. *The Interpretation of the Fourth Gospel*. Cambridge: Cambridge University Press, 1953.

Downing, F. Gerald. *Has Christianity Revelation?* London: S.C.M. Press Ltd., 1964.

Eliade, Mircea. *Image and Symbol*. Translated by Philip Mairet. London: Harvill Press, 1961.

Eliade, Mircea and Joseph M. Kitagawa, eds. *The History of Religions, Essays in Methodology*. Chicago and London: The University of Chicago Press, 1974.

Emmett, Dorothy M. *The Nature of Metaphysical Thinking*. New York: The Macmillan Co., 1957.

Falwell, Jerry. *Listen, America*. Garden City, N.Y.: Doubleday-Galilee, 1980.

Farrer, Austin. *The Glass of Vision*. Reprint. Westminster: Dacre Press, 1958.

———. *A Rebirth of Images*. Boston: Beacon Press, 1963.

Ford, Lewis S. *The Lure of God*. Philadelphia: Fortress Press, 1978.

Foss, Martin. *The Idea of Perfection in the Western World*. Princeton: N.J.: Princeton University Press, 1946.

Foster, Michael B. *Mystery and Philosophy*. London: S.C.M. Press, 1957.

Frankfort, H., H. A. Frankfort, John A. Wilson, and Thorkild Jacobsen. *Before Philosophy*. Harmondsworth, Middlesex: Pelican Books, 1951.

Frankfort, Henri. *Kingship and the Gods*. Chicago: The University of Chicago Press, 1948.

Frei, Hans. *The Eclipse of Biblical Narrative*. New Haven and London: Yale University Press, 1974.

Funk, Robert W. *Language, Hermeneutics and the Word of God*. New York, Evanston, Ill., and London: Harper and Row, 1966.

Gadamer, Hans-Georg. *Truth and Method*. New York: A Continuum Book, The Seabury Press, 1975.

Gellner, Ernest. *Legitimation of Belief*. Cambridge: Cambridge University Press, 1974.

Gilkey, Langdon. *Naming the Whirlwind*. Indianapolis and New York: The Bobbs-Merrill Co., 1964.

Gill, Jerry, ed. *Essays on Kierkegaard*. Minneapolis: Burgess Publishing Co., 1969.

Goen, C. C., ed. *Works of Jonathan Edwards.* Vol. 4. *The Great Awakening.* New Haven: Yale University Press, 1972.

Gordis, Robert. *Judaism in a Christian World.* New York: McGraw-Hill, 1966.

Grant, Robert M. *The Early Christian Doctrine of God.* Charlottesville, Va.: University Press of Virginia, 1966.

Gustafson, James M. *Can Ethics Be Christian?* Chicago and London: The University of Chicago Press, 1975.

———. *Ethics from a Theocentric Perspective.* Vol. 1, *Theology and Ethics.* Chicago and Oxford: The University of Chicago Press, 1981.

Hahn, Ferdinand. *The Titles of Jesus in Christology.* New York and Cleveland: The World Publishing Co., 1969.

Hanson, R. P. C. *Tradition in the Early Church.* London: S.C.M. Press, 1962.

Hartshorne, Charles, and William L. Reese. *Philosophers Speak of God.* Chicago: The University of Chicago Press, 1953.

Hartt, Julian N. *Theological Method and Imagination.* New York: The Seabury Press, 1977.

Hazelton, Roger. *Ascending Flame, Descending Dove.* Philadelphia: The Westminster Press, 1975.

Hendel, Charles W., ed. *David Hume, Selections.* New York, Chicago, and Boston: Charles Scribner's Sons, 1927.

Hepburn, Ronald W. *Christianity and Paradox.* London: Watts, 1958.

Herbert, R. T. *Paradox and Identity in Theology.* Ithaca and London: Cornell University Press, 1979.

Hick, John, ed. *The Myth of God Incarnate.* Philadelphia: The Westminster Press, 1977.

Higman, Francis M. *The Style of John Calvin in his French Polemical Treatises.* London: Oxford University Press, 1967.

Hirsch, E. D. *Validity in Interpretation.* New Haven and London: Yale University Press, 1967.

Hoffmeister, Johannes, ed. *Introduction: Reason in History.* in *Georg W. F. Hegel, Lectures on the Philosophy of World History.* Translated by N. B. Wishart. Cambridge: Cambridge University Press, 1975.

Holbrook, Clyde A. *Faith and Community.* New York: Harper and Brothers, 1959.

Holmer, Paul L. *The Grammar of Faith.* New York, Hagerstown, San Francisco, and London: Harper and Row, 1978.

Hook, Sidney, ed. *Religious Experience and Truth.* New York: New York University Press, 1961.

The Interpreter's Bible. Nashville, Tenn., and New York: Abingdon Cokesbury Press, 1952.

Javalet, Robert. *Image et Ressemblance au Douxième Siècle.* Editions Letouzey et Ané, 1967.

Johnson, F. Ernest, ed. *Religious Symbolism.* New York: Harper and Brothers, 1955.

Johnson, William A. *The Search for Transcendence.* New York: Harper-Colophon, 1974.

Kelsey, David H. *The Uses of Scripture in Recent Theology.* Philadelphia: Fortress Press, 1975.

Kierkegaard, Sören. *Attack on Christendom.* Translated by Walter Lowrie. Boston: The Beacon Press, 1960.

Kraft, Robert A., and Gerhard Kradel, eds. *Walter Bauer, Orthodoxy and Heresy in Earliest Christianity.* Philadelphia: Fortress Press, 1971.

Küng, Hans. *On Being a Christian.* Translated by Edward Quinn. Garden City, New York: Doubleday and Co., 1976.

Lampe, G. W. H. *God as Spirit.* Oxford: Clarendon Press, 1977.

Lewis, C. S. *A Grief Observed.* New York: The Seabury Press, 1961.

Lewis, C. Day. *The Poetic Image.* London: Jonathan Cape, 1947.

Lundeen, Lyman T. *Risk and Rhetoric in Religion.* Philadelphia: Fortress Press, 1972.

M'Clintock, John, and James Strong, *Cyclopedia of Biblical, Theological and Ecclesiastical Literature,* New York, Arno Press, 1969.

McComb, Samuel, ed. *Friedrich Heiler, Prayer.* London, New York and Toronto: Oxford University Press, 1932.

MacCormac, Earl R. *Metaphor and Myth in Science and Religion.* Durham, N.C.: Duke University Press, 1976.

McIntosh, Douglas C. *The Problem of Religious Knowledge.* New York and London: Harper and Brothers, 1940.

McIntyre, C. T., ed. *God, History, and Historians.* New York: Oxford University Press, 1977.

McIntyre, John. *The Christian Doctrine of History.* Edinburgh: Oliver and Boyde, 1957.

MacLeish, Archibald. *Poetry and Experience.* Cambridge: The Riverside Press; Boston: Houghton Mifflin Co., 1961.

McQuarrie, John. *Thinking about God.* New York and Evanston, Ill.: Harper and Row, 1975.

Marcel, Gabriel. *The Mystery of Being.* Ser. 1, *Reflections and Mystery.* Translated by G. S. Fraser and René Hague. Chicago: Henry Regnery Co.; London: The Harvill Press, 1950.

Morse, Samuel French ed. *Wallace Stevens, Opus Posthumus.* New York: Alfred A. Knopf, 1977.

Mowinckel, S. *The Psalms in Israel's Worship.* New York and Nashville, Tenn.: Abingdon Press; Oxford: Basil Blackwell, 1962.

Needham, Rodney. *Belief, Language and Experience.* Oxford: Basil Blackwell, 1972.

Neville, Robert C. *God the Creator.* Chicago and London: The University of Chicago Press, 1968.

Neibuhr, H. Richard. *The Meaning of Revelation.* New York and Boston: The Macmillan Co., 1941.

Oates, Whitney J., ed. *Basic Writings of Saint Augustine.* Vol. 1. New York: Random House, 1948.

Oman, John. *The Natural and the Supernatural.* New York: The MacMillan Co.; Cambridge, Cambridge University Press, 1931.

Otto, Rudolph. *The Idea of the Holy.* Translated by John W. Harvey. London, New York, and Humphrey Milford: Oxford University Press, 1925.

Pannenberg, Wohlfahrt. *Faith and Reality.* Translated by John Maxwell. London: Search Press; Philadelphia: The Westminster Press, 1977.

————. *Jesus—God and Man*. 2d ed. Translated by Lewis L. Wilkins and Duane H. Priebe. Philadelphia: The Westminster Press, 1977.

Paz, Octavio. *The Bow and the Lyre*. Translated by Ruth L. C. Simms. Austin and London: University of Texas Press, 1973.

————. *Claude Lévi-Strauss: An Introduction*. Translated by J. S. Bernstein and Maxine Bernstein. Ithaca and London: Cornell University Press, 1970.

Pedersen, Johannes P. E. *Israel*. Translated by Aslang Møller. Reprint. Humphrey Milford: Oxford University Press, 1925.

Pegis, Anton C., ed. *Basic Writings of Saint Thomas Aquinas*. New York: Random House, 1945.

Peiper, Josef. *The Silence of St. Thomas*. Translated by Daniel O'Connor. London: Faber and Faber, 1957.

Pelikan, Jaroslav. *The Emergence of the Catholic Tradition, 100–600*. Chicago: The University of Chicago Press, 1971.

Perrin, Norman. *Jesus and the Language of the Kingdom*. Philadelphia: Fortress Press, 1976.

————. *Rediscovering the Teaching of Jesus*. London: S.C.M. Press, 1967.

Phillips, D. Z. *The Concept of Prayer*. New York: Schocken Books, 1966.

————. *Religion without Explanation*. Oxford: Basil Blackwell, 1976.

Phillips, John. *The Reformation of Images: Destruction of Art in England, 1535–1660*. Berkeley, Los Angeles, and London: University of California Press, 1973.

Prestige, G. L. *God in Patristic Thought*. London: S.P.C.K., 1952.

Price, H. H. *Belief*. London: George Allen and Unwin Ltd.; New York: Humanities Press, 1969.

Putnam, Hilary. *Meaning and the Moral Sciences*. London: Routledge and Kegan Paul, 1978.

Rad, Gerhard von. *Genesis*. Translated by John H. Marks. Philadelphia: The Westminster Press, 1961.

Ramsey, Ian T. *Religious Language*. London: S.C.M. Press, 1957.

Ramsey, Paul, ed. *Works of Jonathan Edwards*. Vol. 1. *Freedom of the Will*. New Haven: Yale University Press; London: Oxford University Press, 1957.

Richardson, Alan, and W. Schweitzer, eds. *Biblical Authority for Today*. Philadelphia: The Westminster Press, 1951.

Ricoeur, Paul. *The Symbolism of Evil*. Translated by Emerson Buchanan. New York, Evanston, Ill., and London: Harper and Row, 1967.

Robinson, H. W. *Revelation and Inspiration in the Old Testament*. Oxford: Oxford University Press, 1946.

Rowe, William L. *Religious Symbols and God*. Chicago and London: The University of Chicago Press, 1968.

Rust, E. C. *Nature and Man in Biblical Thought*. London: Lutterworth Press, 1953.

Santoni, Ronald E., ed. *Religious Language and the Problem of Religious Knowledge*. Bloomington, Ind., and London: Indiana University Press, 1975.

Schaff, Philip, ed. *The Creeds of Christendom*. 4th ed. New York: Harper and Brothers, 1872; 1905; 1919.

————. ed., *Nicene and Post-Nicene Fathers of the Christian Church*. New York: The Christian Literature Co., 1892.

Schilpp, Paul A., ed., *The Philosophy of Alfred N. Whitehead*. The Library of Living Philosophers. Evanston, Ill., and Chicago: Northwestern University Press, 1941.

————, ed. *The Philosophy of Ernst Cassirer*. Vol. 2. The Library of Living Philosophers. Evanston, Ill., 1949.

Shedler, Norbert O., ed. *Philosophy of Religion, Contemporary Perspectives*. New York: The Macmillan Co., 1974.

Smart, Ninian. *Reasons and Faith*. London: Routledge and Kegan Paul, 1958.

Smith, John E. *The Analogy of Experience*. New York and Evanston, Ill.: Harper and Row, 1973.

————. *Experience and God*. New York: Oxford University Press, 1959.

————, ed. *Works of Jonathan Edwards*. Vol. 2. New Haven: Yale University Press, 1959.

Snaith, Norman H. *The Distinctive Ideas of the Old Testament*. London: The Epworth Press, 1950.

Tagliacazzo, Giorgio, and Donald P. Verene, eds. *Vico's Science of Humanity*. Baltimore and London: Johns Hopkins Press, 1976.

Taylor, A. E. *The Faith of a Moralist*. London: Macmillan and Co., 1951.

Taylor, Vincent. *The Names of Jesus*. New York: St. Martin's Press, 1953.

Thatcher, Adrian. *The Ontology of Paul Tillich*. London: Oxford University Press, 1978.

Thompson, Leonard, L. *Introducing Biblical Literature*. Englewood Cliffs, N.J.: Prentice-Hall, 1978.

Thrall, William Flint, and Addison Hibbard. *A Handbook to Literature*. Revised and enlarged by C. Hugh Holman. New York: The Odyssey Press, 1960.

Tillich, Paul. *Biblical Religion and the Search for Ultimate Reality*. Chicago: The University of Chicago Press, 1955.

————. *Dynamics of Faith*. New York: Harper and Brothers, 1957.

————. *Love, Power and Justice*. New York and London: Oxford University Press, 1954.

————. *The New Being*. New York: Charles Scribner's Sons, 1955.

————. *The Shaking of the Foundations*. London: S.C.M. Press, 1940.

————. *Systematic Theology*. Vol. 2. Chicago: The University of Chicago Press, 1957.

Tracy, David. *Blessed Rage for Order*. New York: The Seabury Press, 1978.

Tupper, E. Frank. *The Theology of Wohlfahrt Pannenberg*. Philadelphia: The Westminster Press, 1973.

Urban, Wilbur M. *Humanity and Deity*. London: George Allen and Unwin Ltd., 1951.

————. *Language and Reality*. New York: The Macmillan Co.; London: George Allen and Unwin Ltd., 1961.

Van der Leeuw, G. *Religion in Essence and Manifestation*. Translated by J. E. Turner. London: George Allen and Unwin Ltd., 1938.

Warnock, Mary. *Imagination*. Berkeley and Los Angeles: University of California Press, 1976.

Warren, Austin. *Theory of Literature*. 3d ed. New York: Harcourt, Brace and World, 1970.

Wheelwright, Philip. *Metaphor and Reality*. Bloomington, Ind., Indiana University Press, 1962.

Whitehead, Alfred N. *Process and Reality*. The Social Science Book Store Reprint, 1941.

———. *Religion in the Making*. New York: The Macmillan Co., 1926.

———. *Science and the Modern World*. New York: The Macmillan Co., 1945.

———. *Symbolism, Its Meaning and Effect*. Cambridge: Cambridge University Press, 1928.

Wieman, Henry N. *Man's Ultimate Commitment*. Carbondale, Ill.: Southern Illinois University Press, 1958.

Wilder, Amos. *Early Christian Rhetoric, the Language of the Gospel*. New York: Harper and Row, 1965; rev. ed., Cambridge, Mass., Harvard University Press, 1971.

Wilder, Amos Niven. *Theopoetic*. Philadelphia: Fortress Press, 1976.

Works of President Edwards. Reprint of the Worcester Edition. New York: Leavitt and Allen, 1843.

Yates, Frances A. *The Art of Memory*. Chicago: The University of Chicago Press, 1966.

Index